CONTENTS

BUSINESS

WITHOUT

BORDERS

A Strategic Guide to Global Marketing

Donald A. DePalma

John Wiley & Sons, Inc.

Published by John Wiley & Sons, Inc., New York.
Published simultaneously in Canada.

This publication is designed to provide accurate and authoritative information in regard to the subject matter covered. It is sold with the understanding that the publisher is not engaged in rendering professional services. If professional advice or other expert assistance is required, the services of a competent professional person should be sought.

ISBN: 0-471-20469-2

Printed in the United States of America.

10 9 8 7 6 5 4 3 2 1

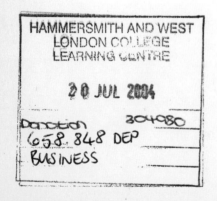

ACKNOWLEDGMENTS

I dedicate this book to my parents, Guy and Meda DePalma, who let me make my own decision about spending my entire life savings to visit the Soviet Union when I was just 16. Their sometimes amused ("Russia? In the winter?") but strong support through subsequent sojourns abroad launched me on my own global journey. I'd also like to thank my family—Karen, Rachel, and Kevin—who endured the long hours and inconvenience associated with research and writing this book.

I'm indebted to Elisabeth Abeson, a globalization expert who read everything that I wrote, provided insightful feedback, and kept directing me back to the bigger issues. I'd also like to thank my other reviewers—Val Ziegler, Dana Tower, Joe Sawyer, Melissa Josephson, Tom Shapiro, and Renato Beninatto—all globalization and marketing specialists in their own right, who contributed thoughtful comments and insight.

I owe another debt of gratitude to the globalization advocates and leaders at the companies that I interviewed for my case studies. They gave generously of their time for interviews and follow-up inquiries, even as they were working hard to make their own global and ethnic marketing investments pay off.

As for the content of the book, many people provided information that I included in my model, but a few of them stand out. Louis Dejoie of McNees, Wallace & Nurick reviewed sections on international legal issues. Adam Asnes, Alex Pressman, and Yann Meersseman helped me make the tough problems of internationalization easier to digest. Andreas Randhahn counseled me on better graphic representations of information. Idiom Technologies' consulting and WorldWise teams, especially Mark Yunger, Louis Carvallo, Anne Ertlé, and Joel Pulliam, supplied background on issues ranging from localization to legal to vendor landscapes. Finally, I want to thank eMarketer for access to its eStats database, the best source that I've found for statistics of and relating to the Internet in all its forms.

And while the contributions of all these people helped me write the book, ultimately the responsibility for what you read here falls on my shoulders. While you're sure to find things that you don't agree with, what I'd like you to walk away with is the importance of communicating effectively to your target markets, wherever they happen to be. With that as your goal, everything else—focused marketing, organizational structures, technology, and budgets—will follow.

Introduction

The Sun Never Sets on the Web

Seven days a week, 24 hours a day, hundreds of millions of people around the world cross national borders without a second thought—and often without knowing that they have done anything unusual. This community scours the Internet for the ideas, products, and relationships that they might not be able to find easily—if at all—where they live.

This borderless community of Internet users comprises a virtual Eighth Continent racing toward a population of a billion inhabitants. It exists wherever a computer, mobile phone, set-top box, or personal organizer touches the Internet. Until the Web pulled together this huge electronic society, its citizens were unreachable without massive investment in local staff and infrastructure in each and every country where a person wanted to do business.

This borderless community confounds legislators and cultural purists worldwide who do not know what to make of the Web-based globalization phenomenon that threatens to make their geographic, political, economic, and cultural boundaries almost meaningless. It places new burdens on companies suddenly confronted with inquiries from far-off places.

Your firm's most visible online channel—the corporate headquarters' Web site—exposes its values and products to the inhabitants of the Eighth Continent every minute of every day. These people challenge organizations to make geography irrelevant in the name of satisfying customers. For many of you within these organizations, the Web has made this international demand transparent for the first time because in the past, their interest was always filtered through the noisy channels of local staff, distributors, and suppliers. With the Web, the denizens of the Eighth Continent can bypass these middlemen and tell you directly what's on their minds—and on their buying agendas. This free-flowing communication imposes hefty new demands on companies that want to stretch beyond their domestic markets and become suppliers to the Eighth Continent.

One of the most common mistakes among companies today is assuming that being on the Web makes you an instantly global success. Despite the Web's potential in opening new channels, presence on the Web also may expose places where your company has nothing worthwhile to say or sell. Being on the Web may very well reveal that your products and services offer no value outside your domestic markets because your company, its organizational structure, and its products are profoundly local. Success on the Web demands that you have worked to globalize your company, its products, and its market. This book is dedicated to getting you to a superior level of globalization, making it possible to market your products worldwide. Most executives spend their days trying to increase revenue and improve customer satisfaction. This book addresses these issues from an international and domestic ethnic marketing perspective, dealing with the market entry, organizational, and technical issues that form the foundation of an international marketing strategy.

Becoming a Business without Borders

This book introduces the best practices of global leaders; it is about the globalization that you do not hear about when the evening news follows protesters in Seattle, Prague, and Genoa. I will not echo the op-ed page of major newspapers and rant about the homogenization of world culture or other things attributed to the global economy; rather, I will investigate the potential ways in which the Web can dramatically affect your business on a global scale. I will investigate the ways in which your company can lead with the Web to create a great experience for international customers, business partners, and employees. But even the best online strategy must touch every part of the company; a globally aware Web site backed by an isolationist business will fail.

Since I first wrote about the borderless world of the Internet while a principal analyst at Forrester Research,[1] I have consulted with companies as an independent strategist, as the representative of a software company, and as an executive advisor to industry organizations. My global inquiries have taken me through many conversations, interviews, and planning sessions with international business aspirants.

- Each discussion started with a fervent commitment to doing some kind of business internationally over the Web, whether it was simply providing information, selling goods or services, or simplifying customer support.
- Each interaction proceeded through a thicket of product, organizational, regulatory, and technical challenges created by doing business first on the Web, then on the global Web operating in other languages, with foreign currencies, and under the laws and regulations imposed by other governments and commercial systems.
- Every consultation ultimately involved non-Web units of the company as we dissected corporate budgets, marketing plans, transaction processing systems, and all of the other operational underpinnings of a modern business. Successful firms viewed the Internet as an integral component of their communication and commerce mix.

There are cases in which companies I consulted for decided not to go global, figuring in most cases that they were not ready to make the enduring organizational and budgetary commitments to new markets. Lacking a steadfast promise to an international agenda, their caution made sense to me in a few of the cases. However, in this book, I focus on the companies that chose to move ahead, recognizing that without international growth, they were failing in their duty to their shareholders—that is, to create more value.

Marketing and Selling on the Eighth Continent

Throughout this book, I highlight the discipline and best practices of these market leaders in setting up and supporting their very visible international Web sites and underlying systems. So that you can learn from their experiences and from that of less successful companies, I also underscore the *worst practices* of globalization.

In the sections that follow, I present two case studies—Travelocity and Eastman Chemical—and the process and practices that allowed them to address the needs of the Eighth Continent. These two companies represent archetypes of corporate efforts to address consumer (Travelocity) and business users (Eastman) on the global Internet. I also outline the domestic marketing opportunities created by global immigration. In all three cases—and in numerous examples of other companies in the rest of the book—you will see how companies have unleashed the global giant within themselves to become businesses without borders.

<u>Selling Travel Dreams to Consumers Worldwide</u>   Travelocity brokers travel and leisure products that, once they are past their use-by date, no longer have any value. Industry wags characterize this business of selling hotel beds and airplane seats as "selling ice cubes before they melt." The owners of the Sabre customer reservation system (CRS) established travelocity.com in 1996 based on the idea that consumers would want to make their own travel arrangements—and that here would be enormous, direct demand to its supply of services. However, Sabre knew that while its CRS offered large inventory of travel products, there was no way that consumers would use its decades-old green-screen approach to booking travel. So Sabre undertook the challenge of creating a new consumer-friendly channel to complement its ability to service 50,000 travel agencies around the world.

From Travelocity's first day of operation, travelers could book seats from an inventory representing 95 percent of the world's airline seats, reserve rooms in more than 47,000 hotels worldwide, and rent cars at any one of 50 rental agencies—that is, of course, assuming that they could speak English and pay in U.S. dollars.

Compared to its online travel competitors such as the U.S.-based Expedia and the United Kingdom's LastMinute, Travelocity boasts the highest rate of converting lookers to buyers. However, this U.S. centricity became an issue when analysts found that 20 percent of the site's looker traffic came from outside the United States—and conversion rates among those travelers were considerably lower than the average of U.S. travelers. Travelocity's planners found these underserved "foreign" visitors very attractive, as travelers in some European markets exhibit an enthusiasm about travel far beyond that of the average American tourist. For example, Germans and Scandinavians travel more per capita than do Americans. These Europeans have more days off and tend to vacation away from home more than their fellow travelers from the United States do.

Determined to improve Travelocity's ability to sell to the well-heeled non-American traveler, CEO Terry Jones undertook a three-step initiative to create a powerful Web experience tailored to potential travelers in specific nations:

1. First, Travelocity let English-speaking lookers pay in their own currencies, a great relief to anglophone Canadians, other denizens of the

British Commonwealth, and bilingual buyers in other countries who no longer had to deal with surprises due to currency conversion.

2. Next, it launched U.K. and Canadian sites, taking advantage of the language commonality and its ability to handle foreign currencies. It partnered with AOL and Yahoo!, both popular in Canada, to increase traffic and patronage north of its border.

3. Then the company scouted out the best non-English markets for travelers—Germany now, Japan and the U.S. Hispanic market as possible future targets—and sought to offer the full Travelocity experience wherever it did business. That meant supporting language, culture, travel purchase behavior, and travel preferences for German travelers; for example, many Germans still do not use credit cards and will not do business unless they can use a bank debit. As American travel sites look to the Japanese market, they will have to tweak their business models. In Asia, for example, 85 percent of the fares are negotiated as "merchant fares" and are hard to find in the dominant customer reservation systems such as Sabre, Amadeus, and Galileo. Similarly, U.S. Hispanics looking to visit relatives back home will zero in on destinations that differ from those of the average vacationer or business traveler.

The opportunities of the Eighth Continent extend beyond consumers to the world of business, where large manufacturers and suppliers sell to other companies.

Producing Plastics for the Whole Earth

Eastman Chemical Company supplies manufacturers around the world with the chemicals, plastics, and fibers used to produce many things that we cannot live without. Spun off from photography giant Eastman Kodak in 1994, Eastman's worldwide revenue in 2000 was US$5.3 billion. The company employs 16,500 people in sales offices and manufacturing plants in over 30 countries.

Eastman started its globalization journey in traditional pre-Web fashion by investing heavily in international operations on the ground. In the early 1980s it established its first sales and marketing presence outside the United States. In the late 1980s Eastman continued its march abroad by establishing manufacturing presence in its key markets. For example, to satisfy international demand for one of its core products, the polyethylene terephthalate (PET) used in making plastic beverage bottles, the company built manufacturing plants in Europe and Latin America, and to support customer needs in those markets, Eastman created physical call centers in many of its individual countries and regions.

Eastman first turned to the Web to support its customers in the United States. It went live with its first Web site in 1995, and in 1999 the company aggressively began to develop its e-commerce capabilities for both customers and suppliers. By 2000, buyers of its chemicals and plastics around the world could get the information they needed about Eastman's products, markets, and applications. Customers could also place orders directly through the Web and track the status of those orders through fulfillment. To support its online commerce plans, the company built an online customer center.

But Eastman's customers around the world could buy the company's products online only if they were willing and able to interact in English. This was a problem: In the second half of the nineties Eastman's Web developers watched international Web traffic grow to about 50 percent of overall visits to eastman.com. They also watched non-U.S. foreign competitors such as BASF, Bayer, and Royal Dutch Shell develop multilingual sites, as well as American competitors such as Mobil offer local-language content and applications to attract business from the Eighth Continent. With its rivals raising the competitive bar outside their home markets through in-language support, in early 2000 Eastman stepped up to the challenge by tuning its online presence to the needs of its international markets.

- First, the company provided critical information, such as its "Responsible Care" doctrine for manufacturing and safe handling, in the languages of its international markets. The company's goal was to make it easier for its customers to get support, regardless of local language, geography, or business practice, while shifting the interaction from expensive human call centers to the much cheaper Web.
- Then the company complemented its customer-facing initiative by providing increased multilingual capabilities for trading partners in its worldwide supply chain. Eastman teamed up with Global Logistics Technologies, Inc., to create ShipChem, a firm that offers digital global logistics services to the chemical industry. Eastman continues to invest internally and in other firms to improve and expedite the flow of goods and information through its supply chain.
- All the while, Eastman uses the Web to increase international awareness of its products and brands. As a company strategist observed, "You can't generate sales from potential customers who have never heard of Eastman Chemical or don't understand what we have to offer. You have to do business in the language of your markets."

<u>Winning Underserved Customers within National Borders</u>   As U.S. companies learned with the release of the 2000 census results, you need not leave your home market to find customers who do not speak your language or whose buying behavior differs from that of your prototypical consumer. This multiculturalism is the human evidence of globalization: As the global economy accelerates the flow of information, investment, and industry across international borders, people with different languages and cultural points of view follow the opportunities.

So this migration means that global markets today are coming to domestic companies. With the ease of migration within regional blocs such as the European Union (EU) and the North American Free Trade Agreement (NAFTA), such linguistically separate but domestic communities will offer growing appeal to marketers looking for new revenue and more share. Marketers around the world will find similar online opportunities in their own backyards.

- Some Canadian firms, especially those in Quebec, have mastered the art of selling on different domestic fronts successfully by offering bilingual sites to serve the needs of the francophone community. However, a surprising number of firms in Quebec ignore this opportunity by maintaining English-only sites. On another front, many Canadian firms look to opportunities in the one-million-strong Chinese community living in Ontario and British Columbia.
- In Germany, companies such as Deutsche Telekom experiment with targeted marketing programs to expatriate Russians and the two million residents of Turkish origin. As in Quebec, though, most German firms ignore this opportunity.
- Brazil's kaleidoscope of nationalities can be seen in its capital of São Paulo. The megacity reportedly has 10,000 Italian restaurants to serve one of the world's largest populations of Italian-surnamed individuals, while a big Japanese population strives for visibility. The country's official language is its own dialect of Portuguese, complemented by significant use of Spanish, English, and French.
- In Hong Kong, both Chinese and English serve as the region's official languages. In Singapore, the population includes Chinese, Malay, Tamil, and English speakers, all active participants in the country's economy. Limiting a business to Chinese in either of these regions means losing access to a significant chunk of the national economies.
- On the Indian subcontinent, English is used for official and commercial purposes, but 30 percent of Indians prefer to use Hindi in their

everyday communication, and Hindustani is widely spoken across northern India. Overall, India boasts two dozen languages with a million or more speakers.

The best-documented multicultural opportunities can be found in the States. In early 2001 the U.S. Census Bureau published some fascinating details about changing American demographics. Hispanics, estimated at 35.3 million, have become the country's fastest growing ethnic community, representing 12.6 percent of the country's total population. This group now comprises the world's fifth-largest group of Spanish speakers, after Mexico, Spain, Colombia, and Argentina.

- These American Hispanics are more affluent than most of their Spanish-speaking peers; in addition, unlike their Hispanic brethren outside the States, almost half work and play regularly on the Internet.[2] Researchers suggest that many crave more Spanish-language interactions on the Web.[3]
- With a 1999 average household income of US$30,735, they trail only Spain in economic prosperity. In 2000 Hispanic consumers in the States spent over US$420 billion, a number that grew to US$452 billion in 2001.[4]

Some of the best-known consumer brands in American business—Procter & Gamble, Sears, State Farm Insurance, Chase, and Capital One—have zeroed in on this market opportunity. Even before the 2000 Census results alerted mainstream businesses to the domestic U.S. Hispanic market, these companies had already begun interacting with their customers en español. They created culturally tuned Web sites that appeal to Spanish speakers, at the same time that they reinforced branding programs. For example, Procter & Gamble promotes its Head & Shoulders brand to the U.S. Hispanic market through an online game featuring the Capitán Cool, the hero of its Spanish-language Mission Refresh game (see Figure I.1).

These multicultural pioneers quickly realized that translating their sites into Spanish was only the first step in appealing to Hispanic buyers. For example, one large catalog retailer retained much of the look and feel of its original site but introduced a Spanish-speaking spokesperson to make buyers feel more comfortable. These companies also understood that they must tailor their products and service offerings to the Latino buyer. Besides featuring products that were of special interest to this community, for example, the cataloger's Spanish site also dropped some big sellers—such

Figure I.1 The Web Can Reinforce Offline Branding Efforts
Source: Copyright © Procter & Gamble

as the English-language King James Bible—that would not interest Latino buyers.

Companies Worldwide Push Aside Borders

Eastman, Travelocity, and the other companies profiled in this book have been early movers whose successes and failures in the global economy hold important lessons for all marketers. Like countless other companies, they sell goods and services to consumers and business buyers, participating in complex supply and demand chains that crisscross the globe. What makes them different from many companies is that they saw growing demand or potential for their products outside their home countries or inside an ethnic community that they previously ignored. They realized that they could use the Internet to supplement existing sales channels with more prepurchase information or to make life after the sale better through in-country support. Then, they did something: They invested what it took to support those markets via the Web.

These companies benefit from the Internet-enabled ability to project themselves and their messages into new markets around the clock and around the world, something that required deliberate planning and multi-year development projects in the pre-Internet business world. Before the Web, only larger companies such as Embraer, McDonald's, Sony, and Volkswagen had enough resources to set up the requisite infrastructure to serve a global community. The Web has removed that requirement of mas-sive scale and resources to enter international markets. Now companies both large and small have learned that their firms are visible to the whole world, just by virtue of merely having a Web site.

How Internet Technology Has Created a New Continent without Borders

This Eighth Continent of e-business and online commerce ex-ists as an overlay on the physical world of brick and mortar, characterized by its reliance and general agreement on a common set of technology rules called Internet Protocol (IP). Without it, the Internet is just a bunch of wires. IP is the electric current that runs the Internet—the necessary ingredient for powering Internet communication, commerce, and collabo-ration around the globe. All of the companies that I have interviewed use IP to manage their internal systems, reach into new markets, or provision their supply and demand chains.

Unlike the unrealized projections about dot.com bonanzas, this Internet electricity has demonstrable benefits that most financial analysts and pun-dits have failed to quantify. Just 10 years ago, getting two companies to trans-fer data between their disparate systems could take half a year and cost millions of dollars, and the notion of global supply chains was unthinkable. Today, because of the widespread implementation of IP and its supporting infrastructure of Web standards by both providers and buyers of hardware and software, a company can plug its external Web site into its internal ful-fillment systems. Because of IP, a teenager in Germany can look at an easy-to-use interface at landsend.com, click once, and have a pair of jeans show up in three days. IP makes it possible for two companies that decide to partner for a project to snap their corresponding applications together quickly. (While not at all a simple task, it is being done every day.)

It is this IP-defined Eighth Continent that has let Eastman and Trave-locity extend their reach around the planet. At least for now, the Eighth Continent imposes fewer restrictions than do the Earth's seven border-girdled continents. In fact, the only real borders on the Eighth Continent are mental ones that keep you from unleashing the global powerhouse in-side your company. Now that you can project your products and services anywhere in the world via this ready-made channel, the next step is to fig-ure out how to appeal to the hundreds of millions of Web-based customers, tempering your plans according to the languages, different buying behav-iors, business practices, and legal restrictions that exist in each customer's nation of origin.

<u>What Should Your Next Step Be?</u>   You can choose to do business as usual—and leave your international prospects to fend for themselves, as many firms have chosen to do. Or you can choose to tune your corporate value propositions to an audience outside your traditional comfort zone of domestic marketing. For most businesses, staying at home would be a mistake. By year-end 2002, Internet-enabled global business will become a must-have for large companies and a critical path to growth for smaller firms anxious to increase their revenue and project their brand around the world (see Figure I.2). The challenge will be to pick the right markets to enter.

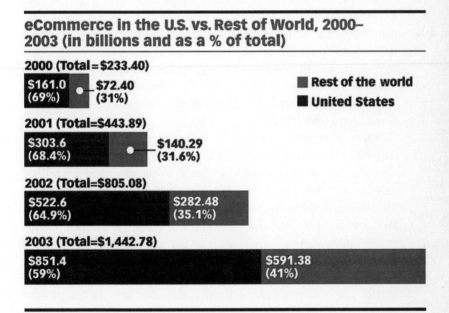

eCommerce in the U.S. vs. Rest of World, 2000–2003 (in billions and as a % of total)

2000 (Total = $233.40)

$161.0 (69%) — $72.40 (31%)

■ Rest of the world
■ United States

2001 (Total=$443.89)

$303.6 (68.4%) — $140.29 (31.6%)

2002 (Total=$805.08)

$522.6 (64.9%) $282.48 (35.1%)

2003 (Total=$1,442.78)

$851.4 (59%) $591.38 (41%)

Figure I.2 Web Commerce Becomes Less Dependent on American Sales
Source: eMarketer, 2000.

Note: Long the dominant player in Internet-based commercial transactions, the United States will comprise a smaller percentage of a much bigger number by 2003.

Navigating This Book

In writing *Business without Borders,* I followed the same journey made by all of the companies that have gone global. Their expeditions began with a realization of the opportunity that was heightened by self-education. They studied the market potential or the benefits of an improved supply chain, and then these globalists educated and "sold" their colleagues, bosses, and directors on the importance globalization. They entered fairly lengthy and involved periods of planning around organizational impact, implementation, and measurement. I, too, have gone through these processes with my consulting clients, and in my experience, the big issues include the following:

- *Education.* For years, many people accepted the notion that being on the Web meant that you were instantly global; what most failed to recognize was the importance of acting global and meeting the needs of local markets. In Chapter 1 I outline the basics of being a global company online and lay out the importance of localizing your value proposition to market needs and detailing successes and failures. In Chapter 2 I discuss the benefits that companies expect to derive from international business, providing the core of a business case for international expansion that you might make to your budget committee or board of directors.
- *Planning.* Few people know where or how to start—after all, "global" is a pretty big topic, and many people are overwhelmed by the prospect. To make the problem more tractable, I have condensed the critical aspects of planning a global journey. In Chapter 3 I give an outline of the debates that you will have on how best to organize for the global Web, on the need for a chief globalization officer to set a course for the company, and on the service level agreements that will underpin successful efforts. In Chapter 4 I detail a tried and true approach to determine which countries are likely to enter on the Web, thus allowing you to target the most appropriate markets. In Chapter 5 I present studies of the legal implications of doing business in other markets, complementing Chapter 4 with detailed information about the exigencies of transnational commerce.
- *Implementation.* The ultimate goal of implementation is to evolve from a company that services only its domestic market in the domi-

nant language to one that can offer a more compelling experience for other countries. I use Chapter 6 to lay out the technical grunt work, describing how your developers and technology partners must technically enable support for foreign character sets, currencies, date formats, and other minutiae that can quickly undermine your best efforts to act global. I continue this discussion in Chapter 7, where I focus on the tough translation and market localization issues that have arisen with global commerce.

- *Organization.* Successful globalization requires the guidance of a strong leader complemented by internal and external resources. I describe an organizational structure in Chapter 8 for optimizing the use of corporate, regional, and local staff. In the next chapter I define the need for external specialists, reviewing the market landscape for translation and localization firms. The assistance of these outside firms has proven essential for the companies that I have interviewed, as I will explain.

- *Measurement.* In this age of too many projects and not enough funding, few globalization efforts would make it past their first year without some structured analysis of the return on investment (ROI). In Chapter 10 I discuss the ways that companies have measured their ROI. The book concludes with the three imperatives that define success: (1) the *rigor* of planning, design, implementation, and deployment for entering international markets; (2) the *reliability* of organization, execution, process, management, maintenance, and enhancements in successfully completing; and (3) measuring the *return on investment* that demonstrates that their efforts were worthwhile.

Finally, one of the themes that you will find throughout the book is that the Internet is a volatile environment that reflects the dynamism of global business. Companies morph and content changes hourly in this vibrant online world. That reality poses a challenge for hardcopy books, so you are sure to find that some companies, Web sites, and other information are no longer accurate. With that reality in mind, I have set up www.businesswithoutborders.info as a place to keep the content of this book as current as circumstances allow.

Meet Mira, Our Globalization Heroine

Each chapter begins and ends with an italicized passage describing the thought processes and actions of a woman named Mira Vozreniya, the chief marketing officer of a U.S.-based company. Mira is a composite character whom I have created to characterize the approach that many of my interviewees and correspondents have taken to international marketing and business.

SHOULD YOU DO EVERYTHING IN THIS BOOK?

This book suggests a lot of things to do before going global, as well as how to do it right and how to demonstrate long-term commitment. The book is meant to provide guidance to the things that you need to think about in marketing to international markets. My goal is to help you consider what you will need, the scope of the endeavor, and the work that it will require, as opposed to creating an absolute, one-size-fits-all plan.

1

Discovering the Eighth Continent

Mira Vozreniya is the chief marketing officer of a U.S.-based company called Acme Widgets Inc. Acme has about 2,200 employees, large sales offices in six European countries, and annual revenues of US$600 million. A longtime manufacturer of backyard lifestyle enhancement products, Acme launched a rudimentary Web brochureware site way back in 1996. Since then, it has added customer support and basic online commerce to the mix. After two years, Acme started personalizing what it showed to registered visitors and created MyAcme for frequent guests. The company is currently exploring integrating its Web site with its customer relationship management (CRM) to draw together information from all the company's sales channels. In the States, the Internet is a strategic channel of commerce and communications that is on its way to full integration with more traditional means of marketing and selling such as stores and distributors.

Meanwhile, Acme's Web developers at its four European subsidiaries have been busy building their own sites for prospects and customers in their home markets. They started their projects later than did Acme's U.S. team, so they're not as far along. While some country units have dedicated Web teams, Acme's online efforts in smaller markets are usually a part-time exercise. Acme's European businesses are anxious to take advantage of what their U.S. colleagues have already learned and developed—assuming that it meets their market needs and that they can squeeze it into their budgets. In some cases, the country units have put up Web sites without any corporate authorization or control and with little attention to managing Acme's brand or to conveying its corporate message.

What the Budding Globalist Faces

This chapter covers the big issues that business globalization advocates like Mira will face, including the following:

- *Terminology.* Globalization means bad things to one camp and good things to another. Make sure that you and your audience are talking about the same thing. To that end, this chapter begins with a discussion of this broad term.
- *Opportunity.* The Eighth Continent represents enormous market potential, both inside and outside companies. No business globalization project will go anywhere without quantifying that advantages to global commerce.
- *Market realities.* Once you realize that there's gold in those global hills, you have to set priorities. Successful international forays mean adapting your message, product, and marketing to the needs of local markets. Given the relative size of economies and the uptake of the Internet, you will soon realize that some countries just do not matter, while others matter a lot. You will also see that many companies have done your homework for you, establishing some precedents that you would do best to emulate and others that you would do well to avoid.
- *Not just the Web.* The consumer-facing Web is the most externally visible part of your company's Internet investment, but it might not be the most important part. Depending on what you are trying to accomplish, supply chain or employee-focused ventures might make more sense. This chapter introduces these other forms of the Net, all of which support effective marketing worldwide. In the next chapter I extend this discussion to the different business drivers behind *Web* (the consumer-facing Internet), *Intranet* (as used inside companies, for employees), and *Extranet* (online integration with business partners, suppliers, and other businesses).

"Globalization": Just What Does that Mean?

Over six billion people live in over 200 countries spanning 24 time zones. These people use hundreds of currencies to conduct business in thousands of different languages and dialects. Their business practices are all over the map, ranging from simple barter to cash to electronic payment to sophisticated arbitrage.

But when you look a bit harder at the concentration of trade in a few economic superpowers such as the United States, the European Union, and Japan, you soon realize that of these, only a few currencies and languages really matter to commerce on the Internet. Whereas in the nineteenth century, the Germans held that language and culture should accompany trade and armies on their march around the globe, in the second half of the twentieth century, modern telecommunications and jet travel have enabled both businessmen and armies to march into new markets and territories with far less trouble. More than anything, the Internet allows companies and countries instantaneously to project their language, culture, and economic might anywhere on the planet. There's no Berlin wall or Ministry of Trade to keep out inconvenient ideas or different economic models; therefore, governments and citizens of less powerful nations worry about their loss of cultural and economic identity.

Bad Globalization Squashes Cultures

International trade and communications have led us down the path to *globalism* or *globalization.* This phenomenon causes large corporations to straddle political borders in their worldwide conduct of production and distribution. Globalization affects whole economies and every individual—and enflames passions everywhere. For example, antiglobalization activists point to shopkeepers in Mexico and Russia who prefer the dollar to their own currencies, and they decry how American English has become the lingua franca of world culture and trade whether it happens on the ground, on television, or on the World Wide Web. Most companies doing business on the Web only reinforce this stereotype as they support trade if—and only if—the customer is willing to speak English, pay U.S. dollars, and accept delivery from Federal Express.

Good Globalization Can Reinforce Cultural and Commercial Practices

Although the United States and its big trading partners dominate the world economy and antiglobalization cadres march against the International Monetary Fund, the World Trade Organization, and McDonald's, the demographics of the Internet economy change daily. The Web draws business users and consumers for whom English is not a preferred language or who do not carry the "right" kind of credit cards. Recognizing a new potential for international commerce, multinational U.S. firms from General Electric to Lands' End have already employed the Web to sell their goods and services in the language, currency, and business practices of their target markets in Europe and Asia.

This Web globalization goes both ways: BMW in Germany and Embraer in Brazil operate compelling English-language Web sites to sell their high-value manufactured goods to buyers in the United States. Countless other companies use the Web to aggregate worldwide demand into a much larger audience for their offerings. Some companies willing to make an investment in translating their site need not even look outside their borders for new markets. Large ethnic populations inside the United States, Germany, and Brazil provide an opportunity to increase domestic revenue share while translated service information can cut the cost of doing business in a multicultural society.

A note on the net: Although I focus on globalization that is tied to the Web, that's only the tip of the iceberg. International activity at your company's Internet site happens to be the most visible manifestation of worldwide interest if not demand, but satisfying that demand will involve every corner of your company. For some firms, such as General Electric and Renault, the Internet is already an active channel of global communication and commerce—and these companies are actively integrating the Web with other corporate media and distribution. Other companies are just starting the journey. In both cases, globalization is a fundamental business issue that will reach far deeper into your company than just your customer-facing Internet marketing efforts. It will touch other distribution channels, integrate with your supply chain, and be plugged into your customer service systems, letting everyone in your company know that you're now a global player.

The Opportunity: International Markets Outstrip the United States

If your firm is like most companies, the Internet has been a largely domestic matter, servicing the information and transaction needs of your home market. The next generation of the Internet promises to be a much more cosmopolitan affair with increased participation by Asians, Europeans, and Latin Americans, all of whom will be transacting in their own languages with their own currencies.

Since the birth of the Web, the benchmark for business and consumer connectivity has been the United States, where over 60 percent of its 285 million inhabitants are already online.[1] As recently as 1998, Americans accounted for 56 percent of the Web's users, but by 2001 they represented only about 35 percent—and sinking.[2] However, by 2004, non-U.S. usage will swell to 70 percent,[3] reflecting the booming 50-percent Internet user growth rates in Latin America and in the 30-percent growth rate in Asia Pacific. In contrast, the growth rate in North America is 14 percent (see Figure 1.1).[4]

Today, 90 percent of Web revenue derives from the English-speaking United States, United Kingdom, and Nordic countries, and most of that comes from the States.[5] While business-to-business revenue numbers for this Internet economy range all over the map, most analysts predict that the pendulum will swing mightily by 2003, with 40 percent of Internet-derived business revenue coming from outside the States, if not from outside the North Atlantic Anglo zone (see Figure 1.2).[6] That increase corresponds to the rapid uptake of Internet technologies as the foundation of many companies' internal systems, connections to their trading partners and supply networks, and the interface to the world in general.

To get a sense of why these numbers are so interesting to American companies, take a look at what is driving Lands' End, the upscale U.S.-based retailer of casual and sports clothing, into global markets. Analysts estimated that the total catalog apparel market in the States for 2001 was

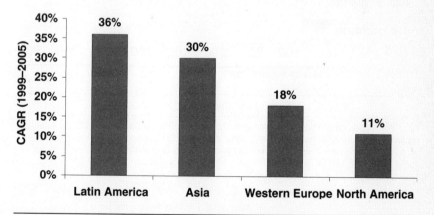

Figure 1.1 Net Growth Outside North America

Note: The compound annual growth rate (CAGR) in Web usage will exceed the increase in gross domestic product (GDP) around the world. The Intensification of Web usage in Latin America and Asia will outpace North American growth.

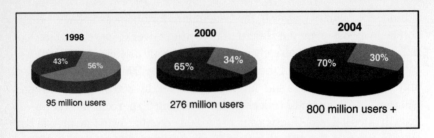

Global B2C E-Commerce Revenue Regional Breakdown, 2000 and 2005

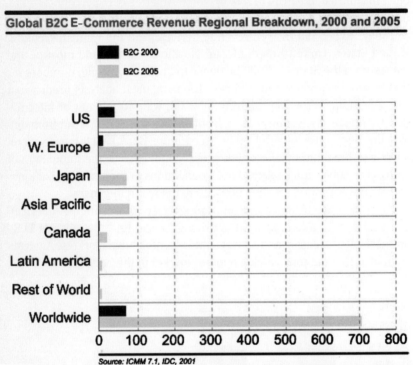

Source: ICMM 7.1, IDC, 2001

Figure 1.2 Internet Population and Revenue Growth

Note: The total world population is growing yearly, and growth in regions outside of North America is causing U.S. users to comprise a smaller percentage of this much bigger pie. Meanwhile, revenue growth in both the consumer and business sectors continues to grow despite the slowdown that began in 2000.

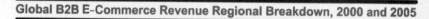

Global B2B E-Commerce Revenue Regional Breakdown, 2000 and 2005

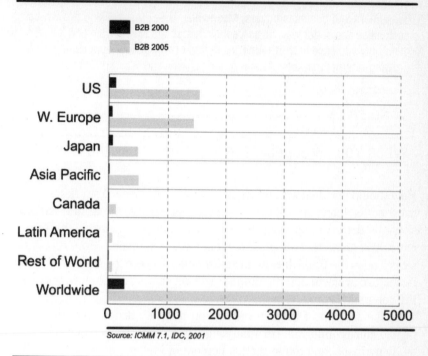

Figure 1.2 *continued*

US$16 billion. The company's top three international markets (the United Kingdom, Germany, and Japan) accounted for another US$20 billion in catalog sales. Furthermore, Lands' End conducted nearly 20 percent of its U.S. business over the Internet in 2001, and more than 25 percent of those online buyers were new customers. On top of that, the online customer is more profitable to Lands' End than its traditional catalog buyer. The company's planners clearly smell profitable new revenue in key markets outside the States.

The Net. Whether online or offline, the United States will remain the dominant economic superpower well into the twenty-first century, but other regions are coming on strong. About 35 percent of all products sold in the U.S. come from outside the country, up from 20 percent in 1990.[7] Thirty percent of the Net population is American, and these customers execute 60 percent of the revenue-producing activity on the Web; therefore, companies in Europe, Asia, and Latin America will continue to target that rich online market with sites that appeal to consumers and business buyers. Meanwhile, U.S. firms seeking growth opportunities and better ways to serve their customers will look beyond their English-only audience in North America to find rich targets of opportunity in the growing Internet markets of Latin America, Asia, and Western Europe.

When Your Prospects Are in Rome, Do as the Romans

How should you deal with this more cosmopolitan Web? Your first step toward better international efforts—more local language at international sites—is already happening. A study of a billion documents on the Web in early 2000 found that about 87 percent were in English.[8] More recent research pegs the English content at just under 70 percent, and consultancy Accenture projects that the number will fall sharply as Chinese becomes the dominant language on the Web.[9]

As the amount of English content on the Web drops, the number of people more comfortable in other languages increases (see Figure 1.3). A study by Ipsos-Reid found that 90 percent of Internet users in nonanglophone countries prefer their own languages over English.[10]

Attracting Customers with Translated, Localized Sites and Support
If you are like most companies, you will translate the marketing part of your sites or your online product catalog. Why? So that customers will at least know what you are trying to sell them. As early as 1998, companies were reporting that buyers tend to spend twice as much time at a site if the language is their own.[11] In-language sites mean that the potential buyer can drill down deeper into the site, gathering more information about your product offerings from posted collateral, product reviews, and testimonials.

The same market studies showed that these better-informed business buyers are three to four times more likely to buy if they are addressed in their own language. How did they come to these conclusions? Some early adopters knew that they would have to demonstrate the return on their translation investment, so some instrumented their sites with data collection software to compare the buying behaviors of users with and without translated text. Others conducted primary research with focus groups.

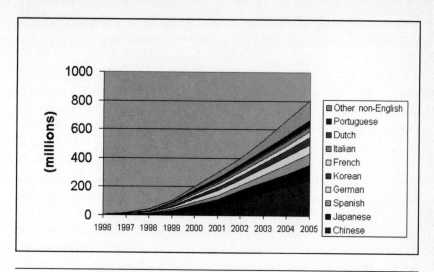

Figure 1.3 English Takes a Second Seat to Other Languages
Source: Global Reach at http://glreach.com/globstats/evol.html.

Note: English, still the dominant language on the Web, will be a less effective means of communication as the percentage of non-English-speaking users increases.

Not surprisingly, both approaches led to the conclusion that an interaction in our native language feels better, safer, and more controllable than does a transaction in even a second language in which we feel comfortable. You have a far better chance of generating leads, engendering trust, and creating buyers if you adapt your value proposition to the ways of thinking and the market realities of your international prospects.

Finally, these studies have shown that business customers addressed in their own language cost less to support. The Japan-based call center expert Prestige International measures the lower cost in terms of shorter call duration and fewer callbacks to customer service representatives. Then, if the customer can be redirected to a frequently asked questions (FAQ) page or an online answering utility such as AskJeeves, the cost drops dramatically. Firms using this software—such as DaimlerChrysler, Ford, and Nestlé—have experienced cost-per-call decreases of 90 percent or more.

Even so, many U.S. technology companies insist that their buyers quite comfortably deal with English; in fact, 66 percent of them do not bother to offer content in any other language.[12] Even those companies that offer other languages focus on marketing only, with no customer support. For example, GE Power found that the highly skilled, U.S.-educated managers of their megawatt generators lost their proficiency in English when faced with major system failures, thus driving up support costs when English-language support online could not answer their questions.

Losing Customers by Not Offering Them a Localized Experience

The corollary to getting more international business is losing business at untranslated sites. Faced with unclear choices or instructions, prospective buyers might just click on to another site that better meets their linguistic needs. Nearly half of the international visitors at anglophone U.S. business sites abandon their transactions due to language, currency, or business issues.[13] Think about it for a second: You're reading this book in English, the language that dominates international trade and the Web. But look at Figure 1.4 and put yourself on the other side of this digital divide. Most English speakers would not know what to make of Toyota's car rental site. Not only is the text unintelligible to anyone who doesn't speak Japanese, but also the design ethic falls outside the north Atlantic model for colors,

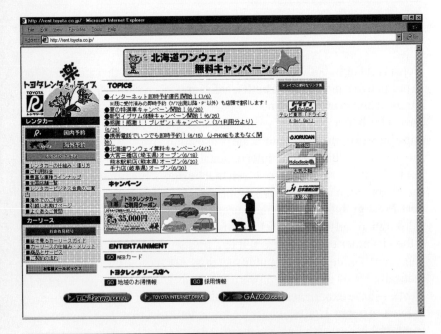

Figure 1.4 Toyota Car Rental Site

Note: Toyota's home-market car rental site put me on the other side of the language divide, since I cannot read Japanese and I am unaccustomed to this type of layout. If this page were all the information that Toyota offered to world markets, it would not be the third-largest auto manufacturer in the world.

images, and layout. If Toyota offered only this site as a way to rent a car, it would not be one of the world's largest auto manufacturers. The translation and localization question ultimately comes down to whether what you offer customers will make sense to their local eyes.

Toyota actually has done a good job in many markets, demonstrating a rare sensitivity to market detail—such as fine-tuning its Dutch Web content for the Belgian Flemish market. Most companies use Dutch when dealing with Belgian Flemish speakers. Dutch (called *Nederlands* in Dutch) and Flemish (*Vlaams*) are essentially the same language, varying in pronunciation (as distinct as American vs. British English), vocabulary (Dutch coins many neologisms, while Flemish is more conservative), and formality (the Belgians are more formal). Both Toyota on the Web and Hewlett Packard with computer manuals in both languages exhibit a strong sensitivity—and willingness to invest—to even these minute market differences for the nearly 16 million Dutch citizens and almost six million Flemish speakers in Belgium.

The Language of Globalization

Not surprisingly, business globalization specialists have developed their own terms and shorthand to describe what they do.

Translation refers to the process of taking information in one language and conveying the same details and thoughts in another language. Most translation is performed by humans, although an increasing number of companies use computers to translate documents and Web sites that have a limited scope and vocabulary, such as those for network switches or telephone equipment. Good human translation is often viewed as an art as much as a discipline, while computer-aided machine translation tends to be much more utilitarian with a focus on conveying merely the gist.

Localization describes a more ambitious task that tailors translated words and transactions to local needs. For example, a German company selling into the States will mark prices in dollars, replace DHL with FedEx as the shipper, and translate privacy statements into English. Localization also must take into consideration technical issues as well, such as knowing the average connection speed of the target audience you are seeking so that the Web production team designs appropriately, keeping load times down to acceptable levels.

Internationalization refers to the behind-the-scenes technical work done to enable translation and localization. This typically involves making sure that a site can support the alphabet of a target market, a problem frequently encountered by U.S.-developed software that cannot handle Japanese characters or even diacritical marks for European languages. Other internationalization tasks involve adapting systems so that instructions, error messages, currency, and measurements can be expressed differently for local markets.

Personalization relates to the online practice of mass customization and the ideal of one-to-one marketing, both enabled by the Web's ability to capture information about visitors and react with appropriately tailored content and data. When applied to ethnic and international markets, this is *globalization,* the term that practitioners use to describe their ability to appeal to buyers around the world.

<u>Companies Worldwide Are Committing to Local Markets</u>   Your competitors have already started to benefit from their commitment to make interacting and transacting easier for their international business customers. U.S. companies expect to serve up to twice as many international Web sites by 2004 as they did in 2000,[14] and many European firms already market directly to American and British buyers. For example, Renault lets British, French, and German consumers browse all of its vehicles and check on availability in real time. Behind the scenes, the Europewide Renault.net network keeps dealers in constant contact with Renault, streamlining communications and giving them insight into customer needs by market as well as the ability to order and track production. By allowing prospective buyers to select and configure their cars in their own language before talking to a salesman, Renault hopes to prompt its customers to make a quick purchase decision, mimicking Eastman's ability to:

- *Eliminate costly human customer service representatives.* For example, knowing that its plastics buyers ask the same question about the molding process for one of the materials it sells in bulk, Eastman has posted a canned response in the form of an FAQ (frequently asked question) in the language of each market it serves.
- *Educate customers online.* By creating FAQs for other common questions and adding more product and safety information in local languages, Eastman can focus its customer service on calls that raise the amount of a purchase.

The same customer service benefits and upside apply in home markets. Discovering that the household income of its Chinese-American customers was more than 50 percent higher than that of the average American, Schwab decided to create a site for consumers in the United States who feel more comfortable transacting in Chinese. Because these customers trade two to three times as much as other investors, customers at Schwab's Chinese-language site are much more profitable than are those at its anglophone site. With 50 million Chinese people living outside China and controlling most of the economic activity in many Southeast Asian countries such as Indonesia, Singapore, and, increasingly, in Canada and the United States, catering to the Sinitic economic community in diaspora could be great business for many companies.

> *The Net:* Ask yourself: would you sign a document without being able to read it? As your Web presence reaches into new markets, your prospects and customers will expect much more localized experiences that they can understand. Business without borders does not mean that local needs will disappear. In fact, they increase because you must serve international markets with the right local flavor. For many people, globalization equates to Americanization. That's too narrow a definition—globalization means good business, wherever you happen to want to sell.

Global Business Does Not Mean Every Country

To paraphrase an old political truism, "All commerce is local." Ideally, a Web site will look and feel like it was built in that market for only that market, whether it was a local company, a foreign business, or a British firm developing an online experience for South Asian inhabitants of the United Kingdom. Because local markets most likely have native players, it is likely that the indigenous sites will be better tuned to the needs of that market than will the foreign ones. To succeed, you will have to be at least as good as the hometown alternative or provide enough value to make that a nonissue. That could be very expensive, especially if you fail to scope the opportunity in a given market against the requirement to offer a quality experience that passes the local smell test.

Many companies have read the analysts' numbers presented earlier in this chapter, have considered their own Web site reports showing the national origins of their visitors, and have decided to use the Web aggressively to do business online in every country. Other less-ambitious firms limited themselves to the 30 countries of the Organisation for Economic

Co-operation and Development (OECD) plus China or the European Union. For example, after a successful showing of its marketplace for flow-control devices at the CeBIT fair in 2000, BigMachines.com vowed to set up shop in every country on the planet. Such hubris is not restricted to new-economy start-ups. Fingerhut, the catalog arm of retailer Federated Department Stores, investigated similar large-scale expansion into international markets.[15] High-tech players such as Dell and Cisco hurried their online presences into dozens of countries.

Both Fingerhut and BigMachines ultimately realized the challenges involved in such an undertaking. Translating hundreds of thousands of words for thousands of Fingerhut products into even a few languages would cost far more than the planners had originally estimated. For example, a large-scale effort to translate a half-million words from French into English could cost US$200,000. Keeping the translation synchronized so that the information remains current and correct can add similar costs depending on how efficient and automated the process is; multiply this amount by the number of languages that need supported, and the costs mushroom. Ultimately, BigMachines settled on a smaller, more manageable cadre of European and Asian markets. Fingerhut took an even more disciplined approach, focusing its online investment to the 35 million Latinos inside the United States on its way to a future global presence.

Through 1999 and 2000 this kind of expansion into every market on the Internet was a common theme of many companies that sought to increase both revenue and share. By 2001 many companies were confused about their next step.

- *Globalization newbies.* Many not-yet-global companies that I speak to are bogged down by their analyses about which market to get into first. They see opportunities, they see costs, and they see the need for a long-term commitment. But like the suitor who fears commitment, they fall into a state where they do nothing but maintain the status quo and continue to worry about losing the race into new markets to more agile competitors.
- *Global cognoscenti.* Companies already involved in international markets online or offline question how they can optimize their existing programs, organization, technology, and sites to meet the needs of their international customers. In precarious financial times, they want to make sure that every dollar, euro, real, or yen that they spend is spent on the right thing.

Where Should You Start? How Should You Continue?

Do not be misled by the numbers, and do not fall for the "go global" mantra. The brutal truth is that when it comes to the Web, there are "have nets" and "have nots." Assuming that the analysts got it right, within a few years the 30 percent of Internet users who are American will be responsible for 60 percent of the Web's revenue. This is great news for anyone targeting the U.S. market—lots of revenue from a relatively homogenous population. However, that rest of the pie is a lot more troublesome. Most globalization boosters point to the 70 percent of the Internet's user and the 40 percent of revenue that they will generate as proof of big opportunities beyond America. What they fail to realize is that hundreds of millions of people live in a variety of countries around the globe, where they speak different languages and engage in commercial activities in ways that are quite different from each other (see Figure 1.5). The challenge for companies looking beyond the rich North American market is to figure out

Population Internet Usage, by Country (in millions)	Dominant Languages	Currency
U.S. 134.4	English, Spanish	U.S. dollar
Japan 33.9	Japanese	Yen
China 22.5	Mandarin, Cantonese	Yuan
Germany 19.9	German	Euro
South Korea 19.0	Korean	Won
U.K. 16.3	English	Pound
Canada 15.4	English, French	Canadian dollar
Italy 12.5	Italian, German	Euro
Brazil 10.4	Portuguese	Real
France 9.0	French	Euro

Figure 1.5 Where in the World Is Your Prospect?
Source: CIA, World Factbook at http://www.cia.gov/cia.publications/factbook/.

Note: The business and consumer users of the Eighth Continent live in geopolitically bounded countries with a dominant language or two as well as a national or regional currency.

which of those international markets comprise enough revenue to make the localization efforts worthwhile. In most cases, even simple translation will not pay the bills.

Look at your own online traffic logs to find out who has been visiting your home-country site and where they come from. More likely than not, the lion's share of foreign visits to French or German sites will originate in other francophone (e.g., Quebec) or German-speaking (e.g., Austria) countries, respectively. Visitation to American and British sites, though, will probably originate from a wider range of locales.

- *Already there?* If you are already committed to a market on the ground, there are probably several good reasons why you should do a good job online in that country. More speculatively, you should look for countries with the high levels of Internet penetration and usage that translate into a population that is mature enough to buy on the Web (see Figure 1.6). The threshold of usage may relate directly to business buyers and consumers on the Web, your own employees or brick-and-mortar investment in a country, or the nature of your supply chain, consisting of development partners, distributors, and suppliers.

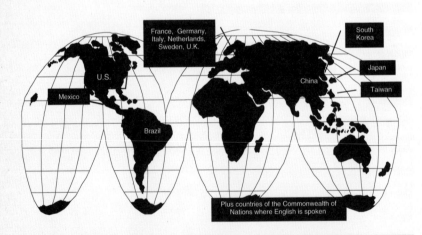

Figure 1.6 Quick Study of Markets That Matter on the Web

Note: In an ideal world, you would support each country on the planet with the language, currency, commercial practices, and cultural sensitivity that it deserves. In the real world, however, your decisions about which markets to support will be driven by the business case that you make. How much new business will supporting a particular market generate? Will targeted investments in certain countries enhance your ability to support customers, optimize your supply chain, or improve the productivity of your employees? Chapter 4 provides some insight into how to pick a market.

- *Looking for new markets?* As you move beyond existing markets, avoid the enter-every-market-tomorrow trap by studying only the countries with the highest visitation to your site. Then analyze the opportunities in those individual markets against market entry characteristics at a site such as CyberAtlas, NUA, or eMarketer.

Once you have a sense of opportunity and size, consider the true cost of entering those online markets with a presence that works. For example, say you chose to support the countries represented by the six languages on the United Nations' home page: English, Arabic, Chinese, French, Russian, and Spanish. You would have to deal not only with the language but also with the business practices and currencies of the dozens of countries where those languages are used. Making sure that your offer and value proposition stood up in each would be difficult enough without keeping your corporate image and brand synchronized across all markets. This investment is not merely a one-time translation, but a commitment to a marketplace for more than a single cycle of your business plan.

The Net: Do the math. More than one country will drive the 40 percent of Web revenue that will come from outside North America in 2003. Your mission, should you choose to accept it, is to figure out which of those countries makes the most sense to support. Focus your energy only on the markets that make sense in terms of a more comprehensive analysis of their globalization investment. Rather than slavishly looking to the top line of revenue growth or to the bottom line of projected savings, you should adopt a more holistic return on investment (ROI) analysis, focusing as well on the benefits that come from better customer service and brand equity. Chapter 2 frames globalization in these terms, tying it to top shareholder concerns. Chapter 10 extends this analysis to include an ROI model for globalization and commonly used metrics.

Realizing That the Web Is Not So Worldwide after All

Most Companies Do Not Carry a Passport on the Web   When foreigners visit a U.S. business online, they will find only English-language information, toll-free phone numbers that work only in the States, and prices

in dollars. Of the top 100 U.S. companies, only one-third offer content in any language other than English. Take, for example, the case of a U.S.-based consumer goods manufacturer, which typifies how most U.S. companies consider but do not act on the international opportunity. These points could be applied to many of the Global 2,000's online efforts.

Through early 2002, the company's home page looked promising with the CEO's global greeting to site visitors: His three-sentence English-language welcome mentioned the "world" three times. The home page backdrop listed Latin America, Africa, North America, Europe, and Asia, but that is where the company's global-savvy pitch stalled. There were no links behind the geographies that enabled Spanish, French, or Japanese guests to read about the company in their own languages.

Nonanglophone (i.e., those who do not speak English) visitors with the patience to navigate the site will be ultimately rewarded with a map of the world superimposed with the company's business regions. Clicking through to Latin America or Asia, though, brings up an English-language list of the products sold in that geography.

To its credit, this consumer goods company has given its business units in other countries free rein to create their own sites for their markets. Unfortunately, their international sites neither link back to the corporate site nor pick up the corporate branding elements. In short, the U.S. headquarters fails to leverage the massive investment that the company has made in global brand management and advertising. Consider what impact a weak or absent presence might have in three consumer economies—Germany, Japan, and the United Kingdom—whose total population of around 269 million comes close to the United States' 285 million.

Enormity of U.S. Market Lulls Many American Firms into Complacence

As mentioned earlier in the chapter, 66 percent of U.S. high-tech companies have not localized. In the general economy, about two-thirds of U.S. firms have not bothered to translate or localize their online offerings.[16] The biggest reason for this is that many have never felt the need to apply for a passport. By offering nothing more than an English-language site, they have access to a market of over 280 million who use the same currency and share the same business practices. In many cases, English is also enough for the highly educated techno elite that buy medical equipment, software, and gas turbine generators. Furthermore, when it comes to international business, many U.S. firms rely on the advice of their sales advisors outside the States, most of whom travel in that rarified anglophone atmosphere of the "jet set." Fluent in English, they assure their American counterparts that there is no need to translate—much less to localize—sites for their markets.

European Firms Know That They Have No Choice but to Localize

Long accustomed to doing business in multiple languages, European companies have a leg up on their U.S. competition (see Figure 1.7). Some multinational firms, such as DaimlerChrysler and Phillips, conduct their internal affairs in English, derive a good percentage of their revenue from anglophone markets, and expect English to be understood by demographically correct customers in other countries. Reflecting these realities, most large European companies offer at least some multilingual content on their sites, most often choosing English to complement their home-country language.[17] This serves them well in the global Internet community, where 30 percent of the buyers will generate 60 percent of the revenue. But even these experienced multilingual players frequently slip up, failing to do much more than welcome their international visitors.[18]

While the creators of these sites mean well, they have failed in their goal to create a credible international presence for their companies, sometimes even alienating their guests in the process. At many other sites in various regions of the world, international callers feel welcome until they get past the mere pleasantries of the localized home page.

These companies are not unique in how they treat international audiences. These first-generation Internet sites push the corporate story to the natives of the headquarters country. Over time they add powerful new

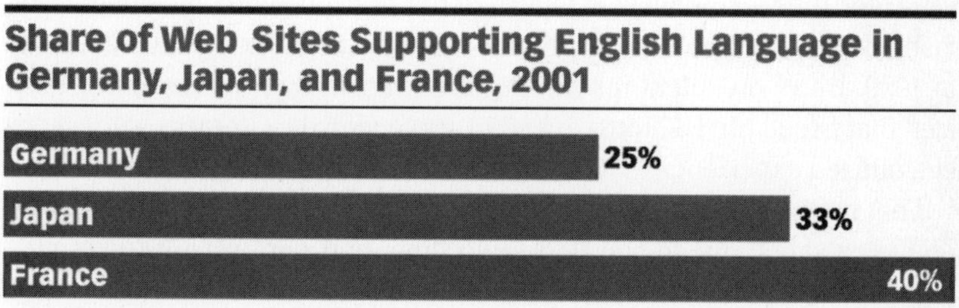

Share of Web Sites Supporting English Language in Germany, Japan, and France, 2001

Germany	25%
Japan	33%
France	40%

Figure 1.7 German, Japanese, and French Support for English
Source: International Data Corporation (IDC), 2000. Retrieved from www.eMarketer.com, 16 May 2001.

Note: European customers expect to be addressed in their own languages.

functions to the site so that visitors can ask questions, arrange for service calls, or make purchases. Knowing that most of their business is domestic, every interaction, message, and commercial capability first targets only their mainstream internal markets. Even large minority populations such as Latinos in the United States or Turks in Germany find themselves left out of the party.

Meanwhile, international subsidiaries do the same thing that their parent corporations do: They create an online experience that makes sense for their majority domestic markets. These in-country efforts usually lag behind the headquarters site in features, depth of information, and interactivity because they lack the budget that the parent corporation pours into its branded dot.com site. Companies that might have their international act together on the ground look fragmented and inconsistent on the Web.

The Net: Most companies have a tough time offering an experience outside their home markets. Either they try to create an internationally branded experience out of Darmstadt or Schenectady, or they rely on local subsidiaries to build a site for their own markets. The right approach will allow companies to appear consistent where it matters—brand, logo, corporate principles—and local where that is needed—the offer and market-specific terms and conditions.

<u>A Passport Does Not Guarantee Success</u>   Even ambitious companies that choose to meet these challenges head-on face significant risk. Consider the well-publicized failure of the first Boo.com, a British-based fashion site that launched 18 country sites from a single London database in 1999. Boo's president for North America said that the company "realized that to sell hip fashion, we had to serve global customers with a very customized experience."

That meant investing nearly US$200 million in complex technology for online catalogs, one-to-one personalization, and hardware to guarantee high levels of performance. In fact, the rollout was delayed nearly half a year as Boo ironed out kinks in the system and sought to meet performance targets. Much of the development budget went also to creating proprietary software to link these sites with suppliers, warehouses, and logistics middlemen around the globe. To Boo's management, this was a natural fit: High fashion demanded a high-tech site.

Despite its ambitious multinational debut, Boo never established a credible value proposition in *any* of the 18 markets it targeted. Boo did too much, too fast, and too expensively. Following its crash-and-burn demise in the spring of 2000, a British Internet technology firm bought Boo's back-office infrastructure for a mere US$400,000, and fashionmall.com acquired Boo's customer list, content, trademark, and domain names for an undisclosed sum.

Even more moderate efforts can run into big troubles. Despite its obvious business model and easily explained value proposition, the United Kingdom's LastMinute had trouble keeping its Italian and Spanish affiliates adequately funded. American travel site Travelocity experienced another kind of international problem when it launched its Italian site several years ago. Volatile content in a consumer market forever demanding to be entertained meant that the Italian variant quickly looked less and less like its branded counterpart, both undermining the brand and causing Travelocity eventually to pull the plug and start over.

The problem that many companies face as they go international is that they forget two things: (1) It's not enough simply to translate your content, and (2) a successful international business requires making a long-term commitment. Boo had the right idea about what would appeal to buyers in France and Italy, but not the temperance to take a less ambitious bite. Most companies lack Boo's understanding of the challenge, so they start by simply translating their domestic site into French and Italian this quarter, then into German and Dutch next quarter, and they never look back. Without active work on a site to keep it up to date, the experience gets stale, uninteresting, and out of sync with the corporate site. The result is that visitors to a derived site cannot count on the information that they find; it may be inaccurate, out of date, and inconsistent because of the cobbled-together processes used by most companies that do have international sites.

This can be a disaster as bilingual customers arbitrage the net for the best experience and current information. Even if your prospects in other countries do not speak your home-country language, they can see easily see the difference between an expensively produced headquarters site and a low-rent effort served up in their market. To paraphrase the international strategist at State Street Global Advisors, "Don't advertise a work in progress, and don't show something that you yourself wouldn't want to use."

Just as you cannot stand still with site content, you must look ahead with regard to technology and design. While the conventional wisdom is that the United States leads the rest of the world in Web technology, the reality is that markets in Scandinavia outpace the United States in certain respects such as wireless connectivity to and transactions on the Internet. So as you roll out your best and brightest technology and features for the U.S. market—things such as one-to-one personalization—other markets will expect the same quality of technology and experience, again underscoring the importance of conducting a rigorous ROI analysis on every market that you consider supporting.

Be sure to consider not only what you offer in your home market, but also what competitors offer in their home markets. Customers will benchmark your site within their country and internationally against the best of the Web, driving observant companies to provide ever higher levels of interactivity and customer service (see Figure 1.8). For example, at Cathay Pacific and United Airlines, you repeatedly hear questions such as "How are we doing in this market against American Airlines?" or "How does Sin-

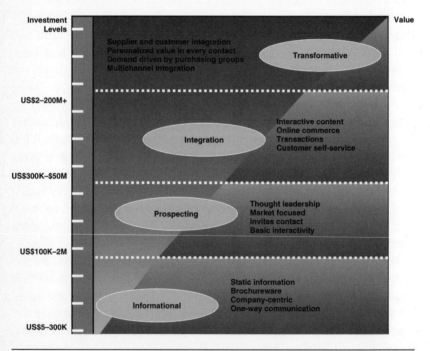

Figure 1.8 Internet Evolution
Source: Gartner Research, November 2001.

Note: The Internet will continue to evolve, both as a technology and as a channel. This figure represents the phases through which companies will pass as they ratchet up their own investments from mere thousands of dollars (US$5K and up) to hundreds of millions (US$200M).

gapore Airlines serve this market better?" These companies constantly monitor the function and technology of their competitors because they are determined not to be on the losing side of a feature-function shoot-out— or, worse yet, losing market share to competitors or being ranked lower than a rival in customer satisfaction.

The net: Be global at every level of your company, technology, and process. A Web site is an organic beast, constantly evolving. A Web site meant to represent a company outside its domestic market must react to stimuli from multiple sources: what's happening at headquarters and, what's driving that site, plus the needs of prospects in the target markets and the ever-present danger of being perceived as an interloper or carpetbagger in the "foreign" market. That means looking, smelling, and tasting as if you were created in that market—not just today, but for as long as you decide to compete there. It means making sure that everyone in the company thinks of your mission in global terms.

Guiding Principles for Going Global Online

To recap, *international* is a relative term. If you are an American company, it means appealing to non-U.S. buyers. For Germans, it means marketing anyplace outside Germany, even in German-speaking countries such as Austria. More broadly, *international* could mean targeting your domestic multicultural or ethnic populations. In all cases, though, it means aligning your entire strategy with your business goals, regardless of the channel.

- *Be realistic about the global market.* While the international Internet economy will be big, no market in the next decade will be bigger than the United States. Accounting today for most of the revenue and still more than half by middecade, the American market will fuel the Internet, just as it does the world's physical economy. This is good news for U.S. companies, but it is great news for Europeans, Asians, and Latin Americans looking for opportunities to sell their goods and services.
- *Do the math.* Just like business or politics in general, on the Internet some countries matter more than others do. In fact, considering

Internet penetration, profitability, or customer service needs, some markets will not even show up on your radar. Making the tough calls, matching product or service to a given market, and managing the cost of fulfilling business in a foreign market are all up to you. Precede all decisions with a rigorous analysis of ROI; that is, business cases should drive decision making. Chapters 2 and 10 discuss ROI issues in more detail.

- *Interact locally.* Remember that your prospective customers have many choices about where to spend their money; the most compelling of those choices will be with companies that ask for their business—in their language, addressing their cultural needs, denominated in their currency, and according to the rules of their market. The least forceful sites will be those that do not even acknowledge these international business realities. Going global really means serving local markets well when you start out and continuing into the future through wireless communications, personalization, content management systems (CMS), customer relationship management (CRM), peer-to-peer networking (P2P), and the rest of the ever-evolving alphabet soup of Web technology.

- *Think beyond consumer Webs.* The meltdown of the dot.com economy dominated the headlines, but it blurred the real benefits behind the scenes. Besides being able to reach out to service customers anywhere, the Internet lets you work better internally and with partners. The ability to integrate a tactical marketing campaign online with your long-evolving customer data warehouse, physical point of sale systems, and direct mail involves the full range of your marketing and sales competence—even before you get to the operational systems that will allow you to fulfill demand, ship products that customers order, and follow up on service needs.

What Mira's Analysis of Acme International Showed Her

As Mira reviewed Acme's online presence around the globe, she realized with some sadness that everything she had read about online failures at other companies' sites applied also to Acme's international efforts. While its U.S. site had won a design award within its industry and was hailed by three Internet weeklies for its superior navigation, Acme's international sites did not bene-

fit from the expertise and investment of its headquarters' site. The sites in too many of Acme's international markets were put up by part-time teams in that country with the requisite local language support and a localized look and feel, but each was a mere shadow compared to the dynamic, information-rich U.S. site.

At an executive team meeting Mira reported on her review of Acme's international sites, some of which did not link back to the corporate site. She remarked that country units had taken matters into their own hands, doing what they felt had to be done to succeed in their markets because Acme's corporate site was so "American." To highlight problems, Mira used Acme's Czech site as an example. Her issues included the following:

- Brand management. *Mira showed PowerPoint screen captures of the Czech and other offending sites. Acme's Czech Web unit did not employ the company's trademark yellow and purple color scheme. The developers also backdropped the company's scimitar logo with the spires of Prague, a nice local touch that unfortunately violated corporate branding standards.*

  Mira observed that the company had not globalized itself. For example, she noted that the company's branding and style guides were written in English, described branding elements in terms of Acme's U.S. site and offline business, and referenced A. C. Nielsen and NPD data about U.S. buying cohorts.

- Product catalog. *This time projecting the U.S. site and its Czech equivalent, Mira pointed out major errors and omissions in product descriptions that would undermine Acme's well-known commitment to safety, the environment, and human rights. She also distributed a focus group study that had been conducted by Acme's regional headquarters in Amsterdam. The results underscored lower consumer trust in products sold through Acme's Czech retail site.*

  How could the Czechs, even with a more localized site, score lower in consumer trust? Mira recounted her conversation with the managing director in Prague. Despite their best efforts with their limited resources, Acme was still seen as a U.S. brand that did little to meet the needs of the local market. There was little that the management of Acme A.S.[19] could do if Acme Inc. in the States failed to build or market products that met the needs of the Czech backyard vacationer.

- Pricing. *Mira projected the American and Czech prices for Acme's top-selling products, noting that the Czech product prices did not reflect an across-the-board price hike necessitated by rising energy prices. Comparing Acme sites managed by business units in adjacent countries revealed that prices varied within the central European region by up to 35 percent.*

Next, Mira discovered that the Czech Web master had not updated the management profiles on the site, figuring that the Czech consumer could not care less about Acme's American management team. Instead, he spent most of his time monitoring the U.S. site to see what product information had changed. The Webmaster knew that he missed a lot of changes because he relied on his memory and his knowledge of both sites to know what had changed.

Mira concluded that www.acme-lifestyle.cz did not represent the same corporate reality as did www.acme-lifestyle.com. In working with the CEO, she anticipated potential damage to Acme's worldwide brand and sales. They consulted with the CFO to calculate what this international imbroglio cost Acme in duplicate headcount, technology, content, process, marketing, distribution, and all other operational attributes of a modern Web site.

The first thing that Mira determined was that inefficient duplication could not continue. The CFO also noted that much of that spending was secreted in local marketing budgets away from his ROI scrutiny, rather than in the information technology (IT) or Web budget, where its effectiveness could be measured. After consulting metrics such as unaided brand awareness and cost of sale, the CFO determined that Acme had been doing a terrible job of projecting its hard-won image for quality and safety and of establishing a unique value proposition in international markets. Mira's next step was to pull together her presentation to the board—why did she think that Acme should spend more on global marketing and the systems and staff to support it?

2

Great Expectations for Global Markets

Back in her office, Mira considered what she learned about going global. Sure, the United States was the 800-pound gorilla on the Internet and probably always would be, but her instinct told her that prospects and customers in markets such as Germany and Japan deserved more of her company's attention. She knew better than to fall for the old canard that the Web made you instantly global; while its Web site made Acme accessible to everyone in the world, who knows what sense Acme's products made to a Czech or a Korean?

In an ideal world, Mira would have a budget big enough to make geography, language, and culture irrelevant for visitors to Acme Online. Certain that the executive budget committee would not go by her intuition, the global sugarplums in her vision looked like they would be squashed by the blunt reality of her limited budget and America-first CFO—unless, of course, she could make a strong business case for going global.

Convincing Your Colleagues to Act

When reviewing her argument for going global, Mira considered the top five shareholder issues as reported by Ernst & Young in the summer of 2001[1]:

1. What is the company doing to retain key employees?
2. How can the company ensure that management produces satisfactory results?
3. How is management handling the risks and rewards of globalization?

4. How is the company leveraging the Internet to increase earnings and shareholder value?
5. What is management doing to increase shareholder value in a volatile stock market?

The third and fourth concerns inspired Mira—and are the heart of this chapter. Given everything that you have to worry about, why should this unproven Web, domestically or globally, be something that you spend any precious budget on? This chapter will discuss some valuable uses of the Internet that will drive many businesses like Mira's to extend their reach beyond domestic markets.

- *Business alignment.* Successful planners align their Web projects with key business goals. The same requirement applies to the global Internet and can take any international project from the status of nice-to-have to must-do. Clever planners will recognize that not all winning projects face the buying public but may support critical internal or business partner functions.
- *Dealing with sophistry.* There are many reasons not to do anything because domestic markets are big enough, sufficiently profitable, or easier to manage. Most such arguments do not stand up to the light of day. Every company needs the growth engine of more sales or greater profitability to meet its shareholders' expectations. The global Web offers opportunity on both of those fronts.
- *Making the call—and the case.* Some arguments for going global work better than others do. This chapter lays out seven effective arguments that go beyond the simplistic "make more money" or "beat the competition."

Where Does Globalization Fit into a Business Strategy?

The prospect of entering new markets around the world and selling products or services to new prospects sounds like a great plan. You can demonstrate your marvelous offerings through the display window of your Internet site and rely on the good people at UPS or DHL to deliver the goods to any customer on the planet. Without engaging a distributor or building out an infrastructure in other countries, you can aggregate the buying power of demographically correct buyers around the world.

This sudden ubiquity is what intrigued many investors during the boom days of the Internet, letting them set up shop anywhere there was a customer connected to a phone line and thus gaining access to book buyers and travelers living far from any bookstore or travel agency. This wired omnipresence enabled Net-only companies to bolt past slower-moving brick-and-mortar firms both in valuation and public perception—at least until the laggards integrated their offline systems with the Web and built their own online stores. For many companies, the Web has evolved into a fundamental channel of commerce and communications, allowing them to enter new markets, extend their brand, and serve their customers better as a complement to traditional face-to-face business. That means offering a wide range of capabilities at their sites, from the basics of product information and reaching out to self-service and commerce (see Figure 2.1).

The same possibilities and needs present themselves on the global Internet, but most companies have not yet evolved their planning past "make lots of money in new markets" daydreaming. What these companies are doing online and why they are doing it is very clear in their domestic markets: Study after study shows that companies are using their Internet channel to be more competitive, improve customer satisfaction, increase brand awareness, generate new sources of revenue, and become more profitable. But when it comes to their international market strategies, their aspirations deflate. They want to remain competitive and increase sales, but few mention major issues such as customer satisfaction, brand awareness, efficiency, and profitability.[2]

The missing link between success on the Internet and winning on the global Internet comes from the lack of practical experience outside domestic markets. Many companies have already deployed their second- and third-generation Internet sites, adding large dollops of interactivity, personalization, and one-click navigation, all intended to win customers and keep them coming back again and again. Few firms, though, have successfully deployed even a first-generation international site that accomplishes much more than welcoming an Italian with a hearty "Benvenuto!" before throwing them back into the language, currency, and cultural milieu of the home market.

Companies have succeeded online in their domestic markets, but they have failed to align their global aspirations with what is driving the success of their headquarters' business online. More experienced companies that have successfully deployed e-business applications laid out not only the expected return on their investment (i.e., competitiveness, new markets, more share) but also the means to get there—specifically, more satisfied customers who buy more stuff more frequently.

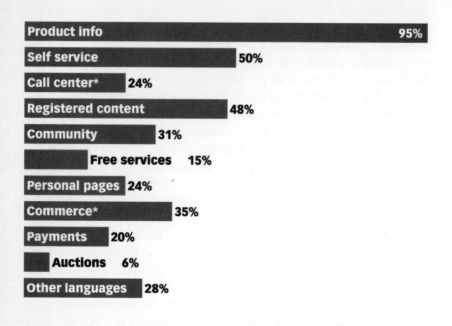

Figure 2.1 Web Site Functionality of Large U.S. Companies, 2001
*13% have both.
Source: International Data Corporation (IDC), 2001. Retrieved from www.eMarketer.com.

Note: Almost every successful customer-facing Web site in the States supports marketing efforts, while about half of them allow customers to self-serve with frequently asked questions (FAQs) and answer utilities such as Dell's Ask Dudley. Internally, companies use the same Internet technologies to improve employee productivity and enhance communication with partners in their supply chains.

The net: It is hard for the early-bird globalists to do much more than state their ambitious goals about making more money for their respective companies. They will aim for simple goals such as more sales, more market share, or staying competitive, while their domestic counterparts have evolved beyond these nostrums to critical differentiators such as creating more intimate relationships with their customers through personalization or improving satisfaction through better support and self-service. Until international Web planners establish these metrics, their plans will be less than compelling.

To Every Company There's a Reason

Unfortunately, there is no list of every company with international Web sites, the business plan that they used to enter new markets, and the technical road map on how to get there. Companies bring different levels of global experience to the table, along with the understanding of the challenges that made them push ahead or stop dead in their tracks. Some, such as automakers, bring decades of brick-and-mortar experience in international markets to the Web. Others such as Travelocity bring online selling knowledge but no on-the-ground expertise. Consider the two extremes—planetary newbies and the globally experienced—with all their permutations. As you read, think about where your company would show up.

<u>Planetary Newbies: Still in the Starting Blocks</u>   Maybe you work for a global organization that has had little experience with the Web, your company just does not care, or it is too risk-averse to do much more than acknowledge that it is not tackling those enticing international markets. In my work with firms looking to kick the tires of global e-business, I've seen three archetypes.

1. *Aware but not there.* Few executives anywhere fail to understand that the Web's "www" means global reach. However, research about top U.S. companies shows that about half to two-thirds are not making the investments that will turn foreign visitation into increased business.
   Action: If your firm falls into this category and you are not happy about that, ask your IT department to start measuring your international traffic and try to gauge the percentage of sales that you lost because prospects could not complete a transaction, much less understand your value proposition. Few firms collect as much data about Web traffic as they should, whether about fellow citizens or foreigners visiting their sites. The data is there—collect it, analyze it, and act on it!
2. *Globally delusional.* Some executives understand that a global market exists, but they will not go the extra kilometer to reach it. Consider a typical American company that attracts 15 percent of its traffic from outside the U.S. market without any translation, adaptation, or appeal to other markets. Five percent of those visitors actually succeed in buying something. Because the company invested nothing to draw global traffic and did little more than contract with UPS or FedEx to handle international deliveries, many executives would be ecstatic

over the bluebird of any non-U.S. business. But no one considers how much higher the look-to-buy ratio would have been had the site been localized for other markets.

Action: Recognizing that you are delusional is the first step in the cure; if you think that your home market language and currency are enough *today,* what will you do when you saturate your domestic buyers with your offerings? What will you do when you find your major rivals mining lots of new business from countries that you ignored? Your next step is to figure out which markets will propel you to the next phase of growth. The same advice holds for U.S. companies looking to augment their top lines or improve their bottom lines.

3. *The stay-at-home crowd.* In all fairness to the delusional, there is a contingent that feels pretty justified in staying at home. It is hard to argue with someone who says that meeting the needs of over 280 million consumers in the United States is business enough for anyone. The same holds true for other large-population markets such as Japan (126 million), Germany (83 million), or China (over 1¼ billion).

Action: No CEO at publicly traded companies has the luxury of addressing shareholder meetings with statements like "We're happy right where we are. Sales are about as high as we'd expect them to be, and we don't pay any attention to our competitors." The notion that a company's revenue is large enough or that it needs no more customers will not last long. Competitors domestic and international will strive to take away share. Ultimately, companies in larger markets will find that they are not so homogenous after all, and that they have been ignoring large ethnic populations such as Latinos in the United States, Turks in Germany, and China's large expatriate population around the world.

Globally Savvy: Companies That Have Cut the Domestic Umbilical Cord

As the planetary newbies evolve, some will see an opportunity to use the Internet to serve their "foreign" customers better, increase their online business in new markets, or push their brand around the globe. Everyone needs the ammunition to convince the budgetary powers-that-be that globalization will enhance shareholder value. Some of that ammo will come from the tales of successful companies that have proactively sought to extend their reach to consumers and business partners around the world.

I see a recurring pattern of successful firms from the high-tech arena—computers, aerospace, and consumer electronics—all of which offer products that cross national boundaries and cultural preferences. However, these globally aware firms represent a spectrum of evolution as well. In working with companies that have burst out of their domestic markets, I have seen the following characteristics:

1. *Toe dippers.* These firms typically react to some event (e.g., a demanding national distributor or an aggressive competitor) when they adapt some element of their site to local market needs. Such localization tends to be incomplete, involving either limited translation of some content or an ability to deliver via local shippers. The prototypical toe dippers often find themselves entering a national market, either accidentally because of new demand for a product that appeals to foreign visitors or more deliberately, though usually without conviction or adequate budget.

   Action: If you are a toe-dipper, some structured research such as focus groups and interviews with customers and prospects will probably show you that you are leaving money on the table and spending a lot more money than you have to because of inefficient translation and localization processes. If you have resources such as local staff in a market, work with them to find some assistance with conducting such research. If you do not have staff in-country, look to marketing and public relations agencies for help in setting up such focus groups. One thing to watch out for: In hard economic times, when companies face proof that they are wasting money through inefficiency or fear that their investment could be better spent in other areas, they sometimes propose the knee-jerk reaction to eliminate international efforts altogether.

2. *Stubbed toes.* Many well-known brands have entered international markets by allowing local business units to set their own agendas, usually divorced from the corporate brand, message, and look and feel. The net result is a fragmented international presence with very little leverage of the assets that make these companies such a powerful force in their domestic market. Nonetheless, they continue investing internationally but without a consistent use of the Net to bolster their physical channels.

   Action: Executives at many such companies wrap themselves around the axle of indecision and regret. Convinced that they are spending far too much to get much too little, they do nothing. It is time to grab the tiller and let everyone know where you want to be globally, even if you decide to hold the course for now. For example, you may decide that your current product line would be useful anywhere on the planet without any modification. On the other hand, you may find that your as-is offering happens to be tied to a single language, culture, country, and ethnic group. Any decision to enter a market requires a systematic analysis of what exactly your products are and how universal or locale-dependent they are. Chapter 3 discusses this issue in more detail.

3. *Second bouncers.* Some companies created international sites in response to real or perceived market needs, often spending enormous amounts of money and manpower creating manual and jury-rigged processes to make their corporate message, brand, and product offerings consistent worldwide. While they failed the first time around to meet customer or market needs, they succeeded on the second try. For example, firms like information system and software provider EMC in the United States and electrical power equipment supplier Weidmüller in Germany have a different agenda than the other categories just discussed: They are actively selling in multiple markets around the world, and they have experienced—and overcome— some turbulence along the way.

Action: Failure the first time around is par for the course. If your first international forays do not work out, analyze the misstep and figure out how to do it right.

The net: Where does your company fit? When it comes to using the Net to go global or bolster existing channels, no two firms are alike. In fact, no two projects or even business units inside a company are likely to have the same experiences on the Web. With that in mind, let us move on to the next question: What should you expect to get out of globalization?

Seven Most Effective Arguments for Globalization Budgets

What should companies expect to net on the Web? Look to the masters, a small but growing cadre of multinational firms such as Cathay Pacific, General Electric, and Microsoft that have evolved their corporate Web sites into critical channels for communicating, collaborating, and transacting with customers, partners, and employees. In the process, they have made the Internet an integral element of the value that they deliver to customers.

This ambitious group seeks the means to create, manage, and deliver their value to global audiences, regardless of the medium, or of whether they are dealing with a consumer or a cog in a global supply chain. Their goal is to become truly international businesses, looking to achieve big returns on their ambitious efforts in revenue, branding, and customer service. Unless you are a dot.com, do not assume that you will make all of your money from just selling stuff on the Web; look to investment on the Eighth Continent as a way to support your ventures in the other seven continents. So when it is time to make the case for a bigger budget to enter international markets, here are seven tried and true reasons that go beyond the top-of-mind reasons such as revenue, the demands of the Dow or the FTSE, or what their competitors say they are doing.

The seven ways of convincing management to globalize shown in Table 2.1 are discussed in more detail in the next sections.

Reason 7: Increase Revenue and Share from Global Markets

Revenue justification for international expansion can take many forms. Here are just four that other companies have used to justify increased attention to the needs of buyers on the Eighth Continent:

1. *Bald-faced pitch for more business.* Dot.coms such as Amazon have the luxury of identifying markets whose citizens buy the most books or CDs. French automaker Renault feels that by making more product information readily available online in key markets, prospects will be more likely to buy a Clio coupe or a Scénic minivan. Italian motorcycle manufacturer Ducati targeted its demographic sweet spot in Germany, Japan, and the United States with specially packaged cycles available only online.

2. *Sales cycle compression.* Some early movers have used the global Web to compress sales cycles across channels. Operating online in 23 markets, EMC uses its sites in different countries to complement the sales engagement model that it employs in its face-to-face marketing. Online, prospects register for events, providing more detail that feeds EMC's profiling tools. This lets the company promote anonymous users to registered users and then channel them to a human sales representative. This personalized approach yields better conversion rates and more loyal customers, ultimately increasing profitability.

Reason Number	Reason
7	Increase revenue and share in global and ethnic markets. Growth will come from selling to new markets and from reaching new communities in existing ones.
6	Beat competitors. Market reconnaissance and time response are critical as you face current rivals and meet new ones.
5	Heighten brand awareness. Your brand may be all that separates your company from commoditization. Make sure that key world markets know your brand.
4	Shorten time-to-market. It may be the case that the customer-facing Web is not where you will realize shareholder value. Besides a basic presence, look for internal and opportunities that could improve your competitiveness.
3	Improve collaborative efforts and knowledge management. The efficient flow of information and knowledge within and between companies will be a major differentiator between you and less data-savvy competitors.
2	Lower the cost of doing business. Taking expense out of both critical processes and customer service will improve the balance, sheet, thus raising the return on Web and global investments.
1	Focus on your customer. Satisfying customers and making each interaction more profitable mean happier shareholders.

Table 2.1 Seven Ways to Convince Management of the Need to Globalize

3. *Hedging revenue bets.* It's all a matter of balance. Planners at successful global companies feel that they have done better than their domestic counterparts exactly because they are international. Besides being able to sell into markets around the world, they can smooth the peaks and valleys of individual markets with their multinational portfolio—complemented by a strong story on the Web that has been localized to market needs, buying behaviors, and, of course, language.

For example, Cisco pays close attention to world markets, recognizing that each region comprises a major chunk of its revenue. That way, when the Japanese economy slumps, Cisco might increase its investments in healthier markets such as Europe or Latin America that might be firing on all cylinders. In addition, goods that do not sell in one market might be wildly popular in another. For example, BMW can highlight its larger, more expensive 7 series models to U.S. prospects who are less concerned with miles-per-gallon than are their European counterparts. BMW strongly invested in its U.S.-market Web sites, determined to tailor its online story exactly to the demographic most likely to buy or influence the purchase of their products.

4. *Meeting a legal requirement.* Canadian law permits the use of both English and French in any forum, while Quebec law gives a primacy to French. Regulation aside, strong cultural and political preferences in Quebec argue for making a Canadian-market Web site available in both languages.

As the Canadian bilingual reality demonstrates to companies based in the Dominion, you do not have to look abroad for these kinds of new market opportunities; an assessment of your domestic ethnic markets should accompany any globalization effort, especially in Germany, Great Britain, and the United States. For example, ethnic Americans online represent a big opportunity as consumers, employees, suppliers, and business partners. The Census Bureau notes that although only 3 percent of Americans are Asian, Web researchers estimate that 69 percent of them already use the Web, compared to 44 percent for the general population (see Table 2.2).

	% Online January 1999	% Online January 2000	% Online January 2001	% of Total Population 2001
Caucasian American	34	43	60	75.1
African American	23	33	36	12.3
Hispanic American	36	47	49	12.5
Asian American	64	69	73	3.6
All households	35	43	57	103.5

Table 2.2 Ethnic Groups Online in the United States
Source: Forrester Research Consumer Technographics™ Benchmark 2001 and U.S. Census Bureau, "Overview of Race and Hispanic Origin." Available at www.census.gov/prod/2001pubs/c2kbr01-1.pdf.

Note: The 2000 census added a new dimension to the U.S. economic and political landscape: Individuals were able to claim ethnicity in more than one group. Because so many of the 35 million people of Hispanic heritage are online, American companies in retailing, financial services, and auto manufacturing began to rethink their English-only Web sites. Meanwhile, larger firms from Spain and Spanish-speaking countries in Latin America started thinking about how to tap this large market.

U.S. Hispanics represent nearly 13 percent of the U.S. population, but 47 percent of them are online. Thus, the same revenue benefits that you advanced for global markets work for the domestic ethnic—or, more politically correct, "multicultural"—markets.

This group accounted for an estimated US$452 billion dollars in buying power in 2001. Retailers such as Fingerhut and PC makers such as Gateway see a big upside in marketing to this population. Gateway adapted cross-selling programs that had succeeded with Anglo consumers: Spanish-speaking marketing representatives often call Gateway customers and suggest peripherals such as printers or scanners that add extra value to the computer—and revenue to Gateway. Similarly, Fingerhut supplemented its printed Spanish catalogs with an Internet retail site dedicated to U.S. Latinos and a partnership with Spanish-language broadcaster Univision that featured Fingerhut catalog items. The opportunity and the need extend beyond consumers. U.S. Census Bureau statistics point out the large growth in minority-owned businesses, especially Asian.[3] Companies such as Microsoft have already targeted these small and medium enterprises (SMEs).

Similar opportunities exist in Europe. According to British government statistics, about one person in 15 in Great Britain is from an ethnic minority, with younger inhabitants more likely to have been born in England than their elders.[4] Some British companies hope to target these younger cohorts that speak English but who are culturally Pakistani or Indian. In Germany, telecom companies such as Deutsche Telekom would like to exploit the market for Slavs and Turks who want to call relatives back home in Moscow or Istanbul.

Finally, the ethnic opportunity can take another form—it can open the door to expatriates. For example, the excellence of Indian higher education has spawned a cadre of entrepreneurs and technology specialists spread across the world. As increasing expatriate investment has demonstrated, many of these émigrés still harbor a strong loyalty to their motherland. In India's growing Internet community, sites dedicated to retail, investment, and content such as khoj.com and eIndia.com can win and retain these expatriates as customers by appealing to their continuing allegiance and the cultural elements that form its foundation.

Reason 6: Beat Competitors to These New Markets

Your counterpart over at your longtime competitor is plotting to take advantage of these same opportunities. This familiar old foe has decided to unwrap a great new program for Latin America. Meanwhile, rivals that you do not even know about from other markets are figuring out how to beat you to the punch, both internationally and in your own domestic ethnic markets.

Everyone remembers how Amazon.com sped past established booksellers to gain critical share in the early days of the Web. Even with the burst bubble of dot.coms, companies such as Barnes & Noble and Bertelsmann are still trying to catch up to Amazon's share. Others, such as Borders, have thrown in the online towel and named Amazon its Web distributor. The Web still offers this quick deployment of a sales channel.

At the very least, you should pay more attention to competitive reconnaissance. Enlist sales reps and trade partners for signs of threats beyond your immediate horizon. Figure out which markets will be most important to your company—and your competitors—and plan accordingly for the right level of support.

Reason 5: Heighten Brand Awareness

Brand is what makes a can of Coca-Cola worth US$1.00 and a can of Sam's Cola worth only US$0.25. Much of the stock market value of companies such as Coca-Cola, Levi, and Nestlé derives from their brands. With such enormous equity tied up in brands, companies both large and small use the Web to increase awareness of brands and the products associated with them into new markets around the world.

Over the last few years the top ten Web sites have accounted for upwards of 60 percent of all traffic. This online traffic comes from the goodwill associated with a brand, a hard-won value resulting from the trust that a strong brand engenders among its customers and partners. Projecting a brand into new markets can increase the equity associated with it, at the same time that this global thrust puts the brand itself in jeopardy.

Most businesses that call themselves global are mere pretenders, not having done as well outside their home markets as they claim. Web channel initiatives bring this to light pretty quickly. Building a brand often takes decades—it is about trust and promises. On the Web, visitors still go to names that they know and that evoke value.

Large companies spend hundreds of millions of dollars annually to manage and refine their brand. Experience has shown that spending more on the Web does not lead to success. For example, eBay's 1999 advertising budget amounted to US$5.5 million, yielding a top-of-mind brand awareness of 22 percent of those surveyed. Ameritrade, however, spent 18 times more than eBay—a whopping US$103.7 million—for a 1-percent awareness.[5] On the other hand, the Web can reinforce branding programs through services that deliver information and manage customer relationships.

With branding budgets in the hundreds of millions, companies want to see their efforts extend beyond the small patch of their headquarters country. They want to see brand attributes correctly and consistently represented in each of their target markets.

All too often, however, global companies rely too much on in-country managers to handle branding issues in each market; these typically drop the ball on corporate branding constancy in favor of their well-meaning but underfunded and often underdeveloped hometown efforts. For example, Royal Dutch Shell saw that local business units around the world were off-brand, using its well-known seashell logo inconsistently and inappropriately.[6] In-country workers simply created their own branding rules and market-specific Shell content as they worked with local advertising agencies. This lack of control resulted in significant new costs as Shell reinvented itself in each market, spending on duplicate staff, messaging, process, and technology.

These Web sites sacrifice a well-defined, enforced global brand, hurting brand integrity. By listening to your country units and incorporating their concerns and needs in your plans, you should be able to steer clear of this all-too common problem.

On the domestic front, the upside of using the Web to push your brand is getting through to ethnic audiences that might not be exposed to your target media (e.g., big city newspapers). Before it actively sought out the Hispanic market, Gateway was a nonstarter in unaided brand awareness. Today, thanks to its partnering with Univision on television and online, advertising in other Latino media, and offering customer support in Spanish, Gateway is vying for top name recognition among PC makers in the U.S. Hispanic market.

Reason 4: Shorten Time to Market
You can use the global Web to get into new markets quickly and establish a strong presence before your competitors do. If your archrivals are already in key international markets, you can use the global Web to initiate an offense more quickly than by any other channel. By investing smartly in a localized presence, you can look, feel, and act more local than even your in-country rivals.

Because of the Web, airlines like UAL Cargo and Cathay Pacific can roll out and publicize competition-motivated revisions to their service offerings much faster through their Internet sites than they can through updating and publishing hardcopy collateral and price lists. For a large U.S.-based medical device maker, the Web has become the primary means of getting product information to its market, closing the gap between delivering a product and marketing it.

Reason 3: Improve Collaborative Efforts and Knowledge Management   Much of the benefit of investing in globalization will come from improvements in moving information around internally to the people who need it and sharing this knowledge with your sales channels. This inward-facing effort may fall under the banner of knowledge management or enterprise information portals (EIPs), both of which are still in their infancy in most companies. An avid user of globally available information is Cisco, whose systems enable employees around the world quickly to locate the right resources in real time and escalate problems appropriately. The company estimates that its worldwide employee directory is used 12 times a day by the average employee to make connections with other Cisco staffers worldwide.

A U.S.-based medical device manufacturer uses its global Web to organize branded materials, digital assets, and other files though an online repository for reuse by local sales representatives and marketing groups. In Europe, it leverages the same technology to communicate with its physician audiences. In Japan, where dealers are the device manufacturer's primary buyer, the firm is developing an Extranet to give its distributors access to digital assets and product literature for reuse, as well as customer-specific data such as inventory, past purchase history, and payment details. The company figures that these online capabilities will deepen its relationships with doctor-buyers and dealers.

Reason 2: Lower the Cost of Doing Business   Once you decide to do business internationally—whether customers find you or you actively seek them out—you will have to market to your new audience, sell to them, and support them after the sale. Early movers have found that these must-do components of commerce cost cheaper on the Web.

Take the cost of market entry. Seeing international market demand for its clothing, catalog retailer Lands' End opted to enter Japan and several markets in Europe. It saved marketing dollars by launching Web sites before printing its branded paper catalog, a pricey publication that accounts for about 40 percent of the company's operating costs. Besides price, catalogs sent to a rented list had low conversion rates. Small sums invested in advertising got traffic flowing to Lands' End sites in its international markets. As those international sites evolve their own followings, the company plans to follow up with a printed catalog that will be sent to previous buyers who are more likely to buy again.

As online penetration increases around the world, demand for customer service in the language of the international or ethnic buyer will rise in lock step. This localized information is a basic cost of doing business, but it can be quite expensive as companies staff call centers to meet the demand. You can use the Web to deflect much of this voice traffic away from expensive call center reps to online resources such as frequently asked questions (FAQs). Ideally, prospects can review product offerings, safety advisories, technical data, and competitive descriptions on their own, allowing sales and customer service representatives to focus on higher value-adding activities.

This online support can dramatically reduce costs and staffing levels in call centers. For example, researchers have found that costs for companies offering local language and self-service capabilities drop substantially when buyers serve themselves rather than speaking with a costly customer service representative.

- Online customer self-service costs a business only US$1.00 per customer inquiry versus US$33.00 for each call handled by a customer service representative.[7] Applied to even thousands of interactions, these savings can be huge. At Eastman Chemical, lightening the load of critical business functions lets the company offer higher service levels to key customers while serving a wider customer base—all without additional resources. Eastman's cost of serving its international customers 24 hours a day is lower because it needs fewer customer service representatives to service calls during what would be—without this international business—off-hours. Over time, it expects customer satisfaction to improve, a crucial driver given the typical five- to tenfold cost of acquiring a new customer over retaining your best customers.[8]
- The benefit of speaking the customer's language extends deeper into the buying cycle. In one study, nearly half of the orders placed by people living outside the United States went unfilled because of process failures.[9] Language difficulties and differences in address formats caused companies to send orders to the wrong address or to ship the wrong items, thus driving up both shipping and telecom costs as customers tried to get what they ordered.

Transferring support and sales inquiries to the Web is just the first step. High-tech manufacturers such as Toshiba, Siemens, and EMC wants to reduce the cost of sale by having business customers and partners serve themselves when they buy upgrades, add-ons, accessories, training, services, or documentation. Further, by automating the buying process, the company hopes to cut costs and speed up delivery by eliminating the manual administration processes and checks that accompany orders taken by error-prone humans.

Behind the scenes, companies can save large amounts by improving their supply chain and materials procurement systems. DaimlerChrysler found that it had saved more than 17 percent of the total cost of parts purchases since it began on-line bidding processes for car batteries, fasteners, stampings, and water shields.[10] The company cut the time it took to send production program information to suppliers from 14 days to 1 day without decreasing the amount of data. The company is now working with suppliers and other DaimlerChrysler units—Mitsubishi and Freightliner—to rationalize its data and document formats into well-defined structures using international formats, allow information to be translated, and thus bring a wider range of suppliers into the auctions. Covisint, the online trade exchange that DaimlerChrysler owns in partnership with other auto companies, and initiatives such as RosettaNet for the computer industry will benefit from efforts to standardize formats and interfaces to allow suppliers and buyers from around the world to participate.

Reason 1: Remember That the Customer Is at the Center of Everything

All of the benefits of going global ultimately come down to satisfying the customer, whether it is a consumer buying a travel package or a procurement clerk buying 10 tons of plastic. While many customers on the Eighth Continent are fully capable of meeting your demands for them to speak in English and spend dollars, that will not be the case forever. Successful companies will extend their personalization schemes to be more sensitive to the realities of other markets.

The net: Returns on globalization are not static or global. They will be different from company to company, from project to project within a company, and even from market to market for the same company. Returns will also vary over time, as a company's needs may change over time from simple market entry to a GE-like desire to be number one or two in a given market.

Case Study: Getting Closer to Your Customer

Italy's Ducati.com is an online community for the fans of the stylish, high-performance, expensive motorcycles made in Italy. In late 1999 Ducati chose this gathering point not only to introduce its retro-futuristic MH900e motorcycle, but also as the only place in the world where you could order this highly desirable bike named after Mike Halewood, winner of the 1978 Isle of Mann Tourist Trophy.[11] It did two smart things along the way:

- In a smart nod to its dealer network, the company chose to deliver all the new motorcycles through its Ducati dealer network.
- The company sold its entire first-year production run of 500 motorcycles in 31 minutes, each priced at €15,000, regardless of where the buyer lived, thus removing some traditional nation-by-nation pricing differences.

Within three weeks Ducati sold its second year's run of 1,500 bikes. Nine months later, the company repeated this online success by selling out its entire 300 run of the high-performance 996R motorcycle, again charging the same €26,000 price anywhere in the world. In race trim the 996 led the 2001 Monza Super Bike race series, pushing the manufacturer's plan to "win on Sunday, sell on Monday."

Who bought the MH900e? Motivated fans thronged to country-specific sites for America, Germany, and Japan. Forty percent of the MH900e bikes went to Japanese *Ducatisti;* 35 percent were snapped up by Americans; and the rest were sold in smaller percentages to Ducati customers in Germany, France, the United Kingdom, and other countries around the world. With its Internet product launch strategy, global pricing equality, and sites tuned to the interests and language of its aficionados, Ducati created a borderless community of motorcyclists intensely loyal to its brand.

On the financial front, analysts were concerned that Ducati would have to absorb some hefty losses by charging the same amount regardless of the currency. However, the company felt that the pricing would help its dealers in their marketing efforts and push Ducati gear, a high-margin part of the business. Ducati's accessory sales accounted for 5.7 percent of its €379 million in 2000 revenue, up from 3 percent of its 1998 €240 million.

Finally, Ducati has embraced the Web as a way of doing primary product research as well. Because it continually publishes new content at ducati.com, it has been able to count on a steady stream of repeat visitors.

Seeing this, the firm has started to ask registered buyers for their opinions online. For example, when Ducati was considering an entry in Grand Prix prototype racing—a category above super bikes such as the production-based 996 racer—it asked its buyers whether the company should get involved in this exotic end of the racing circuit. Five thousand owners responded, giving Ducati a great sense of how buyers would react to an even higher offering. This data fed a 400-page report, a core element in Ducati's decision making process.

Looking to duplicate Ducati's online success, other personal transportation companies such as Volkswagen have weighed in with similar strategies. In July 2001 Volkswagen launched its eGeneration Golf subcompact, which it billed as the first mass-produced Internet-ready auto. Sold online, the car comes with computer, cell phone, and MP3 player. The car retailed online for US$19,319, about US$1,800 more than the Web-less Golf you could buy down the street. What Volkswagen intends to do is appeal to the demographics of the Web, enhancing the profitability of each car sale in the process.

Making the Case: A Summary

Effectively using the Web domestically and globally topped shareholders' wish lists for 2001. A successful global strategy will adopt the metrics of the Web, striving to meet the same business goals set for the Internet in general:

- Increase revenue and share in global and domestic ethnic markets.
- Deat competitors.
- Heighten brand awareness.
- Shorten time-to-market.
- Improve collaborative efforts and knowledge management.
- Lower the cost of doing business—both operationally and in servicing customers.
- Focus on the customer.

Of course, these goals are relative. Telling the Budget Committee that you want to increase revenue from international markets is only a third of the story. The other two thirds are metrics (your target improvement) and cost, the basic ante for getting into a market and the continuing cost of com-

peting in that market. Chapters 6 through 9 will lay out the logistical requirements of entering international markets. Chapter 10 ties up these discussions with a more detailed discussion of return on investment (ROI).

Mira's Log

*Having just closed her PowerPoint presentation for the meeting of the board
of directors, Mira had a better sense of what would play well in the boardroom
when she went hat in hand asking for a bigger budget. Her intended cost-
benefit analysis for Acme international would closely mirror what the company has already realized on the e-business front: Better customer service, more
revenue, and stronger brand top the list. Her search for the golden nugget of
truth about returns on globalization showed her that there was no such
nugget, but rather a set of possible outcomes that would vary by company, by
business unit, by market, and even by project. Mira also found that the returns
she would present had to be organic, able to evolve with the rest of the company's initiatives. She had a few jobs to do before she could put numbers on
the table—which international markets should Acme enter first? What investment would it take? And what internal and external resources would she
have to call on? Her first step was to figure out which markets mattered most
to Acme.*

3

Navigating the Global Journey

Mira spent an afternoon surfing the Web to study the online offerings from well-known brands in the United States—Ford, Coke, Sony, Toyota, Shell, McDonald's, and BMW. For the non-U.S. companies, she considered both their home-country and international sites to gauge the effectiveness of each in telling the company's story, selling products, and reinforcing brand. She also looked at a number of lesser known international companies such as Bombardier, Embraer, and Vivendi. She found a wide variation in the quality of the sites, in the amount of information at each, and in the consistency of branding.

At many of the sites she reviewed, she wondered whether anyone from the home office had ever looked at how the company was being represented in other markets. Acme's own efforts around the world reflected the individual country units that built them, but not always in a positive way. While she could see that some countries devoted a great deal of their marketing resources to how they presented themselves online, other countries could not care less about the Web. Of course, standing above everything was the company's U.S. site, chock-full of every interactive aid, thoughtful navigation, and content so fresh that it was still steaming—all because of a corporate decision to build a showcase branded site.

She knew that Acme could do better for its international prospects, customers, partners, and employees, so she began to think about how to get everyone up to a consistently better level. She knew that this effort would require better leadership, sufficient funding, and a rationalized organizational model. She suspected that this would mean getting executive-level buy-in, putting someone in charge, and communicating regularly with affected groups both domestically and internationally.

Issues over Which Mira Would Lose Sleep

This chapter discusses the various organizational models for globalization that someone in Mira's position would face, starting with the best practice of putting a powerful person with executive backing in charge. To gain the support of local and regional subsidiaries, *service level agreements* (SLAs) for content and interactivity should be created. An SLA is a service organization's commitment to certain deliverables within specified time frames for promised levels of service. These agreements remove ambiguity from relationships, clearly laying out the scope of what each party expects of the other. Other key issues discussed are the need to

- *Anoint.* Too many companies do not have anyone in charge—or they have too many who think that they are in charge. You have to break the ownership logjam by putting someone in charge, then backing him or her with the mandate, resources, and advisors to make it happen.
- *Organize.* The most revisited discussion in e-business globalization is whether you should centralize globalization efforts around your corporate site or let your country units manage their own businesses online. This is not a binary decision. Because the Web means so many things—Internet, intranet, extranet—and touches so many pieces of your offline business, no single model will suffice for any globalization effort.
- *Circumscribe.* Because any one of your Web-based initiatives could be so enormous, precise definition is critical. Get consensus on what you are doing in each area, secure the resources to do it, and set expectations appropriate to your plans.
- *Inspire.* Make your country units feel confident that you have their best interests in mind. Avoid the corporate drive-by approach by soliciting their input about their markets' needs and the best way to meet them. Work with them to specify the scope of your support and, wherever possible, push decisions and work down the chain.

Job Number One: Designate a Leader

Too many companies expect operational staff to make their globalization wishes come true. This rarely happens without putting a senior executive in place to direct and oversee the job. Consider, for example, the following cautionary tale:

Too Many Leaders or the Wrong One Can Derail International Plans

Over the course of a few months in 2000, I met six people from the same very large, U.S.-based, high-tech company. I learned from our conversations that each represented a group that was "singularly responsible" for the globalization of the corporate site—that is, creating country-specific paths from www.the-company.com with information appropriately translated and adapted for those markets.

Some of these globalizers did not know that the others existed, while those who did claimed that the others were merely responsible for a very small, specific slice of the corporate site—but no one agreed on which piece. In short, this multinational company lacked a coordinated corporate plan to reach the Eighth Continent. It was spending a large amount of money for these six groups to duplicate the same organizations, business processes, and technologies.

Meanwhile, the company supported operating units in many countries around the world. These business divisions were telling their stories to their local audiences, filtering corporate information through locally colored glasses. Their local Web sites promoted the corporate brand, published information online that they had created themselves, translated useful information that they found at the headquarters site, and duplicated the various "helper" tools, such as personalization, that the corporate group had created to make its site friendlier.

All told, this was an expensive problem with an easily recognized cause: No one was really in charge. Its half-dozen international advocates lacked high-level sponsorship and consequently the authority to do what needed to be done. In the absence of corporate leadership, each country felt compelled to manage its own destiny online. The company's managing directors in different geographies fell into one of two groups:

1. *Countries did it just because they had to.* Each country set about creating its own Web site to meet its local needs. In their rush, they paid little attention to corporate branding guidelines, service-level standards such as 24-7 availability, sharing marketing and design expertise among country units, or reusing complex software technology such as content management and personalization.
2. *Countries did it because they wanted control.* Individual countries needed to flex their self-governance muscles in their continuing

struggle for what some call *internal constituent control*. This approach led them to establish sites without corporate authorization or checking, figuring that they could always ask for forgiveness after the fact.

This polycratic chaos prevented the companies from developing a corporate strategy, from making any coherent assessment of its global plans, and from properly allocating resources by market opportunity.[1] The corporation lost critical time in solidifying its brand worldwide and spent dearly to duplicate efforts in each of its geographies.

<u>Globalization Needs a Champion</u>   While this company represents an extreme case of global dysfunction, it is by no means an exception among the firms that I have interviewed and consulted with over the last 10 years. Your organization can bypass this balkanization by putting a senior executive in charge and giving him or her the authority to make this happen. Some companies call this position the *chief globalization officer* (CGO). Others have a vice president for new or international market development, a vice president of international commerce, a global business czar, or a globalization strategist.

Let's call him the CGO to save space. This person will be responsible for transforming your global Web presence from today's separate channel for each country and business function into an integrated component of your company's growth strategy. Does it sound ambitious, if not impossible? It probably is, but achieving this cross-channel, cross-market symbiosis is far more likely if someone explicitly owns the issue and is accountable for it— than if no one does. To make sure this happens, the CGO might be part of the group that manages your company's Internet operations. For example, Citicorp's Internet Operating Group oversees its North American Web strategy, provides technical support, and manages its back-end operations.[2]

What should be in the CGO's job description?

- *Global Internet strategist.* The Internet Protocol (IP) electricity is breaking down the artificial boundaries that the technology industry set up with labels such as "Web" for consumer interactions, "intranet" for employees, and "extranet" for procurement, supply chains, and marketplaces. Information flows in and out of your company, crossing these boundaries as easily as they fly across international borders without stopping at the checkpoints. Consulting and collaborating with other executives at the corporate and country level, the CGO defines the company's globalization strategy—not only at the consumer level but also internally at the level of employee and business partner interactions.

- *Producer.* The CGO works with resource owners at various levels. In this role the CGO must keep things happening, constantly talking to the "investors" at the board, executive, and country level to reinforce the importance of international markets to shareholder value, continued growth, and even the survival of the firm.

- *Expectation setter.* The CGO draws on resources from corporate marketing, engineering, and other operational groups, especially for corporate-branded sites. He also works with managing directors and Web teams in each of the countries. Working with these corporate and national groups, he develops the general globalization architecture for the company, along with marketing goals and plans. To ensure consistent levels of Internet function and to build a foundation for trust with the national units, he defines SLAs for successive tiers of online activity.

   The SLA commits the CGO's team to delivering certain capabilities or content within specified time frames for tiered levels of service. For example, you might define tiers such as "basic market entry" for smaller markets such as the Czech Republic or Singapore, "full-scale assaults" for more lucrative markets such as Germany, and "procurement system support" wherever the supply chain goes. Later in this chapter I take up the question of SLAs in more detail.

As you review your corporate roster to figure out the best candidate for this position, remember that aligning international expansion with corporate goals is a key factor for globalization success. The CGO should be a senior executive with the authority to direct the globalization initiatives. That means that the CGO must understand the business implicitly so that he can align the international efforts with core business objectives. To succeed, he or she needs a strong awareness of—and preferably experience with—international management issues, the power and limitations of technology in addressing these issues, and the ability to come to grips quickly with a wide range of operational issues. The CGO should also be familiar with and respectful of the company's culture, knowledgeable of processes to "get things done," open-minded to opposing views, and diplomatic, and he or she must be an able negotiator, a great delegator, and a strong evangelist.

Keep reminding yourself and your candidates that the Internet is not merely the Web; there is a whole range of IP-powered systems serving customers, employees, partners, shareholders, and a dozen other external constituencies. Whoever you appoint should understand that the Internet forms the communication and application bedrock for the whole company.

Where did some other globalizing companies find these amalgams of St. Patrick, Paul Bunyan, and Noah Webster? In the case of larger companies with a physical presence in many different countries, they came from the corporate ranks. At others, they were brought in from other companies because they met these core criteria.

<u>Successful CGOs Will Have a Patron</u>   Given the scope of this job, the CGO will experience many trials, not the least of which will be continuing challenges to his authority. One way to disarm such parries will be to consult proactively with all of the corporate and international powers. Another tactic is to equip the CGO with an executive-team board mandate, thus establishing the CEO or the office of the president as the *patron* for globalization and the CGO as the *means* for that to succeed. This mandate will help the CGO as he encounters common problems. For example, this executive will have to work with business units and geographies that are quite accustomed to autonomy in their online decisions.

Organizing Your Company for Global Success

Organizing for the global Web is not a simple matter of putting in place a cookie-cutter business model. The companies that have gone global have found that organizational flexibility is a big factor for international success; no two markets or, for that matter, no two applications on the Internet are the same. Having someone like the CGO work closely with corporate, business units, and your managers in different geographies will provide this worldwide oversight and perspective.

With this in mind, your CGO will quickly find out that the first item on his agenda is the question of *centralized* or *decentralized* control. Do not get sucked into this turf battle. In the typical company, the entrenched corporate bureaucracy rolls out arguments for why you should centralize all Internet activity at the corporate site, while country managers advocate the power of local, decentralized control. Both groups will point to the same chart and argue that it supports their point of view (see Figure 3.1 and Table 3.1).

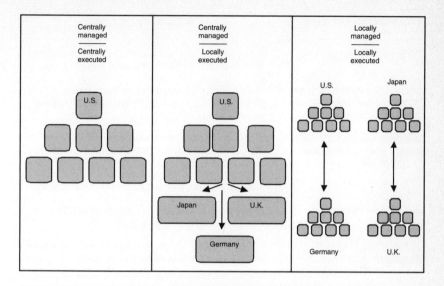

Figure 3.1 Models for Global Organization
Source: Jupiter Media Metrix, January 2000.

Note: This figure represents the classic decision matrix for a centralized versus decentralized organizational approach to the Web. The centrally managed but locally executed model, called the *hybrid,* usually wins out because of its focus on centralizing what should be centralized and distributing the work to the countries. However, given how most companies use the Web, this is only a starting point, rather than the destination.

- *Centralize everything.* This contingent sees great benefit in consolidating staff, technology, spending, and every other aspect of the online business in one place, thus realizing enormous savings in time and money. To them, local anything means inefficiency, duplicated effort, and bigger budgets.
- *Decentralize.* This group points out that the only way to get close to your customers and suppliers is by devolving all control to the local businesses. In their opinion, all corporate does is get in the way of doing business at the local level.
- *Hybrid.* These appeasers in the middle of the diagram contend that both groups are right. They will push for consolidating investment in technology and basic Web services like security at corporate. Countries or regional business units can employ that technology if it meets their needs.

This flexibility is key. However you organize your Internet teams, content, and technology resources, they must be able to respond to the full

Who sets the strategy?	Arguments against
Corporate headquarters	They are usually too autocratic and unresponsive to local market needs and time frames.
Individual country units or regions (often called "geographies")	This laissez-faire approach leads to loss of brand identity and eliminates any economies of scale.
Business units or product groups (they often span geographies)	They are tactical and product-centric. They frequently exhibit the "lead-country" problem, in which the dominant country in the business unit begins building an empire, thus putting it in natural conflict with corporate or local efforts.
Information technology (IT) group	They are too focused on technology and care very little about the actual content
Outsourcers and system integrators	They are divorced from the corporate decision makers and mainstream businesses.

Table 3.1 Shortcomings with Typical Organizational Structures

Note: There are many ways to organize internationally, and this table lists the arguments against the typical approaches. The right way to organize is the one that makes sense for each case. You may have a default preference, but successful efforts require collaboration from each stakeholder listed in the table. The hybrid approach comes closest to the ideal. By centralizing the development, staffing, and management of things that every country needs, you can realize big economies of scale in purchasing software and in developing applications. In reality, none of these approaches meets everyone's requirements. The internet is a hydra-headed beast serving many masters in different geographies and business units, so the right model is the one that makes the most sense for the application.

range of needs—without relegating your business to a one-size-fits-all model (see Figure 3.2). One way that companies have managed this diversity is by looking beyond simple control and execution, laying out instead a plan that emphasizes strategy, tactics, and operations able to morph to meet market needs (see Table 3.2). Strategy needs to funnel down into tactics; many less experienced managers coming from the dot.com world tend to focus more on technology-driven plans, thus requiring them to retrofit strategy to technical tactics.

In all cases, the globalization business advocate at corporate works with teams around the world to establish corporate platforms, processes, and guidance. Other executives may drive this definition directly, as happened at Mexico-based Cemex, where the chief information officer (CIO) led a team to outline its version of this three-pronged strategy.

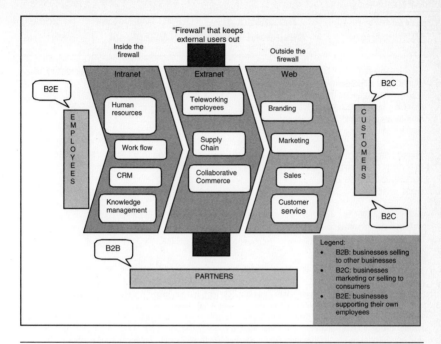

Figure 3.2 One Size Does Not Fit All on the Global Internet
Source: Elisabeth Abeson, IBM presentation at IQPC; various infrastructure vendor presentations.

- *Strategic platforms.* The globalization leader lays out the corporate business strategy, architecture, and support technology for its international efforts. This allows units worldwide to leverage the company's performance in financial, commercial, and operational tasks such as supply chain, inventory, and marketing analysis. This approach leads to more reproducible results, lower costs, balance of control, and measurability. Besides defining the platforms, a corporate group provides technology procurement, integration, and training services for any Web application in the company.
- *Tactical.* Next, the CGO and his global team define a set of standardized processes, interrelated best business practices, and tools—broadly defined as software tools, systems, and work flows—that will be used by a group of people with the right skills at the corporate, regional, and local levels. A corporate "process librarian" or team captures the relevant processes. This activity will dovetail nicely with corporate programs pushing knowledge management and collaboration.

Corporate Headquarters	Transnational Business/Brand	APAC-EMEA-LA-NA Regional	Local Markets
Guidance for how the company presents itself, works with third parties, and delivers services around the world	Follows corporate guidance and recommendations		
Responsible for defining corporate-wide processes and best practices	Uses processes and systems to develop content and applications		
Responsible for setting corporate direction, defining investment strategies	Consulted in development of strategy		

Table 3.2 Let the Organization Structures Meet the Business Need

Note: The hybrid model will evolve into a more flexible response to individual application and market needs. Global market leaders have developed a strategy based on a foundation of strategic, tactical, and operational elements that allow them to offer the right support for each market. Where the work is done or where a site is hosted matters less than does the ability to leverage marketing, project development, and decisions that have already been made after consultation across all corporate entities.

- *Operational.* Finally, they create a rule book—style guides, directives, and operational procedure manuals—that facilitates, clarifies, and allows employees to perform specific tasks using standardized IT, processes, job-related tools, and best practices. This step has been used for years in the automotive and aerospace industries, where enormous amounts of information flow from engineering and original equipment manufacturers (OEM) suppliers to buyers, technicians, service personnel, pilots, and drivers. Chapter 7 discusses these guides in more detail.

The CGO Solicits Input from Corporate, Regional, and Local Colleagues

One of the CGO's most important jobs is keeping the lines of communication open between and among corporate, business units, product groups, regions, and individual countries. As part of this task, the CGO relies heavily on the insight of other executives and on input from the geographies. These advisors include those shown in Table 3.3.

For the sake of this discussion, assume that your title is on this chart, so you are a natural advisor to the chief globalization officer with a stake in

Advisors to Globalization Officer	Responsibilities
VP/director of marketing:	Corporate strategy for international markets
International	Thresholds for entering new markets
Regional	Individual market needs
Individual country units	Resources available for each market
Managing directors	
Chief operations officer (COO)	Budgets
Chief information officer (CIO)	Branding
or corporate director of IT	General marketing
Chief financial officer (CFO)	Conflict resolution
VP/director of operational	Standards for content, technology, staffing
functions	Regional integration
VP/director of product	Plan integration with other channels
management	Benchmark online efforts vs. competitors
Director of research or market	Globalization risk consultancy
intelligence	Focus groups, usability studies
	Work flows, processes, matrixed operations
Legal counsel	Legal issues in other markets

Table 3.3 Strategy Advisor Titles and Functions

how well he or she does the job. You must help the globalization czar keep international projects aligned with the corporate strategy. The effective CGO will consult with these advisors regularly to refine the strategy, deal with conflicts, and manage the dynamic integration of the online business. They will help him prioritize the need for online services by market, both inside and outside the company.

Besides this high-level advice, the CGO also needs tactical guidance to navigate the innumerable fine points, nits, and problems associated with multiple markets. Nineteenth-century strategist Carl von Clausewitz called this *friction,* the countless small things on a battlefield that a commander cannot control but which may come together and have a cumulative, devastating effect. For this kind of advice, the CGO turns to the leaders of globe-girding business units and individual country units (see Figure 3.3).

To help this corporate strategist understand what needs to be done, companies have taken different steps to help him or her do the job depending on how much of an investment they have in a market. Companies that have already moved toward this more flexible model worked within the confines of existing organizational structures, such as the following:

- *If you have a physical presence in a country.* For example, State Street Global Advisors designates an individual in each country to be the person accountable for everything dealing with the Internet. This per-

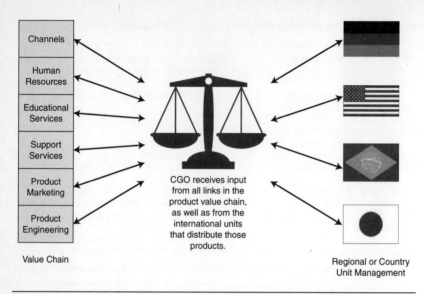

Figure 3.3 Other Key Advisors Sit in the Business Units and Value Chain

Note: Supplement executive advice with directorial and managerial input from business units, product lines, and operational groups. These sources provide critical information on how companies actually work—what it takes to build a product, market it, and get it to market. Ideally, the CGO would be able to solicit input from every market; at the outset of his work, however, it may be only major regions.

son is recognized as the go-to person for all Web activity, both locally and in representing that country's needs to State Street's CGO and his strategic advisors.

Another approach could follow Cisco's model: Several years ago Cisco launched a "Globalization Affirmative Action" program in which the company seeded employees with the word "globalization" in their titles around the company. Through management-by-objective (MBO) compensation packages and training programs, these global provocateurs got everyone in the company thinking about international markets as a core part of their project plans, thus feeding the company's strategy from the bottom up. These individuals kept pushing "international markets" as an agenda item until it became part of product planning, at which point Cisco felt that there was no longer a need for the positions.

- *If you are just entering a market.* You need some in-country knowledge, whether it is your staff—the ideal situation—or a representative such as a distributor or a local marketing agency. U.S.-based

Hoover's entered the European market by hiring a small group in the United Kingdom as the core of its regional headquarters. Because the company wanted to guarantee the integrity of its product offerings in Europe, this core team imported some company DNA from the United States. Hoover's has found that its director must regularly get in front of the headquarters' staff in Texas to keep the international agenda fresh in their minds.

- *If you work through partners.* Third parties such as distributors typically allow the least amount of control and provide the most variable input to the CGO and his or her advisors. To get around these realities, Autobytel arranged for regular communication with its international joint venture partners. Conference calls take place frequently, with a set topic introduced by a subject-area expert who explains the topic and what Autobytel is doing in that area and answers questions. The company has also instituted a CEO Summit, the results of which are posted on an external Internet site dedicated to partners.

This Local Information Might Be Unreliable
The CGO will often find international input to be a noisy channel. Some high-tech companies in the United States have complained that their in-country distributors or expatriate staff rarely reach beyond the jet-set crowd who know English, so they report little or no need to localize for a given market—"English is enough." The CGO should be on the lookout for cases in which the conventional wisdom might be suspect as the Internet reaches deeper into markets and thus beyond the zone of English competence. In these cases, the CGO should go to the source and poll target audiences directly via focus groups and usability studies.

"Every buyer can read English." Some of State Street Bank Global Advisors' international offices believed English to be the universal language of the investment business. However, within months of stating that English-language information was sufficient for Japan, its Japanese office changed its tune when focus groups found that investors—when given a choice—preferred to transact in their own language. Similarly, senior managers in State Street's German unit saw no need for a Web-based application at all because they were not using the Web that much. But younger staff members—the future asset managers—rely on the Web to their job. And even if they are bilingual, they prefer to do their jobs in German, too, because they understand the nuance of the language better than they do English.

<u>Build Trust through Service Level Agreements</u>   A big part of the CGO's job is to stay close to what is happening in the field and to build trust with transnational business units, brands, regions, and local markets. Besides this regular consultation that proves that the CGO is listening to his colleagues, he must prove a commitment to the service levels that will satisfy their markets.

The SLAs support tiers of online activity with increasing amounts of content and function. These pacts unambiguously lay out the services that the corporate group will supply. An example of an SLA in your business today is IT's commitment to round-the-clock support for e-mail. The next section lays out some of the tangible pieces of a service level agreement, namely, how much functionality and content should be supported for a given site.

The net: Many international online business projects fail because they are too authoritarian, too tactical, or too decentralized. Many companies assume that globalization is a *new* set of tasks that must be added to everybody's existing task list—things such as translation, Japanese character support, offering a front-loading rather than a top-loading washer, or putting a North American plug on a DeLonghi espresso maker. However, the right way to think about globalization is that it expands the scope of each of these activities, from product development to marketing to distribution. Success requires executive-level buy-in, someone in charge, and regular communication with all affected groups both domestically and internationally.

Define Project Goals for Each Country and Application

Know why you are entering new territories or enhancing the online support in the markets that you already support. As discussed in Chapter 2, successful globalists have aligned their efforts with their company's business goals (e.g., cost cutting, more revenue, knowledge management). You will find a more receptive audience if your international initiative is tied to mainstream business targets and has metrics against which its success and return on investment (ROI) will be measured. By doing so, you will avoid another area where many companies fail; without a strong business case for entering a particular market and metrics to which to aspire, international sites become nice-to-have projects that are canceled when economic times get tough.

As you lay out your strategy, remember that the Internet encompasses a range of internal and external networks, each focused on delivering services to a particular audience, whether employees, customers, business partners, shareholders, or other business constituencies. Each of these networks supports a variety of critical business applications. However, few companies can support everything for everybody in every market.

You must make the cut and decide which markets to support. This can lead to a very political, testy environment, all the more reason to ensure that you have solicited all views. Furthermore, your company's goals will likely be different for different markets, but in all cases you should reinforce the notions that

- *Second-tier does not mean unimportant.* While Mexico and Poland will not show up as first-tier targets on many companies' list for online retail this year or next, they could be crucial links in your supply chain. Thus, you might decide to translate critical logistics information into Polish and Spanish for your supply chain while your marketing group spends its money targeting consumers in Germany and Japan.

  It will be easier to mollify your representatives in second-tier markets if you employ a methodology for choosing which markets and if they know that their input was considered in the process. This will test the CGO's multicultural management skills. Even for lower-tier markets, treat every market or geography's representative with the respect that you pay to top-priority market reps. Consciously seek out their opinion and collaborate with them on strategy and practical implementation.

- *Every application needs to reinforce the company's branding agenda.* Planners typically relegate marketing and branding sites to the customer-facing front of the Internet, a digital channel to the market. While the focus of such sites is brand for the consumers, other applications on intranets and extranets must present a consistent image as well—especially as the distinctions between the Web, intranets, and extranets disappear. If you do not brand consistently, deeply, and ubiquitously, sooner or later the narrowing gaps between external and internal Internet applications will expose a customer-visible chink in your brand that shows up where you do not want one.

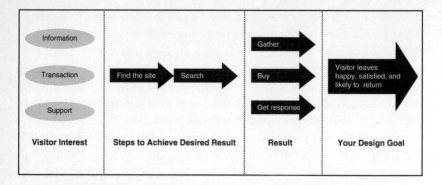

Figure 3.4 Help Visitors in Target Markets Accomplish Key Tasks

Note: Consider three different scenarios for prospects and customers: learning about a product, buying it, and receiving after-sales support. While these situations share several steps, the end game differs substantially. By putting yourself in the place of a visitor to a site, you should be able to fill in the steps along the way to a successful interaction.

Once you decide on which audience and which applications make sense for the markets that you need to support, do not skimp on the quality of implementation. Early movers have found that success comes from providing online visitors with the same high *quality of experience* that you offer domestic users, regardless of where those users live, what language they speak, and which business practices they subscribe to, or their Web connection speeds and cultures (see Figure 3.4). Without such a commitment, your "foreign" customers and corporate buyers will feel shortchanged if they compare the experience that you provide to them to what you offer visitors at your home-country site.

How can you achieve this consistent level of quality? The best place to start is to put yourself on the other side of any service that you offer to international visitors so that you can experience first-hand what they see. As companies develop their second- and third-generation corporate sites, they now have a wealth of data and feedback from users via primary research such as focus groups and interviews on what does and does not work online. While this information comes from your domestic experience, much of it will apply directly to designing great international sites.

For example, many firms are trying to get over the major stumbling blocks of online design that they have found in their home markets. These problems typically include hard-to-find product information, inadequate search capabilities, over-the-top marketing language, obstacles to completing a transaction such as payment options, accessibility concerns for handicapped individuals, and confusing or misleading information.[3] For example, if information is the goal or if you want to get someone to make a decision that is favorable to your product, what data and applications would be required? As always, it is a matter of common sense: What must people do to get information from your company or to buy from you? Put yourself in their shoes and design accordingly. Some companies do this internally by polling associates, while others conduct primary research campaigns in their target markets.

The net: Know what you want to accomplish and how that goal fits into the overall scheme of things. This will ensure a greater return and more resilience against cancellation of your international initiatives. To make sure that your international customers remain loyal, set a goal for your top-tier markets that you will offer them a quality of experience that is commensurate with what you show domestic customers. Of course, each of your markets will want that high-quality experience, but one of the CGO's tough jobs is determining which markets will and which will not, as well as how to fund it.

Set Limits on Quantity of Experience: Living within a Budget

Once you decide on your target audience and objectives and on the outcomes you expect, determine what it will take to meet expectations. Of course, every goal has limits set by money, time, resources, market pressures, and a host of other variables. For instance, considering the thousands of pages and enormous amounts of software development support at successful Web businesses such as IBM and Renault, it is hard to envision meeting that goal of uniform quality in every market or in every business unit as well. At this point, you have to be realistic, understanding that you will never have enough resources to do a great job in every market. Your challenge is to figure out how much of what you do so well domestically is required to convince foreign customers that you are serious about meeting their needs on their terms. This test applies whether you are talking about customers, employees, or business partners.

Instead of offering everything on your domestic site to everyone in the world, determine what it would take to make a credible presence in their own countries. Then balance this against the investment needed to provide that capability and against the return that you expect on that expenditure. In an ideal world, you would translate and adapt everything from your domestic market. In the real world, you have to calculate the ROI for each and every new market.

Witness consumer-facing efforts such as GM BuyPower or Renault, both business-to-consumer projects tasked with gathering leads, providing enough information to consumers to help them make a major purchase decision, and reinforcing their respective brands in the process. The balance of this chapter focuses on external consumer audience, but the same issues apply to greater or lesser degrees to business and employee audiences. What do you want from consumers living on the Eighth Continent? Online marketing and sales embrace a wide range of online activity (see Table 3.4). Most companies start at the informational end of the spectrum, investing in more ambitious integrated marketing and transactional support as they evolve their Internet presence in a market.

The net: Know what you want to accomplish and what it will take to accomplish it. First, study what makes your domestic effort so successful by assessing which information is required for each market. Next, transform this information, making it appropriate to the market that you are in, relying on primary in-market research to know what is expected. Finally, adopt a philosophy of continual change, improving your offerings in a gradual and orderly manner but fast enough to match the velocity of change in your home market.

Study and Assess: What Content Should Be at Which Site?   Get
used to a term bandied about in Internet circles—*content.* What you find at Internet sites is also content, but the interactivity of the Web makes it trickier. Online businesses deliver content tailored to a visitor's activity or to personal details that they provided at registration. Examples of such dynamically generated content include the familiar recommendations at booksellers and music sites, measurements that you provide to a clothing retailer, or seat selection and meal preferences that you give to a travel company.

So, content online is a more slippery concept that includes much more than text. When Web masters and other specialists talk about content, they not only embrace text but also consider a site's appearance (known as *look and feel*), navigation, and usability. They also rope in applications such as the collaborative filtering that personalizes content based on visitor pref-

	Information	Marketing, Prospecting, and Supporting	Integrated Sales & Marketing	Transparent Channels
F U N C T I O N S	Publish company and product information online. The basic goal is to represent the company and its offerings online.	Market the company's wares, creating demand that will be satisfied through other channels (typically through physical stores or face-to-face meetings with sales representatives). The online goal is to create prospects for these other channels and, in more advanced instances, actually sell the product.	Draw in prospects online, create demand, and satisfy it via the Web.	Provide customer with a consistent view of your business regardless of how they choose to interact.
O F F E R I N G S	• Corporate data like mission, executive management, and financials • Address, telephone, and other contact details • Product line details • Answers to frequently asked questions (FAQs)	PLUS • Basic interactivity like e-mail, chat, and webcasts • "Contact us" e-mail • Registration for more detailed information or for a sales contact • Newsletter and product updates • Basic customer support	PLUS • Content tailored to customer action or profile • Features like mortgage calculators or Lands' End virtual model for clothing fit • Customer self-service.	PLUS Cross-channel information sharing, both about products and customers
E X A M P L E S	First step for nearly every e-business on the planet	Current state of affairs online for most large companies More advanced commercial sites sell bulky or expensive goods such as Ducati, GM, and GE Power	Online and catalog retailers like Bertelsmann, Dell, Great Universal Stores, Lands' End, and Travelocity	Online Olympus—what every firm aspires to

Table 3.4 Consumer-Facing Business Channels

Note: Outward-facing Web sites provide information to prospects, whether they are consumers at home or business buyers at other companies. Most e-business activity starts at the informational end of the spectrum and adds more interactivity and commercial support over time. Early movers have found that it is expensive and difficult to roll out feature-rich Web sites simultaneously in more than a few markets, so some segment their international market plans into two or more tiers. Top-tier markets usually receive the same level of support as does the headquarters' country, while second-tier markets might be a generation behind in capability.

erences, the databases that feed product comparisons, and even data about the data that set the rules of engagement (often called *metadata*).

The CGO, in consultation with his or her advisors and country-unit managing directors, must figure out how much of this content—broadly defined as text, images, and applications—is required to create a credible story for a company in a given market. For a company like eBay or Yahoo!, online persona is the extent of its business and its brand: Everything is important. For less transactional companies, though, market needs will be focused more on basic information. In general, more developed markets will demand more content than will smaller or less lucrative markets. How can you deliver that high-quality experience to lesser markets with much less content than your domestic site?

- *Basic market entry.* Companies like EMC and Eastman Chemical have found that by determining which content is absolutely essential for their customers, they can systematically translate and adapt core information for each market they choose to enter without breaking the bank (see Figure 3.5). More established markets get more attention, content, and investment.
- *Other Internet applications.* Internal systems and supply chains will need other content to be effective. This notion of a core set of content applies just as much to those other uses of the Internet. For example, employees worldwide will need access to your corporate human re-

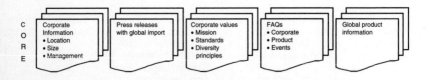

Other content types that could be translated for a demanding market:
- Supporting content: More detail about products and the company, such as product reviews, and company and executive profiles.
- Additive applications: Calculators, wizards, personalization, and CRM that enhance the experience, all typically requiring adaptation for other markets.

Locally produced content types:
- Information about the company as it operates in the country, including local staff, contact information, and press releases
- Locally published product reviews and stories about the company

Note: Most companies do not answer foreign mail to their "Contact Us" link. Do not follow this worst practice.

Figure 3.5 Content Basics for Entering a Consumer Market

Note: Successful globalizers have found that they can create a credible presence in other markets by providing a core set of information about their companies. This figure lists the basic information types, which might add up to 100 pages that must be translated and adapted for each market where the company sells its wares. Differentiating applications that enhance the brand, such as the Lands' End virtual model for sizing clothes, will migrate into the core over time.

source policies and various operational procedures such as expense reporting and procurement. Similarly, your manufacturing organization will likely need essential bits of process and catalog content adapted and translated for its international suppliers and subcontractors. Whether consumer-facing or intended for employees and partners, the same principles still apply about creating a well-defined set of basic content that meet user needs in each relevant application.

This inventory of your basic domestic content establishes the assets that are critical to your brand and that paint a positive face for your company. Consider how this core content catalog must be adapted for each market you enter:

- *Use it as is.* Details like the corporate logo and many product images—those without text and giveaway faces—typically do not have to change by market, but make sure to test them in focus groups to ensure that they are localized into acceptable terms in each market. Some corporate logos may well have to change; for example, Xerox had to change the digital red X in Russia because one of the most obscene words in Russian begins with this letter and is often abbreviated to just this letter in graffiti on bathroom walls.
- *Translate directly.* You can usually have product descriptions translated into complete, semantically equivalent translations in French or Japanese. Remember, though, that because they describe a product that you are trying to sell, it could be part of a legally binding contract representing features or functions. Do not translate product catalogs indiscriminately—some products may not be available in all markets.

   The product names themselves often pose a real problem, as they rarely translate well from language to language. Consider the fine products of the Paxan Corporation in Iran, which I first encountered on offer in central Europe (see Figure 3.6).[4] For the non-Farsi speaker, "barf" means "snow."
- *Adapt to local market needs.* Prices should be in local currency, and phone numbers should reflect national conventions. You will have to change special offers such as discounts; or, as Lands' End discovered in Germany, you might even have to alter something core to your value proposition. Until the law was changed in 2001, German regulators determined that Lands' End's familiar lifetime, no-questions-asked guarantee broke local laws regarding unfair competition. Chapters 4 and 5 address such issues in more detail.

Figure 3.6 Would You Buy This Laundry Detergent?

- *Avoid certain content.* Things like national flags will not play well in some markets. For retailers like Dell, the offer to customize a product makes no sense if all they sell is off-the-shelf computers in a given country. Images of women sans chador—the head-to-toe covering for women in some Islamic countries—will not fly well in some Islamic states. Test the advertising campaigns and photographic images intended for use on the site on local audiences—not just on your employees in those countries who may be inured to such images.

Because companies that establish a core content model know exactly what they will translate in order to enter a new market, the cost of entry plus maintaining a site in that market becomes a simple mathematical formula. In EMC's case, core content equates to so many words translated at so many cents a word by its translation outsourcer, thus giving the company a solid number to use in budget projections. Whenever the core content changes, EMC's internal systems ripple the modification out to its translation bureau, where whatever has been changed is retranslated. I discuss the content model and its interaction with the process of translation in Chapter 7.

Globalization Is a Fact of Life in Many Market Segments

State Street found that its non-U.S. customers wanted U.S. news and views as well as their own. In planning conversations with international offices, its Boston-based planners found a local tendency to overstate the national flavor so much that they pulled out all the American information. But they found that Australian clients, for example, wanted both global and local views, telling their Boston colleagues that "You manage the Australian market, and I want to know what you tell the rest of world about us." Investors and buyers of networking gear care very much about what is happening in the U.S. market.

The net: A core content catalog will help you understand the costs of entering a new market, getting you away from finger-in-the-wind budget estimates. As your ambitions in a market increase, the amount of content you must offer will rise correspondingly. This content core is dynamic, requiring periodic review to ensure that it continues to represent your company and meet the needs of international audiences. Meanwhile, the application side of content will expand as well, with more advanced markets such as the United States, United Kingdom, and the Nordic countries demanding all the bells and whistles of modern Web design. Finally, if you are already operating on the ground in a country, expect that country's management to lobby heavily for the highest level of support for that country. But the CGO and his advisors must stick to their methodological guns and apply the same metrics across the board.

Transform: Determine the Right Level of Adaptation for Each Market

Denizens of the Eighth Continent have lots of choices. They can click away to a competitor or even to another one of your sites. With the core content catalog in hand, your next decision is to determine which markets get platinum-level service—what I call *full-context personaliza-*

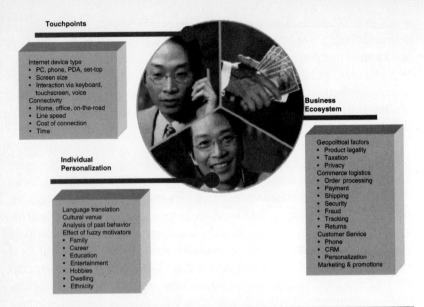

Figure 3.7 Globalization Means Full-Context Personalization

Note: Successful global e-businesses recognize that they must adapt their offers to customer needs, modify their ways of doing business so that they make sense to international customers, and support Web access by using the devices preferred by those customers.

tion, reflecting their individual motivators, the ecosystem in which they do business, and the means that they use to access the Internet (see Figure 3.7). I discuss the three major slices—individual personalization, touch-points, and business ecosystem—next. The figure represents the complete palette of full-context personalization. If you did it all for more than your home market—which no company has done yet, though many aspire to—then you would create an experience that feels right at home for those international users. This ideal does not apply just to consumer sites, either. As you build out Internet sites to improve the productivity of your employees and optimize the efficiency of your supply chain, you will have to address each of these three slices to some degree.

1. *Individual personalization: Localize the experience for each market.* When I went to buy *Harry Potter and the Sorcerer's Stone* at Amazon.com, the site recommended Louis Sachar's *Holes.* But what would it suggest to a Japanese consumer interested in the same Harry Potter book? Would its recommendation engine be sensitive enough to detect the buyer's .co.jp (Japan) domain extension on his e-mail ad-

dress? Each consumer and every corporate buyer is driven by a complex set of psychographic motivators that determine how he reacts to a marketing message, brand, or online selling process.

Therefore, translating product descriptions is not enough. Successful global companies will take the next step and adapt their online marketing techniques to account for national differences in fuzzy motivators such as career, education, and family factors. In the process, their marketing teams will create psychographic profiles that segment their international audiences in each market and in each demographic swath just as they have done domestically. A business site might choose to personalize not to an individual, but rather to a company, perhaps dynamically generating screens for all purchasing agents at BMW or Schneider Electric using the same company-specific profiles.

Ask yourself: Can your target audience read your message? If they can, does it make sense to them in their cultural context? For example, French sites would dump cultural nods to Astérix,[5] a cartoon character as well known in France as Mickey Mouse is in America.

2. *Business ecosystem: Adapt to the buyer's way of doing business.* Online commerce does not happen at dot.com sites; instead, it takes place behind the Web screens on servers, databases, and corporate transaction systems inside your business ecosystem. This complex, entrenched foundation runs your business but typically must be adapted to deal with country-specific issues such as taxation and with basic logistical issues such as shipping and customer service.

Ask yourself: Could a visitor to your site actually buy something? Would he have the means to pay you? Could you deliver his order, getting it through customs? Do not rely on your own faculties to answer these questions, but go to the source and poll people in the markets that they are targeting via usability studies. Chapters 6 and 7 discuss these questions of business system and geopolitical adaptation in more detail.

3. *Touchpoints: Let visitors use what is customary in their markets to interact.* Traditional Web marketing in the States assumes PCs or Macs running AOL or Internet Explorer. The Europeans and Japanese, however, are more open-minded about Web access and ambitiously look to a future Web that is accessible through cell phones. While the sedentary American Internet user will continue to exist, lots of retail, travel, financial, and even business applications will have many users dialing in from cell phones. These points of access affect design and execution; for example, Flash animations will not work on a cell phone,

and in some markets, limited bandwidth, expensive dial-up, and weak telecom infrastructure will spoil your best design efforts even on a fully loaded PC.

This will not be a case of just simple reformatting, but rather a question of offering different services and targeting appropriate audiences. Your Web designers and transaction specialists must dramatically rethink how they interact with their global customers—whether they are consumers or corporate purchasing agents.

Ask yourself: How will you deal with access by non-PC users? Can you manage to serve technology-deprived areas that have slow networks or bad connections? Chapter 7 discusses these translation and infrastructure issues in more detail.

The net: Don't expect to reach this ultimate level of personalization for every international market. Your CGO, advisors, and budget will reserve this Four Seasons class of service for only the top-tier target countries with the right Internet and economic demographics. However, for any market that you enter, visitors will expect a top-rate treatment of the core content that you do offer along with some linguistic, cultural, and political sensitivity to the unique needs of their market.

Kaizen: Commit to Service Level Agreements

Web sites, whatever their purpose, are never completed.[6] The volume of content increases year over year. The content changes imperceptibly by the hour and traumatically by the year, the volatility driven by changes in the business. More and more types of information—memos, animation, presentations, chat, spreadsheets—find their way from every corner of the company to the corporate site. Truckloads of new technology arrive regularly, belying the idea that a company has a standard for managing corporate data and content management.

That is just the domestic situation with which your company's technologists and planners are already struggling. As you move into international markets, they will have to manage these four *V*s—content volume, volatility, variety, and technology variability—across dozens of international sites. Because the Web is such a dynamic channel, your domestic sites change frequently and instantaneously. International sites have to follow suit, or they will quickly become inconsistent in presenting corporate information, in time leading to incorrect or outdated data.

This demand for consistency is a function of the online mobility of the Eighth Continent. The combination of bilingual visitors, machine-generated translation offered at sites such as Google and AltaVista, and even just a simple eyeballing of two experiences—what you offer your domestic market versus what you offer a foreign market—will be enough to demonstrate substantial differences in treatment. It's only a matter of time before this divergence becomes apparent in the form of different prices, product descriptions, and representation of your brand. In the best of cases, this deviation will result in simple confusion. In the worst case, it can lead to legal liability and loss of credibility in international markets.

The best way to deal with this reality is again by developing service level agreements between headquarters and your international subsidiaries or distributors (see Table 3.5). SLAs remove ambiguity from relationships by clearly laying out rights, responsibilities, and remedies. The service levels should be dynamic agreements that are renegotiated depending on changes in situations. These SLAs should exist between divisions of the same com-

Market Tier	Level of Support	Content Update Latency	Lag Time for Adding One-Plus Features
Headquarters country	All corporate content and personalization applications	None	None
Tier 1— Top 2 or 3 markets	Corporate core translated into local language plus locally generated content	24 hours	90–120 days
Tier 2— Next 6–10 markets	Corporate core translated into local language	48 hours	Not applicable
Candidates— All other markets	Watch list to determine when they reach established thresholds for support	Quarterly reviews	

Table 3.5 Sample Service Level Agreements by Market

Note: This table amalgamates market entry plans from several online retailers that sell also through catalogs and physical stores. Each defined several tiers of market support and committed to content levels, to the frequency with which content would be updated, and to the amount of time that would elapse before major interactive features would be available in the other markets. Your service agreements, of course, will reflect your own needs, internal systems, processes, supporting vendors, and other factors.

pany—for example, between the CGO's budgetary organization and local business units—and with the third-party suppliers discussed in Chapter 9. Here are some characteristics of a typical service level agreement:

1. *Basic information.* Characterize the level of online development that you will provide, specifying the core content catalog and the kind of market adaptation or localization that corporate will provide. Basic hygiene issues such as brand integrity and security should be high on this list for first- and second-tier markets.
2. *Responsibility.* Be specific about where each service will be performed. Some companies have set up technical development or marketing competence centers at the regional or even national level, thus complicating the management.
3. *Service levels.* For each tier, lay out the service level basics such as site performance and reliability. If the corporate group will host national sites, issues like 24-7 coverage, five 9's reliability (99.999%), and response time for downloads will be major factors. Be specific about the intervals between minor updates—for example, translating press releases or changes to product descriptions—and major revisions to the site. For countries that host their own sites, the requirement flows in the other direction, as corporate should demand consistency and responsiveness, all in protection of the corporate brand and reputation.
4. *Measurement.* To deal with the political reality, describe the conditions that would allow a country to move up to the next tier of support—for example, increased Web usage in a given country, better brand recognition, enhanced support for brick-and-mortar projects, or heavier local competition. Conversely, identify what could cause corporate to pull the plug on a given market strategy. Causes for cancellation could include significant changes in the economic situation of a country, a decline in the Internet demographics of the market, legal changes that make a continued presence impractical, and so on. Basically, the SLA means that you will have fewer surprises.

   The service level agreements that you reach with your national business units or distributors should reflect market reality. For example, Hoover's emphasizes the importance of local responsiveness, but recognizes that because of market size, the United States will always have the most functional and feature-rich site. Its U.K. site will be functionally superior to its continental European sites, but its European team expects that over time the United Kingdom and Europe will become roughly similar.

These differences stem from both market demographics and technical factors. For example, Hoover's European content database is neither as big nor as capable as its U.S. database. The functional differences cut both ways, leading Hoover's to enhance wireless access in the United Kingdom before the United States with its multiple cell phone standards. The company expects this wireless access to be a success factor in southern Europe with its lower PC penetration.

Chapters 7 and 8 will outline the technical, process, and organizational best practices for fulfilling the promise of this SLA approach to international markets.

The net: Even with service level agreements, many companies will find themselves fighting a constant rear-guard action by local business units to set up autonomous sites. Companies exerting a strong central brand presence have shut these sites down as soon as they have found them. Local and regional representation on the strategy council will go a long way toward making this happen.

Balancing Quality of Experience against Corporate Realities

Globalization doesn't just happen by itself. Successful international efforts require leadership and cooperation among the various stakeholders.

- *The chief globalization officer.* Whatever you call it, you need someone who can afford to take an overarching view without worrying about low-level managerial details. The CGO will complement his or her efforts with the close cooperation and advice of other executives at corporate, in the regions, and in individual countries.
- *Flexibility.* The right organizational model for these efforts is not cast in stone tablets under the statue of "Our Founder" in the lobby at headquarters. The right model is the one that works for the application. The CGO will drive the company to define and support the strategic platforms, document the tactical procedures, and create the operational guidebooks for this to happen correctly.

- *Quality.* Each prospect, employee, and partner comes to your company's Internet sites with expectations about what he or she will find there. How the sites live up to this anticipation will define your success in the market. Deliver what is expected of you in the markets that are important to your company.

- *Trust building.* So that business units and geographies feel comfortable that their needs are being considered and met, the CGO must actively seek their opinions and provide service level guarantees for any functions that corporate assumes as its own. Experience shows that individual countries with limited Web resources will appreciate the support straightaway, but transnational business units may take more convincing since their revenue is on the line and they have the bodies to do the work to their satisfaction. The CGO must provide value to these people as well. Chapters 6 and 7 discuss service and procedure aspects of this commitment, while Chapter 8 outlines the corporate support organization for these efforts.

Mira's Log

Mira worked with her executive counterparts to set up a strategy council for Acme, drawing its membership from both the vice presidential and director ranks in the United States and in each market where the company had a presence. She also made sure that each product line was represented in the international planning effort. Because she stepped forward with the idea, the CEO thanked her for volunteering for the "critical but challenging role" of leading the council.

Then Mira set up a subcommittee of the strategy council to work on assessing what content was basic to Acme's online success. Another group considered the requirements of ultimate personalization, while still another blocked out service level agreements. Her next step was to get the strategy council working on which international markets made the most sense for Acme's product line.

4

Deciding Which Markets Matter

With a list of expected benefits in hand, Mira next considered where and how it made the most sense for Acme Widgets to invest its limited budget in creating a local Web presence in international markets. Initially, she was tempted, as are many American and British companies, to take the easy way out by first pursuing only those anglophone (English-speaking) markets that account for most of today's online commerce. But she also read that in less than five years the linguistic balance of the Eighth Continent would tip, making buyers in English-speaking countries the minority. As she caucused with operational teams in different markets, she learned that an increasing number of Acme's employees did not speak English fluently, if at all, and the company's supply chain now crisscrossed the planet in Gordian knots of technology, language, and regulation.

With some 200 countries to pick from, she knew that Acme could not support them all, so Mira had to figure out where the buyers were online, as well as what products they wanted to buy. This Web-politik would require quite a bit of research, a methodology to separate the international wheat from the chaff, and a lot of diplomacy to mollify affiliates in second-tier markets.

Next, Mira called colleagues in Acme's offices around the world and her business school buddies at other companies. She wanted to conduct her own primary research on buyer demographics by market, on how Acme's product might map to needs in each market, and on how the decisions of different polities—nations, states, churches, nongovernmental organizations (NGOs)— might affect the company's chance to expand into a given market.

Mira also pulled up research from the usual suspects—eMarketer, IDC, Gartner, Forrester—along with that of some other firms studying international and ethnic opportunities—Ipsos-Reid, Cheskin, GeoMarkets—to get a taste of how global markets were faring. She also called down to Acme's competitive intelligence group to get a sense of the competitive position of Acme's top rivals in other countries and to take a look at the group's early warning list of potential threats.

Deep in her thoughts and research, Mira took a call from the CEO, who asked whether she had a current passport. It was official: The Board had formally named Mira Acme's chief globalization officer (CGO). Now her mission was to find the best international investment opportunities for Acme.

Forces that Drive an Investment in Localized Sites

As Mira discovered, deciding where you should offer translated, localized information and how much of it are basic international marketing functions. This chapter discusses the major decisions that you will face in moving beyond your home-country markets.

- *Globalization is not an all-or-nothing proposition.* This is not a binary decision. Some markets make natural sense to support because you have a significant customer base. Others will be less obvious and might involve localizing your internal operations or a behind-the-scenes supply chain before tackling the consumer-facing Web site.
- *Language plus country make a market.* Most globalists start out by reviewing the countries or the languages that are important to their business. Here I outline the more evolved notion of *country-language pairs,* also called *locales.* For example, supporting the German language for Germany is such a pair that I would characterize as a discrete market or locale, just as Spanish for U.S. Latinos or French for Canadian francophones are unique markets. I call languages like Chinese, English, and Spanish that are spoken by people in different countries *megalanguages.* Some companies go global by first creating an international site for all English or Chinese speakers regardless of where they live.
- *Seven guideposts for global marketing.* Just as we have the traditional four Ps of marketing (product, price, place, and promotion) to guide us, we can look to similar guideposts for moving into international markets. Here we discuss the three Ps: product portability, Internet penetration, and the polities that you must consider for each market. These discussions will always revolve around return on investment

(ROI) factored against the benefits discussed in Chapter 2. Don't forget to document the process for deciding how and when you will adapt your corporate site and its underlying systems to local market needs.

- *Tiered support lessens the burden.* Too many globalization aspirants want to enter every country at once and offer phenomenal levels of service in each one. Here I lay out the notion of a multitier approach to entering only the markets that matter.

When Supporting a Market Online Should Be a No-Brainer

One thing that I have learned over the last few years of talking to companies is that globalization is not a binary decision. You can indeed be a little global—and some of the best thinkers in this space have gone global incrementally. This step-wise approach means picking the right markets to offer the appropriate level of localized support. The first moves of these market leaders may have been to reach out to established customers in strong markets, while others have worked at the problem from behind the scenes, striving to improve the efficiency of their Web-based internal operations and supply chains. There are a few cases where most companies will not hesitate to go global:

- *Make relationships in an established market more profitable.* If you already have a significant brick-and-mortar presence or a healthy customer base in a market, you might choose to short-circuit the evaluation process and go directly to creating a branded site for that country or improving the locally built site that you already have. For example, both BMW and Sony get a significant share of their revenue from the American market, so they pushed their U.S. subsidiaries to invest heavily in localized sites. Any of the expected benefits of a global online business—better support for local customers, competitive pressures, and so on—could steer you to online investment where you already have a physical presence.

Localization or nationalization? Some companies talk of *nationalizing* their Web sites, an unfortunate term in some markets where government edicts have removed companies from the private sector. The term that many use to describe the tailoring of a site, a document, or a business to national markets is *localization*. This term is actually more correct than *nationalization* in its broadest sense because it incorporates the sense of locale plus language. For example, that lets you talk about localizing to the U.S. English or Latino markets, two different activities.

- *Increase the productivity of international employees.* You might choose to localize only the inward-facing part of your company in order to sustain internal manufacture—for example, to support *maquiladoras* in Mexico or offshore software development in India or Russia. This may take a simple form. For example, Germany's Siemens uses automated computer translation to give employees around the world the gist of e-mail communications in other languages, thus improving the flow of information between business units.

  These internal considerations are often more straightforward than any other decisions. Review your in-country staff and its fluency with your corporate language and determine whether nonlocalized information stands in the way of productivity or progress. Some global companies may not even realize that not all of their staff speaks fluent English.

- *Extend supply chains to new geographies and opportunities.* If your international supply chain suffers from a lack of local language or market logistics support, you might look at localization as a way to increase efficiency. Multinational firms like DaimlerChrysler now envision broader, multilingual procurement systems. This international, multilingual supply chain will be a growing concern for companies that have chosen English as their lingua franca. And as the Web insinuates itself into more small- and medium-sized businesses around the world, the guarantee of English-speaking users will become null and void, thus driving up costs or increasing the time it takes to get a product to market.

These are the easy cases. If you are like many globally branded companies that sell directly to consumers, you have already got a pretty good sense of which markets might make the most sense for further investment in a more localized experience. But you are probably also somewhat behind where you want to be on the question of more local supply chain and internal operations over the Internet.

Now it is time to approach the question of which market deserves your next round of investment.

It Takes More Than a Border to Make a Market

On the Eighth Continent, the political entity of a country combines with language, culture, legal systems, and business practices to create a distinct market. If you went by language alone, you could expose your firm to some nasty legal problems and consumer reaction to the wrong language.

Languages Mapped against the Countries Where They Are Spoken
Let's map a language to a country in the three most common variants:

1. *One country, one language.* These are linguistically simple markets with a one-to-one correspondence of language to the political entity—for example, Japan or Korea. Once you choose to enter such a market, you must render your message in their language and localize the experience to national currency, practices, and expectations.
2. *One country, multiple languages.* More complex markets involve multiple languages used in a single polity, such as French and Flemish in Belgium. In these situations, the sound business approach is to pick the country-language pair that makes the most economic or political sense. For example, Quebec's Bill 101 made French the official law of the province. Combined with subsequent Canadian federal legislation, doing business in English sometimes mandates operating in French as well; therefore, English-only sites might not be an option.[1]
3. *Multiple countries, one language. Megalanguages* such as Chinese, English, French, Portuguese, and Spanish are spoken in different countries around the world. Even languages with smaller populations can span national boundaries, as Dutch does with the Netherlands and Belgium.

Should you enter individual markets or the more universal megalanguage market? The business case that you will establish as you work through the issues in this chapter will drive your decision one way or the other. Many companies start their international push by supporting multinational languages with no reference to any single country (see Figure 4.1). They use the country-agnostic support for a megalanguage as a first

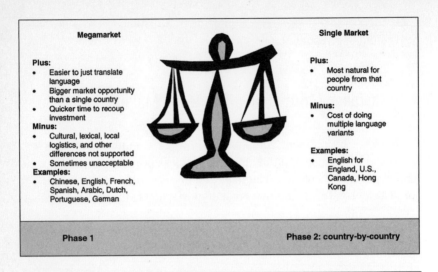

Figure 4.1 Individual Markets versus Megalanguage Markets

Note: Choosing to enter one market in one language and localized logistics and legal support or an international language market without such adaptation is one of the first decisions that you will be asked to make. There are arguments for both approaches—on both the cost and the time-to-market ledgers. Many companies start with the universal variants and incrementally add individual country support as the business case justifies.

step to get accustomed to the idea of managing translation projects and synchronizing content between the home-country site, as well as the raft of process and organizational issues that will come up.

Without exception, companies that have taken this approach adopt the megalanguage dialect used in the biggest, most lucrative markets. For example, Sony might target Parisian French before supporting smaller countries with lower Internet densities, figuring that francophones in Quebec and elsewhere could understand the language well enough. Besides addressing the needs of a large population speaking another language, this approach lets a company get its feet wet with technology that will allow it to manage the more complex content that will come from managing content for multiple countries.

Cultural adaptation might be more appropriate than translation. An adaptation in which you pay homage to religious and cultural differences might be sufficient for some domestic ethnic populations that can operate in the mainstream. For example, informational sites in the United Kingdom might list religious and national holidays that are important to its South Asian residents and remove certain content that is offensive or not germane. U.S. firms might do the same for Hispanic visitors. Some Latino-focused sites have even added "Spenglish" content—the wedding of English with Spanish words. However, this adaptation comes with a price. You still need to keep the culturally tuned site synchronized with the corporate mother ship so that information remains current, consistent, and correct.

Portability, Penetration, and Polity Determine Which Single Markets Win

Once you advance past the megalanguage step, you must determine which individual market makes the most sense for you. Many companies start their analysis with the traditional four Ps of marketing—product, price, promotion, and place. In my conversations with many early adopters, I have isolated the three Ps of global marketing (see Table 4.1) that drive them to the next step of analysis: (1) the "portability" or suit-

Portability	• Does your product travel well, meeting international requirements and market expectations? • Can you deliver products to that market? • Can you promote your products in those markets? **Action:** Consider individual products and whether each has any appeal or serviceability outside your current trading areas.
Penetration	• Are there enough people online to make an investment worthwhile? • Are prospects fluent in your language? • Do they use your currency or means of payment? • Are there secondary markets that might be more interesting? **Action:** Determine whether consumers or business buyers in those markets have the funds, means, and inclination to buy.
Polity	• Can you legally sell your products in a given market? • Do your products violate local sensibilities or cultural taboos and shibboleths? **Action:** Ascertain whether you're legally entitled to sell and support that product in each country-language pair, heeding not only governmental regulations but cultural and religious sensitivities as well.

Table 4.1 Three Ps of Global Marketing

Note: You are probably already familiar with Kotler's four Ps in discussing markets. Rather than limit the discussion to the channel or shelf placement, the three Ps extend it to the readiness of a given product to be sold into a community. Issues of people having access to the channel, means of payment, and simply desire to buy vary by country.

ability of products for international markets, (2) the online "penetration" in a given market, and (3) the "polity" (i.e., the oversight of national, church, or nongovernmental organization) within which online activities must occur.

Portability: Does Your Product, Service, or Content Travel Well?

Successful international marketers have found that it is easier to establish a value proposition for products and services at the core of the Internet economy—retailing, travel and leisure, entertainment, and financial services—than for other market segments that deal in bulkier, more complex, or market-specific products. In short, what looks like it might sell on the global net is usually what sells on the domestic net (see Table 4.2).

The next step is to map product and service offerings to the needs of other markets. The CGO will work with executive advisors, business unit

Category	Characteristics	Example
Physical products	Easily transported goods	Books, CDs and other electronic media, clothing, electronics, repair parts
Product information • Presales marketing • Product information • Postsales service	Information about any kind of product or service, and the actual customer service	Chemicals, motorcycles, cars, generators, computers
Virtual (or bit) products	Ownership of bits exchanged between two or more parties	Financial services, electronic tickets and other travel reservations, downloadable entertainment
Corporate information	Corporate information, branding, messaging	Internet extends corporate branding to anyone with a Web browser

Table 4.2 What Sells on the Global Net

Note: The information, goods, and services delivered over the Internet vary little from country to country. As you plan your international adventures, consider the basic Net-ready categories against your product catalog.

directors, and country unit managers around the world to determine the suitability of products. Together, these will (1) determine whether your products can be sold outside your home market; (2) resolve whether there is a need in other markets for your offerings; and (3) figure out whether you can promote, sell, deliver, and support them beyond your domestic markets.

Step 1: Are Your Products International?   Thumb through your catalog to see which items or services might have appeal outside your domestic market. This is the beginning of an exercise that will require the active collaboration of your colleagues in individual markets around the world, systematic analysis of individual products, and deep research into market needs and logistics. What you will establish here is the *global readiness* of your offerings. Any decision about international business in general—including using the Web to reach anybody online anywhere on the planet—requires a major analysis of your products and how universal or locale-dependent your products are.

- *Few products are ready to travel today.* Some products are very generic and would be useful anywhere on the planet without modification. Few products other than a pencil, or a mousetrap, come to mind; the function of each is fairly obvious.

  For virtual products such as media, you might find that formats are wrong. And with any bit product other than entertainment, it is likely to be in the wrong language. Hoover's, the U.S.-based business information company, employs a single database worldwide, but it must provide a different linguistic persona and additional content based on the country from which you sign on. The British Hoover's speaks the Queen's English and includes U.K. content tuned to English events, companies, people, and news. And while media such as CDs or books might "work" anywhere, they might violate the cultural taboos discussed later in this chapter. As I noted earlier, this is a synchronous exercise.

- *Many products are tied to a market.* Most products are somehow tied to language, culture, country, or an ethnic group residing in one or more countries. Perhaps because of their intrinsic design, in their current form they are unsuitable for sale abroad. This is a research task for your product management staffers worldwide. For physical products, features that you do not even think about—such as power supplies and plugs—might stand in the way of export. As you dig deeper into the box, you might also find that the documentation needs to be translated and printed on A4 paper and that measurements must be converted from inches and pounds to their metric equivalents. Signs of trouble include the need to redevelop, reengineer, or repackage a product; to run it through rigorous market certification tests; or to subject it to stringent ISO9000 manufacturing and process controls.

• *Some products could be quickly repackaged for global markets.* Sometimes, especially in the case of the bit products and corporate information shown in Table 4.2, simple translation or a more sophisticated market adaptation could make the product globally ready. Some physical products, such as consumer electronics, might require minimal packaging changes and a translated owner's manual. Still other products might be suitable as-is for a given demographic. For example, a Taiwanese company could ship its domestic-market goods to a friendly audience, such as the large Chinese population in Indonesia.

For existing signature and high-volume products that cannot be sold as-is, you should figure out whether any adaptation would be warranted in its normal life cycle. Typically, you will find that extensive modification makes no sense unless there is a dire need for it. Most often it will make sense to build global requirements into the next version, rather than try to retrofit an existing product and then do it a second time with the next instance of that product.

Looking forward, the CGO should lobby to change how your company specifies, manufactures, and supports products so that the next generation might be more suitable for export (see Figure 4.2). Making international support an integral part of the marketing requirements and subsequent development is what I call *bred-in-the-bone-globalization.*

For many firms, bred-in-the-bone globalization will require a fundamental change in policy. Looking ahead to new product development, remember that it is easier to design products for global markets than to deal with international requirements after the fact. To make this happen, companies with significant international sales—Cisco in hardware and Xerox in office products, Oracle and Microsoft in software, BMW and Embraer in manufacturing—have made global design an integral part of their market requirements planning. For example, Xerox views globalization as an essential and systemic process. This has also led Xerox to make changes in the way employees work—not just how its office gear is designed and how code is written, but also how it does quality assurance, testing, and product certification. This bred-in-the-bone approach to globalization lets

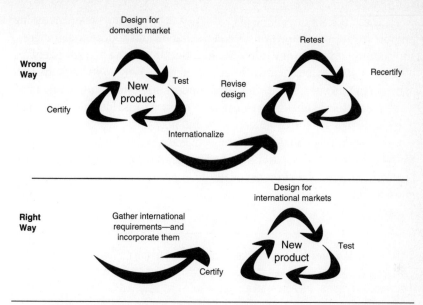

Figure 4.2 Wrong and Right Ways to Build International Products

Note: Many companies build products the wrong way: by adding international support well into the development process. A far better approach is to breed global support into the bone, ensuring that each iteration or variant is globally ready.

Xerox get its products to each of its key markets faster. BMW takes a similar approach, building its cars to meet the world's most stringent safety and emissions standards so that it can sell them anywhere.

Finally, beware of simplistic investment formulas that would block most international forays. Let's consider a fairly typical worst practice that you can avoid. Most U.S. software companies have a tendency to develop their products based solely on requirements originating in the States—from customers, sales, support, marketing, and so on. This has been the case with some very visible products in the content management space, where leading products from firms such as Interwoven and Vignette were well into their fourth generations before systematically supporting something as basic as non-European character sets.

Even when the U.S. planners solicit input from regional organizations, they blindly applied simple formulas for calculating ROI that failed to consider the broader range of benefits discussed in Chapter 2. Must-have features such as support for Japan's kanji characters and developer interfaces with instructions and messages in Japanese were abandoned until sales increased in Japan, a classic chicken-and-egg ROI problem.

Typically, the sheer volume of U.S. sales outweighs the benefit of tuning product features and functions, implementation and educational services, and documentation to any other market. Because of the market size, U.S. requirements for these software vendors almost always outweigh the ROI of international ones, so international support is left for future versions. In some cases, local subsidiaries develop work-arounds. In others, they just don't bother to sell the product or grin and bear it.

I have seen this short-term perspective applied to Web localization as well—with the same solutions applied by local business units. In fact, this problem is one of the big reasons for the fractured brand issue discussed in Chapter 2.

The net: Make sure that your products are suited to the country-language pair into which you want to sell them. That may involve some redevelopment of current products. Ideally, make international salability a criterion for future projects.

Step 2: Do Your Products Meet Market Needs?   Research local market demands to see if a match exists for any of your international product candidates. Look to research from your in-market staff and distributors, from analyst firms that are based in that country or that cover it extensively, from groups such as the International Retail Forum (IRF),[2] or from primary research that you might have conducted with local polling, marketing, or public relations agencies. With this information you can determine the needs of specific markets, begin to quantify the market opportunity for your offerings, and calculate the impact of new or existing competitors in those arenas. If your budget permits, you could go further and fund directed research or focus groups in a potential market to determine the fit for your products. For example, U.S. based Whirlpool would find that washers and dryers it makes for North American distribution do not appeal to Italians looking for smaller, more efficient machines. Similarly, General Motors and Ford have a tough time selling many of their larger U.S.-market autos to Europeans, just as BMW knows that Americans have little interest in luxury cars with four-cylinder engines.

Rather than offering your entire product line to a new country, pick a few products that travel well and push them hard with localized marketing. Success with these products will establish your beachhead in new markets. Use this subset of your catalog to determine trends, understand market needs, and begin to build your presence and brand in international markets.

- For Germany's Bertelsmann, this meant creating a catalog of books that would appeal to each market. For Texas-based PC maker Gateway, it meant offering Latino buyers in the United States the option of buying a Spanish-language version of Windows and keyboards with the diacritical characters used in Spanish.
- For its German site, Travelocity required obvious changes, such as not selling Oktoberfest packages to Germans, eliminating Eurail passes that could only be purchased from outside Europe, and highlighting weekend getaways to Malaga instead of Jamaica. For its U.S. Hispanic customers, it meant offering Dream Maps with destinations across Latin America to offer these consumers a chance to visit their relatives back home.

This exclusion of products is not a one-time action, but instead requires constant vigilance to make sure that offers in the rapidly changing travel and leisure markets are appropriately tuned to each of the markets in which Travelocity sold. Chapter 7 discusses the expectations of international markets for information quality and the tools to ensure it.

Finally, don't make the age-old mistake of carrying coal to Newcastle. The value proposition of selling American-made brie to French consumers, for instance, would not meet the needs, expectations, and supply of the target market. Unless your product has a strong differentiator, pick something else to sell. In some cases, with a strong brand, enough spending, product localization, and sheer panache, companies have overcome national stereotypes. Starbucks joins a number of European coffee shops pushing into Italy, the birthplace of cappuccino.[3] The U.S. company is expected to do well with its appeal to the active lifestyle of younger, time-strapped consumers. McDonald's has localized its products to meet each market's sociocultural expectations, for example by offering beer in Germany and a beef-free menu in India.

Step 3: Can You Deliver and Support the Goods?   The sale doesn't begin and end with a transaction. Before you sell anything, you have to market it and promote it. Once you have sold it, you must deliver the product or service, handle anything that a customer might choose to return, and support it.

Firms with an established distribution and support channel in a country or region have a leg up on companies just starting out. Ideally, you could repurpose those mechanisms to work with your online channel. Companies without the luxury of an established infrastructure can build it out or turn to international logistics providers such as UPS and DHL or to call center operators such as Prestige International. Corporate operations often involve a detailed analysis of heavy-duty back-office systems, which is beyond the scope of this book. What you see in this book is a framework for thinking about how to approach global markets—the possibility of selling into new markets, the legality of sale, the implementation detail, the requirement for translation, new organizational models, and how to measure effectiveness.

Penetration: Is the Population "Have Net" or "Have Not"?

Most companies looking to enter an international market start with a simple question: Are there enough people online to justify entering that market? As they get deeper into their analysis, though, they realize that the issue is far more nuanced than just sheer numbers. Follow-on questions should determine whether those who are online are demographically correct for your products: Do they buy products online? Do they have enough disposable income? Can they pay online? These questions will help to establish whether those consumers are in a have-Net or have-not economy.

Volume: Market Size and Online Penetration   The combination of market size and the number of people online yields a pretty good filter for starting your analysis of which markets to enter first. To get to a short list very quickly, consider using the 30 countries of the Organisation for Economic Co-operation and Development (OECD)[4] plus China, Brazil, and emerging Internet powers such as India as a baseline. The OECD bases its membership on a market economy, pluralist democracy, and respect for human rights, thus ruling out countries in the former socialist bloc and others that are in transition. Most of its members also happen to be fairly large industrialized countries with well-developed telecommunications infrastructures. Paced by the United States, these countries lead the world in Internet usage (see Table 4.3). With the OECD as a baseline, you can

Region	Country Population as % of World Population 1998	Internet Users as % of Regional Population 1998	Internet Users as % of Regional Population 2000
United States	4.7	26.3	54.3
OECD excluding U.S.	14.1	6.9	28.2
Latin America, Caribbean	6.8	0.8	3.2
East Asia and the Pacific	22.2	0.5	2.3
Eastern Europe, Commonwealth of Independent States (some republics of the former Soviet Union)	5.8	0.8	3.9
Arab States	4.5	0.2	0.6
Sub-Saharan Africa	9.7	0.1	0.4
South Asia	23.5	0.04	0.4
World totals	100	2.4	6.7

Table 4.3 Regional Internet Penetration
Source: NUA, United Nations 2001.

Note: The Organisation for Economic Co-operation and Development (OECD) countries can serve as a starting point for your analysis. These countries tend to have the largest Internet penetration and the most appropriate demographics for online commerce. However, if your goal is to optimize your supply chain or internal operations, you might find yourself looking outside the OECD.

take into account the unique dynamics of your company, your industry sector, and target audience to determine top-tier targets for your company.

As you look at the OECD and other lists, do not make the mistake of looking only at market size or at the percentages of a population online. You might inadvertently dismiss a potentially good market or support the wrong one.

- *Big populations with low penetration.* Although researchers assure us that mainland China and India will ultimately support huge Internet populations, the commercial potential of these markets for e-commerce or branding is too far in the future for all but the biggest companies.

Although you should not spend a lot on these markets today, do keep them in your sights—especially given the importance to your supply chain and the large expatriate populations of both countries. As countries like these evolve their telecommunications infrastructures and increase the number of people online, they will be significant players in the global Internet economy, from both demand and supply perspectives.

- *High penetration in tiny populations.* It looks like Iceland with its 60 percent Internet penetration is the place to be online (see Figure 4.3). However, that 60 percent translates into fewer than 200,000 people, the size of a medium city in the United States. Focus your attention instead on the largest industrialized countries with the highest Internet presentation.

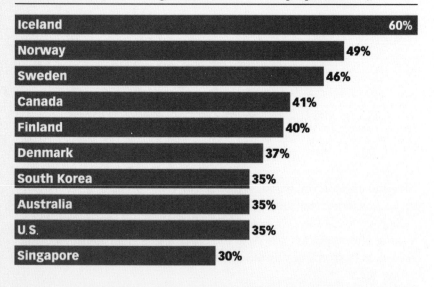

Top 10 Countries Worldwide by Internet User Penetration, January 2001 (as a % of population)

Iceland	60%
Norway	49%
Sweden	46%
Canada	41%
Finland	40%
Denmark	37%
South Korea	35%
Australia	35%
U.S.	35%
Singapore	30%

Figure 4.3 Top 10 Markets by Net Penetration
Source: ITU Telecommunication Indicators Update, 2001. Retrieved from www.eMarketer.com.

Note: Look at total populations as well as the percentages of them that are online. For example, if all you did was look at percentages online as your threshold for support, you would find yourself translating your site into Icelandic for a very small return on your investment.

- *Misleadingly low penetration.* Bertelsmann's online unit removed Brazil and China from its first tier of international markets because their Internet penetration was too low. Depending on your product or service, however, that decision might not be right for your company. Exclude Brazil's rural areas and the huge Amazon rain forest. Focus instead on the large connected urban populations that stretch along the Atlantic coast all the way from Rio de Janeiro through São Paulo into the southern states of Brazil, all the way down to Buenos Aires. Viewed from this perspective, the Brazilian market seems much more viable—not as a country, but rather as a city-state like Singapore or Hong Kong.[5]

The net: There is no single formula for whether you should localize your online efforts for a given country. Working with the executive team at headquarters and in countries and regional offices, the CGO should develop a set of documented procedures that describe how and when your company will support a market—whether for a consumer-facing site, for employees, or for business partners and supply chains.

- *Business-consumer mismatch.* Analysis of your supply or demand chain might reveal an opportunity to sell to businesses but not to consumers. For example, a company like Weyerhauser might target Finland for an Internet supply chain application because of the large number of forest products companies there, but it would not offer a consumer Web site to the relatively small Finnish market.
- *Secondary markets bigger than some countries.* There are also instances in which it makes sense to support a market's secondary languages. The online penetration of certain secondary markets in some cases can surpass the mainstream population, as Asian Americans and Latinos do in the United States. But it's more than just a question of how many are online, but legal and buying behaviors, too. Consider Canada, with its demographically desirable English, French, and Chinese buyers: Legally, you must support English and French, but the immigrant Chinese market appears to be potentially lucrative. For example, Schwab, the U.S. brokerage, found that the household income of its Chinese American customers is more than 50 percent higher than that of the average American.[6] Furthermore, Schwab's Chinese

American customers trade two to three times as much as the average investor.

Some companies view domestic multicultural communities as stepping-stones to the countries from which these domestic ethnic buyers came. For example, Fingerhut created its Spanish site as a venue to learn about the Hispanic customer before entering new markets in Latin America. Firms have taken this domestic, language-only localization approach to grease the skids for international expansion.

As multicultural communities grow both organically and through immigration, these secondary markets will offer an increasing opportunity to grow revenue and share. This option exists not only for companies incorporated in those countries, but also for Spanish or Mexican firms that market to Latinos in the States and for Indian and Pakistani firms that appeal to South Asians living in the United Kingdom.

> *Caution:* As soon as you narrow the field down to a set of target countries for further analysis, expect that your managing director in one of the bypassed markets will explain in great detail why the company should invest in his market for the first tier. This is the kind of tough decision that the CGO will have to face all the time—and it is yet another reason why you should produce a documented approach to market entry along with a well-defined service level agreement to describe what each market gets.

Maturity: Comfort in Online Buying and Propensity to Buy

Just because a population is online does not mean that its members buy online. Their surf-only behavior may mean that they prefer dealing with a human. Each culture has its own level of comfort. Cross-cultural market researchers regularly report that people do not purchase online mainly because they do not feel secure in giving credit card or personal information. Fear of being defrauded online also dissuades potential buyers (see Figure 4.4). Other factors, such as different national experiences with data collection, usage, and government monitoring, have also made them less tolerant of such online interactions.

Fear of fraud keeps consumers from shopping, but what makes them abandon their carts mid-transaction? In the United States, 67 percent of users abandon a Web site when asked for personal data.[7] Twenty-eight percent said that they would be "much more likely" to give personal infor-

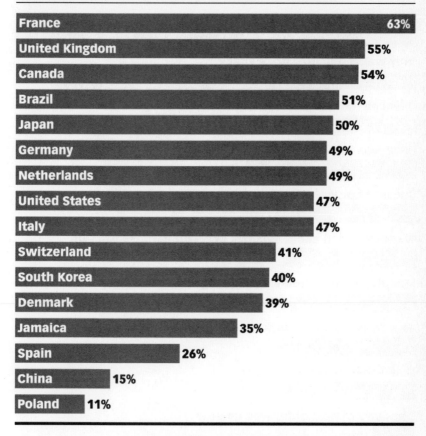

Figure 4.4 Worldwide Fraud Concerns
Source: Ipsos-Reid Global Express Survey, February–March 2001. Retrieved from
www.eMarketer.com.

Note: While half or more of the Internet users (8,583 adults) in the most Web-dense countries fear being defrauded online, the Ipsos-Reid study showed that the actual incidence of fraud is much lower. However, perception is almost always greater than reality, so fraud stands in the way of some purchasing.

mation if the site indemnified them against credit card fraud. Consumers around the world echo these concerns, giving online companies some direct guidance on what they need to feel comfortable buying online. Figure 4.5 presents the results from a poll of Germans and Canadians.

Looking at the data that signals online buyer wariness, other companies

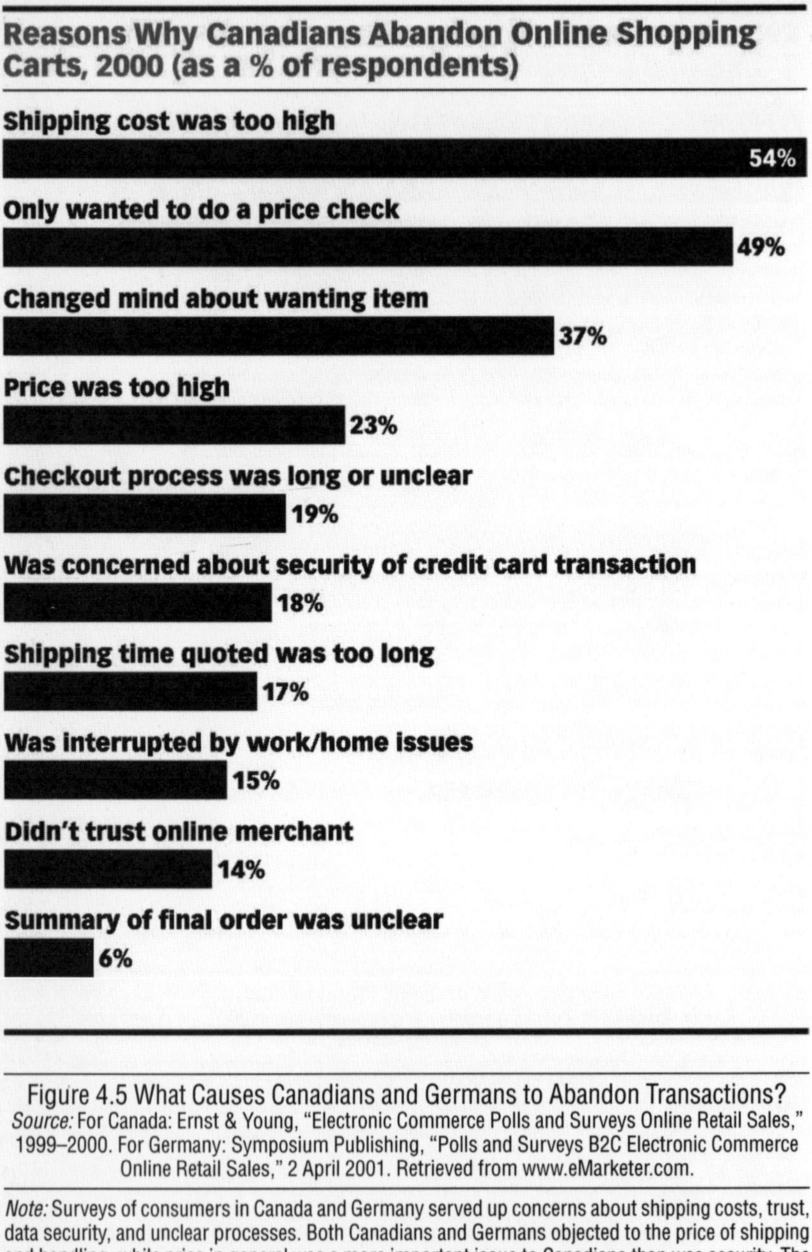

Reasons Why Canadians Abandon Online Shopping Carts, 2000 (as a % of respondents)

Shipping cost was too high

54%

Only wanted to do a price check

49%

Changed mind about wanting item

37%

Price was too high

23%

Checkout process was long or unclear

19%

Was concerned about security of credit card transaction

18%

Shipping time quoted was too long

17%

Was interrupted by work/home issues

15%

Didn't trust online merchant

14%

Summary of final order was unclear

6%

Figure 4.5 What Causes Canadians and Germans to Abandon Transactions?
Source: For Canada: Ernst & Young, "Electronic Commerce Polls and Surveys Online Retail Sales," 1999–2000. For Germany: Symposium Publishing, "Polls and Surveys B2C Electronic Commerce Online Retail Sales," 2 April 2001. Retrieved from www.eMarketer.com.

Note: Surveys of consumers in Canada and Germany served up concerns about shipping costs, trust, data security, and unclear processes. Both Canadians and Germans objected to the price of shipping and handling, while price in general was a more important issue to Canadians than was security. The disparity of these results demonstrates that you must consider each market on its own.

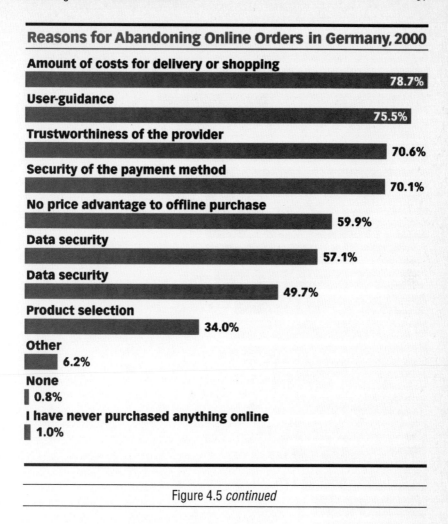

Reasons for Abandoning Online Orders in Germany, 2000

Amount of costs for delivery or shopping — 78.7%

User-guidance — 75.5%

Trustworthiness of the provider — 70.6%

Security of the payment method — 70.1%

No price advantage to offline purchase — 59.9%

Data security — 57.1%

Data security — 49.7%

Product selection — 34.0%

Other — 6.2%

None — 0.8%

I have never purchased anything online — 1.0%

Figure 4.5 *continued*

have responded by pushing to establish trust, improving the way their systems operate, and trying to offer good values online.

- Travelocity has found that over the last few years its Canadian and English visitors have gone from mainly being lookers to completing more transactions. Comfort in many cases comes from trusting the company that operates the site, a trust that it earned by delivering to customers what it said it would—travel services at a great price—in a convenient online process.
- Larger companies such as Coca-Cola and Ford have worked to en-

Future Online Shoppers in Selected Countries, 2001
(as a % of internet users)

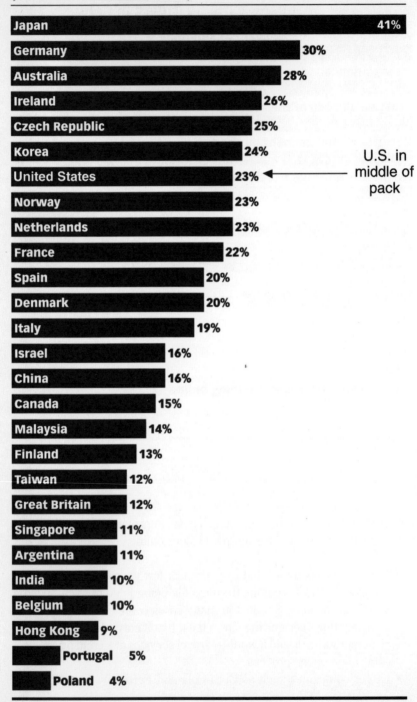

Country	%
Japan	41%
Germany	30%
Australia	28%
Ireland	26%
Czech Republic	25%
Korea	24%
United States	23% ← U.S. in middle of pack
Norway	23%
Netherlands	23%
France	22%
Spain	20%
Denmark	20%
Italy	19%
Israel	16%
China	16%
Canada	15%
Malaysia	14%
Finland	13%
Taiwan	12%
Great Britain	12%
Singapore	11%
Argentina	11%
India	10%
Belgium	10%
Hong Kong	9%
Portugal	5%
Poland	4%

hance their trustworthiness online by integrating their offline branding and marketing strategies with their interactive efforts. For example, they welcome their online visitors into a customized, heavily branded environment that evokes elements used offline—logos, slogans, colors, and campaigns. They highlight the value of their products, and through extensive amounts of content and large dollops of interactivity such as product configuration, they help customers make their purchase decisions.

In most cases, higher degrees of comfort and a feeling of safety translate into more buying. In 2001, 15 percent of Internet users around the world shopped online. Plans to buy on the Web were even higher: 41 percent of Japanese Internet users, 30 percent of Germans, and 28 percent of Australians intended to buy something online in the six months following their interviews (see Figure 4.6).

Geopolitical Woes Can Hamper Web Trust

Hard-earned trust can be lost offline by external events. For example, popular protests against the May 1999 U.S.-led NATO bombing of the Chinese embassy in Belgrade combined with anger over the April 2001 U.S. collision of a spy plane with a Chinese fighter jet spurred attacks against American companies online.[8]

Chinese attacks led to retaliation by U.S. hackers, resulting largely in defaced sites on both sides of the Pacific. International incidents like these, protests against the increasing globalization of large companies, and even traditional bilateral animosities could lead to diminished trust for an international company and could extend to denial-of-service attacks and destruction at sites that is more malicious than simple defacement. Inhabitants of the Eighth Continent are never too far from the politics of the other seven.

Figure 4.6 Online Buying Maturity
Source: Taylor Nelson Sofres Interactive, Global e-Commerce Report, June 2001. Retrieved from www.eMarketer.com.

Note: Consumers in the leading Internet economies plan to buy in the future. Note that buyers in the United States are in the middle of the pack.
This survey was conducted March–May 2001 via telephone and face-to-face interviews with 42,742 people across 36 countries around the world. "Future Online Shoppers" is defined as an Internet user who plans on buying or ordering goods or services on the Internet within the next 6 months.

<u>Method: Paying for and Receiving Online Purchases</u> Allowing customers to pay according to local terms and conditions will also be critical to your international success (see Table 4.4). For example, most American sites complete a transaction by having the customer type in his or her American Express or MasterCard card number. This causes three problems for international customers, none of which is their fault.

1. *Which currency is dominant?* The listed price was $19.99, but the customer is German. Does he pay in euros or dollars? If you let him pay in euros, he will be happy, but you will have to assume the currency hedging risk. If he pays in dollars, then he assumes the risk.[9] Most companies put the burden on the customer's shoulders, giving him a rough idea at payment time what the purchase will cost in his currency based on currency exchange rates at that moment. Barring major fluctuations, this approach works for both parties. Of course, with

Payment	National Preferences
Checks sent via regular mail	French and Dutch consumers prefer to shop online, but pay by check.
Invoices	Swiss consumers can choose to receive an invoice by mail so that they can pay by check, money order, or credit card.
Payment on delivery	Germans like to have the option of paying upon delivery or with a bank debit. Chinese online buyers also prefer COD, but also pay cash at a post office or use a debit card.
Cash transfer or debit cards	Swedes are most comfortable paying online with debit cards, while Australians prefer credit cards.
Payment to a bricks-and-mortar intermediary	Japanese consumers prefer to order online, but pay cash at *konbini,* local convenience stores such as 7-Eleven, where they pick up their purchases.
Wire transfers	Business users prefer to stick to their tried and true means of payment, although employees use credit cards for smaller purchases.

Table 4.4 Sample Payment Preferences

large-scale business procurement through auctions, any variation could be very expensive, so the price is usually set in dollars or euros.

2. *Which payment mechanism should you support?* Without support for local credit cards—such as the Eurocard or Japan's JCB—there would be high numbers of abandoned shopping carts. For example, many Germans have no credit card, preferring instead to pay on delivery or use bank drafts.[10] In fact, many international customers expect a hybrid transaction in which they select and order products, but pay for and pick them up offline. This is the case in a number of countries regardless of their Internet penetration. In the Netherlands, for instance, where Internet penetration has reached more than 30 percent, almost half of all online purchases were paid offline in 1999 with bank drafts.

   To do business internationally, you must arrange for alternate payment means; the right credit cards, smart cards, phone cards, installment, invoicing, and personal checks are some commonly used payment mechanisms outside the States. Business transactions have their own established set of payment schemes, including SWIFT,[11] Customer Direct Access (CDA), other forms of wire transfer, letters of credit, and more traditional forms of exchange, such as barter.

3. *Who pays international shipping and handling?* One question that comes up frequently is whether people in any country would pay outlandish shipping and handling charges to have things shipped from halfway around the world. Even in-country charges turn off consumers: 63 percent of U.S. online shoppers abandoned transactions because they distrusted shipping and handling charges.[12] Seventy-three percent of consumers calculated the entire cost of a product with shipping and handling as part of their purchase decision.

So how do international consumers feel about more expensive international shipping rates? It depends. If products are woefully expensive, some people will gladly pay the added charge as Japanese consumers have long done to arbitrage their country's distribution system for software, cosmetics, and golf clubs.

What should you charge in a given market? Once again, look to your local colleagues, ask customers, and see what your competitors are doing. Let the market tell you.

Product Politics: Things That Can Land You in Jail

Once you decide what products you will offer to people in receptive markets, you will have to determine whether it is legal to sell them there. You will find yourself researching laws that regulate how your product operates and how you sell it. Stop! Pick up the phone right now and call your in-house counsel or retained legal advisors, both in your headquarters country and wherever you intend to sell.

Let the lawyers help you with the arcane legal and regulatory nits that show up where the Eighth Continent intersects with the physical world (see the following box). You will also have to deal with tariffs, taxes, privacy laws, the business climate and environment, and other minutiae that affect sale in a given market. I discuss these geopolitical aspects of doing business internationally in Chapter 5. The balance of this section deals with product legality.

Welcome to Free Trade—Sort Of

Following is a handful of geopolitical issues exacerbated by the Internet. Feel free to use them as I do: as boardroom ammunition and cocktail party chatter to emphasize the importance of getting a good attorney to accompany you on your globalization journey.

- *"Leave my culture alone."* Canada restricts the amount of news and entertainment from its neighbor to the south. Saudi Arabia's government blocked citizens from seeing Yahoo! clubs that published content that it found offensive or pornographic.
- *"Let's play by my rules."* Protectionism, retaliatory tariffs, and plain foolishness underlie many international spats. For example, in early 2000 the European Parliament did away with "The Two Chocolates Policy," a 25-year old ban on British chocolate that used some vegetable fat in place of more expensive cocoa butter. Brazil charges a 200 percent duty on imported CDs, even if they are purchased by Brazilians through eBay.
- *"Keep my people healthy."* The U.S. Department of Agriculture bans raw milk cheeses, a tasty but potentially lethal treat. Mad cow disease and foot-and-mouth disease together excluded British beef from European butcher shops. In addition, many countries object to U.S. agricultural products that have been genetically engineered.
- *"Don't trade with the enemy."* Cold War policies and a vocal immigrant community block U.S. trade with Cuba. Until recently, Iranian caviar was off the

menu for American diners. Encryption software and supercomputers—including the Apple Mac G4 graphics workstation—cannot be sold to U.S. enemies, real or imagined, for fear that they could be used to build advanced weapons or crack secure databases. Even graphite golf clubs cannot be shipped to certain countries because they could be ground down and used for ammunition.

Potential Illegality Where the Eighth Continent Meets the Other Seven

If you think that you do not need legal assistance, consider some more examples of what you can and cannot sell online. Besides limiting what you can actually sell, these exclusions and exceptions will affect various bits and pieces such as your corporate information page laying out what your firm sells and your online product catalog:

- *Dominant components define the relevant laws.* Eastman Chemical found that North American Free Trade Agreement (NAFTA) regulations restricted what it could sell in Mexico. One U.S. retailer ran into regulations wherever it turned. Some products were manufactured from components sourced in different countries, thus causing its lawyers to determine which piece was "dominant" so that it could pay appropriate tariffs. For example, the company sold salt and pepper shakers made from inexpensive crystal sourced in one country and tops of pure silver from another country.
- *Watch out for dual-use products.* The U.S. government restricts the export of dual-use items; for example, you might sell a computer that is intended for weather predicting but that can also be used in the manufacture of missiles and nuclear warheads.

In Addition to Counsel, Where Can You Turn?

Unfortunately, there is no international registry of all laws that could affect your plans for global sales, but there are some excellent resources that you can turn to. Even with these sources, though, you would be well advised to retain a law firm with international expertise.

- The U.S. Department of Commerce's Bureau of Export Assistance (BXA) provides detailed information about many countries in the world, its business practices, and guidance about export restrictions. Other countries and major cities offer similar resources, such as London's Chamber of Commerce and Industry.

- The International Chamber of Commerce provides general information as well as links to its units in countries around the world. Contacts
  in the individual countries should be able to provide basic advice on
  getting started.
- Law firms around the world have recognized this opportunity and can
  provide counsel for individual markets. Contact your local bar association
  to find law firms with international expertise and in-country affiliates.

Tally the Scores—Then Make Your Decision

Once all three Ps are in alignment (see Table 4.5), you must deal with the
classic questions of marketing—the four Ps of price, promotion, placement, and position—and your ability to meet the conditions and expectations of the people to whom you want to market. For each product, you will
build a matrix that says, for a U.S.-based company, "Go to market" or "Yan-
kee, stay home." Companies that have not yet developed a systematic approach to entering international markets will find this section useful. If
your firm already has a global presence, you will find that this information
complements common methodologies for setting revenue targets, dealing
with competition, and meeting other business goals laid out in Chapter 2.

Develop Tiers and Waves of Support   Globalization is not a binary
thing; furthermore, you should not view it as a monolithic "do everything
immediately" kind of task. Because each international market is different
and has its own needs, your approach should be sensitive to those requirements as well as to your own budget and resources.

As many of the early movers have gone global, they have adopted a
tiered strategy to make sure that they do not bite off more than they can
chew (see Table 4.6). With this approach, these firms have laid out a ra-
tional movement into new markets, offering equivalent levels of content
and functionality for companies in the same tier. These early globalists
have also staged their rollouts into new markets, making sure that they include systematic test and validation suites. Chapters 6 and 7 evolve this notion of tiered support, adding in the service level agreements introduced
in Chapter 3.

Port-able	Pene-tration	Polity	Action	Example
√	√	√	All axes are aligned for your global success.	You sell travel and leisure products to Canadians, or books to the English.
√	∅	√	The product and politics line up, but the population just isn't ready to buy on the net.	Online penetration is too low for the demographic that might buy your product.
∅	√	√	The product isn't right for sale outside your traditional trading area, although it would be legal to sell and the population does have the means to buy it.	You want to sell genetically modified brie to the French.
√	√	∅	The product and demographics are right, but legal or logistical issues hinder success.	You want to sell missile parts to countries formerly categorized by the U.S. government as rogue states.

Table 4.5 Decision Matrix for Product Offerings in Individual Markets

Note: As you consider the three Ps (product portability, Internet penetration, and the polities) of each market as they relate to your product offerings, plot the results on a chart like this. List all of the decision criteria and use the chart to document your decision. You may wish to get more scientific and use a numeric score instead of the simple √ for "Go for it" and ∅ for "Forget about it."

Accelerating Your Global Journey

Any journey requires planning and provisioning. This one is no different. You have to consider the destination—here, your country-language pairs that equate to markets. You have to work with your colleagues around the world to determine which of these destinations make the most sense for your company. And once you choose these markets, you have to figure out how and when you will get to each. Upcoming chapters will lay out the gritty work around building an international presence in more detail.

Market Tier	How many?	Level of Support
Mother ship (corporate HQ)	Just one: headquarters	• All corporate content • Interactive systems including personalization • Logistics, legal compliance, and other local elements
Megamarkets (markets where languages are shared with other countries)	English, Chinese, Spanish	• Basic corporate and product content in several megalanguages (multi-national languages) • Customs and commercial practices seen at the Web site are not specific to any one country where that language is spoken • Generic logistics relying on DHL and UPS, which can ship anywhere in the world
Tier 1	Top 3 or 4 markets	• Top few levels of corporate content translated into local language • Locally generated content • Major interactive functions such as personalization and sizing calculators • Logistics, legal compliance, and other local elements
Tier 2	Next 6–10 markets	• Basic corporate information translated into local language • Locally generated content
Candidates	All other markets	• Watch list of markets to monitor as you determine when a given country-language pair should be promoted to the next tier up; SLAs should include criteria for promotion

Table 4.6 Tiered Support for International Markets for Year One

Note: This table represents the archetypal strategy for a number of companies with which I have worked. Individual detail and numbers differed by company size and appetite for globalization, but this table gives a general idea of what is required. Note that this table deals with externally facing sites. As noted earlier, internal employee and supply chain support might take a quicker path.

Mira's Log

Mira initially felt that anything less than a full-scale assault on the international Web would put the company in a net negative position several years out, but she soon learned that she had to be more strategic in her choice of

markets. Her analysis of the opportunities yielded a thorough country-by-country understanding of how individual products could help Acme meet its goals and objectives without breaking the bank. She relied on in-country expertise for her analysis, finding that having resources on the ground painted a much more realistic portrait of the target countries than did just reading analyst reports.

Now she had a handle on the most demographically correct markets and on which Acme products might make sense for those markets. She would continue her work with in-country staff and her executive advisors, documenting a process for picking a market that Acme would support, specifying the level of service that it would be given, and placing that country-language pair in a matrix laying out its expected availability, resources required, and cost.

Her next step was to figure out how to sell the products themselves. This involved digging deeper into the legality of Acme's online plans for international commerce—once again with her old friend, the corporate counsel.

5

The Laws of the Eighth Continent

Mira now had a pretty good idea of which products Acme could reasonably and legally sell in markets around the world. She realized that her customers on the Eighth Continent have dual citizenship: Because they live in countries with different legal and business requirements for commercial trade, Acme's efforts to sell to them online would be subject to the laws of their governments.

Her next task was to probe the legality of how Acme might sell its wares to customers in her target markets. Tops on her list to research were legal issues such as jurisdiction, taxation, privacy, contract law, and content itself—as well as equally vexing religious beliefs with the force of law in some of Acme's target markets. She picked up the phone and called the company's general counsel in Boston and set up a meeting to review Acme's legal challenges as it sought to improve its online presence in markets around the world.

You're Not in Kansas Anymore

As Mira prepared to bring Acme's products to the global market, she quickly learned of the wide array of legal issues that she would first have to address. These include the following:

- *These legal issues affect your relationships with consumers.* The issue of privacy has an immense political, cultural, and personal effect on people, such that it could turn them off from dealing with your company. Similarly, taxation—or lack of it—is one thing that draws individuals to buy on the Net. With that element removed or in jeopardy, you might find fewer people willing to buy.

- *The same issues shape your relationships with employees and partners.* These issues apply to your internal network as well. For example, on the Intranet, collecting information about employees and sharing it globally poses problems for multinational companies.

How should you approach these problems—and this chapter?

1. *Educate yourself.* Read this chapter to gain some basic familiarity with the hottest, most relevant issues that you will face as you look beyond your home markets. I did not intend (here is my legal disclaimer) for it to replace the most essential component of your global legal strategy, which is sound legal advice.

2. *Get a lawyer.* There is far more nuance and precedent to the law than any single book could provide, and the laws, as you will see as you read this chapter, are in a constant state of flux and interpretation. Call your corporate legal counsel and get him or her on your team. If you have business units in other countries, involve them as well. Your internal and external counsel may not have the requisite experience, but they can call on their networks and affiliated firms that do.[1]

   You should look for both Internet savviness and international expertise. On the Web front, look for general experience in laws governing e-commerce transactions and interactions, especially as they relate to your market sector. Internationally, narrow your list to your law advisors who have a multijurisdictional practice, a network of contacts, intellectual property expertise, and country-specific expertise in laws regulating whatever it is you plan to do in that market.

3. *Organize.* Besides adding legal talent to your international team, make sure that employees who produce, edit, and approve content get educated as well. This chapter suggests best practices including the adoption of a high-road approach to privacy and a core content catalog that has been certified for world consumption. Along with a service level agreement that guarantees updates and resources, this is one way that early movers have found to keep their content, policies, and procedures legally compliant for the markets in which they operate.

As you read this chapter, you will note my Eurocentrism. It is deliberate: Over the last few years the European Union has defined a comprehensive legal foundation for the Eighth Continent, predicated on a strong belief in individual privacy and the rights of the consumer. I believe that this model is one that both companies and other governments should leverage as they appeal to new markets worldwide.

<u>Why Worry about Laws in Other Countries?</u>   You work for a U.K. company, running your Web site out of Slough. Why should laws in other countries concern you? By virtue of your company's international selling activity, it could be sued in a foreign court for a number of causes of actions, including such things as defamation of character, copyright infringement, or illegal content, such as Nazi memorabilia in France or pornography in Singapore. Take the example of a foreign customer who is injured by a defective product she bought at your Web site: In today's rapidly evolving Internet legal climate, you may find yourself the defendant of the suit not only at home if a foreign court asserts "personal jurisdiction," but in the foreign court as well.

Courts and legislatures around the world continue to grapple with the problems caused by cross-border commerce. Until now the European Commission has taken the position that the laws in the country where the consumer lives should govern online transactions, but it is now reconsidering that position.[2] The Hague Convention on Jurisdiction and the Recognition and Enforcement of Foreign Judgments intended to establish the idea that judgments in one country should be enforceable in another. However, this does not work when consumers live in nonsignatory countries. In certain cases, one country's courts may decide that a particular law or judgment of another country is inconvenient or otherwise not worthy of enforcement. Add to this the fact that international judicial bodies such as the World Court have no way to enforce their judgments. At the same time, people around the world have been trying to turn the U.S. courts into international arbiters.[3]

In this confused state of affairs and potential for legal exposure, you have no choice: You must worry about the legality of your products and Web presence in every market where you have a customer.

<u>Answering to a Higher Authority</u>   Business on the Eighth Continent must contend also with regulation by nongovernmental bodies such as international organizations and churches, two of the other polities introduced in Chapter 4. Although they do not carry the force of law, religious and cultural taboos can get in the way of business at an international or ethnic site. For example, women featured in European and American advertisements

and Web sites will be viewed as offensive to Muslim piety unless they are entirely covered by a chador. Financial sites that deal in interest paid or received will violate the Koran's stricture on *riba,* usually defined as usury. At the Vatican, Roman Catholic leaders in early 2001 fretted publicly about the accuracy of translated papal edicts, especially for countries that take a more egalitarian approach to gender than does the patriarchal Church.

<u>Nongovernmental Activity</u>   Several leading American and European business organizations do not want to leave consumer protection up to the governments.[4] The U.S. Better Business Bureau, Federation of European Direct Marketers (FEDMA), and the Association of European Chambers of Commerce (Eurochambres) are creating a *Good Housekeeping*–like seal of approval for online commerce. Their goal is to create a retailer's code of conduct that will remove the anxiety of buying from a foreign retailer by specifying a consistent standard for customer service and dispute resolution.

The bottom line: International and ethnic sites must be sensitive to the religious, cultural, and government-regulated legal expectations of a market.

Prepare for the End of the Tax-Free Internet

If the governments of the world had time to deal with only one Internet issue, taxation would be their unanimous choice.

- In the United States, where commerce over the Internet is typically taxed only if the buyer lives in a state where the seller is physically located, state governments feel the pain of lost sales tax revenue on big-ticket electronics and innumerable books and CDs.
- In most other industrialized nations, value-added tax (VATs) and other consumption levies account for about one-third of the tax base. In Europe, these taxes average 20 percent of overall tax receipts for each EU member state and pay about 44 percent of the total organization budget.

The World Trade Organization (WTO) and the Organisation for Economic Co-operation and Development (OECD) actually succeeded in convincing member nations to refrain from imposing taxes or tariffs on the Internet—at least for now.[5] What has thus far baffled legislators is the same thing that terrifies many of the online businesspeople with whom I have spoken: the wide diversity of taxing schemes. In the United States alone, 50 states, thousands of counties, and tens of thousands of municipalities have the authority to levy sales, use, and excise taxes on their citizens' purchases. How much they charge and which goods escape vary from state to state. American online retailers and other distance sellers such as 1-800-Flowers and L.L. Bean, faced with the prospect of supporting each possible permutation, advocate no tax or the same tax scheme everywhere. The same unitary logic applies to their international initiatives.

Listening to their constituents and following the lead of a 1998 WTO resolution, the U.S. Congress imposed a moratorium on any taxation of the Internet, including taxation on access or transactions.[6] In its April 2000 report, the Advisory Commission on Electronic Commerce (ACEC) recommended that the taxation moratorium should be extended another five years, that the WTO tariff resolution should be made permanent, and that any taxes placed on Internet access—whether federal or state—should be permanently banned.[7]

Avoiding Permanent Establishment

Many countries have agreed to abide by the U.S. tax-free approach and the principles outlined in the WTO resolution while congressional aides and European bureaucrats study the issues. While they ponder, though, you should be careful about how you enter a given market. Member-states of the European Union can tax e-commerce indirectly through their VAT. The payment depends on what, where, and to whom goods and services are sold. Any physical presence—such as locating your Web server, becoming a local ISP, or keeping computer hardware in place long enough in an EU country—could lead to what tax attorneys called *permanent establishment status* of your company in that country. Again, consult your legal counsel.

On the tax front:

- For an American company selling in Europe, permanent establishment status means that you would be liable for collecting VAT from your customers in Europe. While you would be able to credit any VAT that you pay against your U.S. income taxes, you still end up bearing the fairly substantial burden of collecting, administering, and paying VAT in Europe. U.S. tax regulations concerning these credits are highly complex. Because of the differences in tax rates between the United States and Europe, some American companies find themselves having to carry foreign tax credits from year to year, thus effectively losing the time value of their money.

- Non-American companies selling into the United States get a pass—for now—and do not have to worry about collecting taxes. However, that changes if you set up a physical presence in the States, thus changing your status to that of permanent establishment. As with Americans selling in Europe, though, you should check with your own tax law advisors and accountants.

The net: International taxes can be complex and potentially very expensive, so engage tax experts with country-specific expertise and knowledge. They will thoroughly research VAT policies for any country you intend to enter, determine whether your company is likely to be judged a permanent establishment, and develop the procedures to keep you from having to collect taxes. You should also retain these experts to watch for and help you plan for the day—and you can be sure that day will come—when the Internet tax holiday ends.

Define a Holistic Policy for Protecting Consumers

Prospects in any country will not buy if they do not trust you, your products, or your selling practices. Some markets, especially the United States, rely on the goodwill of companies to police themselves or adhere to Better Business Bureau practices—at least until there are flagrant violations of basic consumer rights. In other markets, governments have regulated the selling process, the contracts, and the use of customer information that companies collected before, during, and after a sale (see Figure 5.1). Whether there is a legal obligation to do so, if you want to succeed online, you have no choice but to develop a modus operandi that makes buyers feel comfortable, safe, and secure in their purchase.

Selling internationally creates a conundrum for companies that previously sold only to a domestic market with at least a commonly agreed-upon approach to dealing with customers—if not a well-defined set of regulations. Because the Internet exposes your practices in any given market to scrutiny by customers in any other market, though, it will be tough to justify lesser quality or fewer rights in a market just because the government requires less protection in those markets.

Instead, the best practice of market leaders is to provide a similarly high

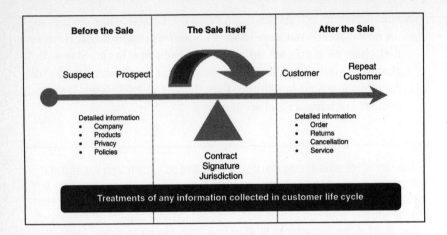

Figure 5.1 Journey from Suspect to Loyal Customer

Note: A sale on the Web is more than just the monetary transaction itself. Someone interested in what you have to offer visits your site. If the interest warrants, this "suspect" becomes a prospective buyer. When the sale is completed and a contract is signed, your company now has a customer that you hope will turn into a repeat customer. To make that happen, often you must provide good service to the customer after the exchange of value. The EU directives mandate proper use of any data collected during that arduous journey from suspect to repeat customer.

quality of experience and protection in every market in which they choose to operate. You can do that by standardizing based on the regulations of the most rigorously regulated market in which you operate—in much the same way that many automakers build their cars to stringent U.S. emission and safety standards. In the case of the Internet, that will mean adhering to the European Union's Directives on Distance Selling and Privacy.[8] Initiatives such as the Better Business Bureau's online efforts to improve Web site reliability promise to be a subset of the EU directives.[9]

Information That Must Be Provided before the Sale

More than any other body, governmental or otherwise, the European Union has taken the lead in protecting the rights of online consumers and business buyers. Its Directive on Distance Selling is meant to increase consumer confidence and so strengthen the single European market by providing an agreed minimum level of consumer protection. The directive applies to companies selling goods or services on the Internet, by digital television, by telephone, by mail order, or by fax.

As with any EU directive, the Distance Selling act does not have the force of law. Instead, each member country must pass its own national law

Required Information	Details
Company	Your company's name Your address
Pricing	The price including VAT and other taxes Any shipping, handling, or other delivery charges How long the price will remain valid Any payment options that are available
Delivery	Delivery details—the default is within 30 days
Cancellation	A statement of the customers' right to cancel within seven days of delivery if they don't like the product or have changed their minds. The idea behind this cooling-off period is to give consumers the same opportunity to examine products or services that they would have if they bought them in a brick-and-mortar shop. Downloaded books, audio, and films are not subject to this provision. Other obvious exceptions include personalized items, perishable items, services delivered within the cooling-off period, and sealed items such as audio or video products that have been opened.
Duration	The minimum period that the customer is obligated to a contract for a continuing service. For example, a cell phone contract typically lasts a year.
Substitution	A statement that you will ship a substitute product if what the customer specified isn't available. You must also note that you will pay return shipping charges if the customer doesn't want the substituted item.

Table 5.1 Information That Must Be Available before Placing an Order

Note: The European Union's Directive on Distance Selling specifies the information that you must provide to the buyer before an order is placed.

to implement its provisions. Although each variant will differ in wording and nuance, you should be able to craft a policy for your company that adheres to the spirit and letter of each country's law by adhering to the directive. The presale provisions are pretty straightforward, outlining the basic information that a consumer needs to decide whether to buy form you (see Table 5.1).

<u>What Is Required during the Contracting Phase</u> "Click-through" agreements—the "I Agree" button present on many Internet sites—form the most common contract between an online buyer and a seller or be-

tween a reader and a content provider. Because it is impossible to negotiate separate agreements with every user, click-through agreements are the most widespread type of Web-based contract. However, both click-through agreements and the contracts governing a purchase pose many problems. This is where you need to bring in lawyers for basic contractual hygiene.

To assist in contract formation, the European Union passed the E-Commerce Directive to remove any legal impediments to the enforceability of electronic contracts.[10] This directive provides for the following:

- *Electronic agreement.* All member states must ensure that contracts can be signed electronically (see Table 5.2). Available forms of electronic signatures include certificates, biometrics such as fingerprints, and encryption.[11]
- *Statement of compliance with national laws.* EU member-states must maintain restrictions on electronic contracts only with regard to contracts requiring, by law, the involvement of the courts, public authorities, or professions exercising public authority. What this means is that you can engage in e-commerce in all EU signatory countries as long as you comply with the laws in your member state or in the member state in which you are legally established.
- *Contract enforceability.* The E-Commerce Directive also states that click-through agreements are enforceable and calls upon all member

Use of e-Signature	What It Does
Authentication	Confirms the buyer's identity
Authority	Determines whether the other party has signing authority
Integrity	Guarantees that the contents of the document have not been changed or altered in any way
Authenticity	Verifies that the electronic file has come from the claimed party
Legal commitment	Legally binds the buying or selling party
Nonrepudiation	Ensures that the original signing party cannot later claim not to have signed

Table 5.2 Uses of Electronic Signatures

states to reflect this fact in their national statutes. However, because individual countries might have more stringent measures than what the European Union mandates, make sure that your online contracts comply with all consumer protection laws.

- *Private autonomy.* Within the European Union, a contract is governed by the law chosen by the parties to the contract in what is called *private autonomy,* as long as this choice does "not have the result of depriving the consumer of the protection afforded to him by the mandatory rules of the law of the country in which he has his habitual residence." This choice is normally designated explicitly in the contract. If it is not, then the governing law is that of the country in which the consumer normally lives. If your click-through agreement specifies U.S. law, though, it will likely be overridden to the extent that the consumer's home country provides greater protection.

Obligations after the Sale   Once the transaction has been completed, your responsibilities under the more stringent European regulations do not end. Besides shipping the order or delivering the service, you have to let the customer know how to cancel the order (see Table 5.3). You also need to provide a physical address to which the consumer can complain if there is a problem. In addition, you must make a statement of any postsale guarantees or service availability, and you have to indicate who is required to pay for any returned goods.

Required Information	Details
Cancellation	When and how to take advantage of the cooling-off period. If it's a service agreement with no stated termination date, details on how to cancel.
Address	A physical address where the customer can complain. This cannot be an e-mail address or the Web site's address (URL).
Guarantees	Statement of any post-sale guarantees or service availability.
Fees	Statement of who pays for any returned goods.

Table 5.3 Information That Must Be Sent with an Order

Note: The European Union's Directive on Distance Selling specifies details about the transaction that you must provide to the buyer along with the order.

Best Practices for Contracts

1. *Engage the services of counsel with international expertise.* Laws are tricky, constantly evolving, and subject to interpretation. While this section outlined some major contractual issues, it by no means captured all of the detail that you need to play nice in other countries.

2. *Translate your contracts, if not your entire site.* The first thing you should do is make sure that you translate your click-through agreement into the language of your target market, employing local counsel both to ensure accuracy and to add any pertinent local rules and regulations.

   For example, a German court will not enforce a click-through agreement that was not available in German. A consumer could argue that he did not realize that he was entering into a legally binding contract because he could not read it. The scope of translation could become an issue as well if the court interprets your entire Web site as constituting the contract with the consumer, meaning that your failure to provide translated presales information, product detail, all transactional detail, and postsales follow-up could invalidate your contract with your customers.

3. *Create a generic international contract.* To protect yourself in markets where you have not yet translated your agreements, develop a contract that will serve as the default until you do. To the degree that your resources allow, have your legal counsel review that generic agreement for its enforceability in markets that generate measurable traffic but do not yet justify localization.

4. *Specify whose laws apply.* Note in the contract that any disputes will be resolved according to the laws of your country. Lawyers suggest that you clearly indicate where your business is located on every page in order to make it entirely clear whose rules you operate by.

The net: What the European Union means to convey with these directives is the need to communicate clearly to your customers the nature of your business, where it is located, what you sell, how you sell it, and how you will serve them after the sale. You must make sure that your online business in each market complies with the governing law. One way to do that is to adopt the regulations of your most stringent markets as your corporate baseline.

Protecting Customer Privacy

User profiling—tracking Internet browsing and buying habits—underlies the highly personalized experiences offered by companies ranging from Amazon to Renault. This personalization depends on powerful software that matches a marketing offer with a visitor. Information can be gathered from the user's e-mail address, from a registration with voluntarily provided information, or from a cookie, a small file on the user's computer that tracks previous behavior.

These identifying tokens allow the software to observe specific users, analyze their behaviors, and then interact with them by offering choices that make sense in that context and by responding with appropriate offers. Ideally, the software "learns" enough from the customer's interaction to improve the experience the next time around (see Figure 5.2). The software may anonymize visitor data, making recommendations based not on an individual but rather on behavior common to people with similar characteristics.

This profiling presents a dilemma for Internet users and raises serious concerns about how that information might be used. For example, what

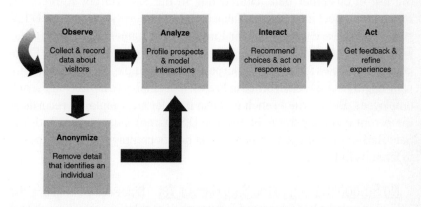

Figure 5.2 Personalization Cycle

Note: Personalization on the Web mimics the work of a good salesperson in the real world. Over time, the seller observes the behavior of an individual prospect, perhaps categorizing that potential buyer into one of several general categories: impulse buyer, looker, family-influenced, and so on. By continually analyzing and comparing recommendations against behavior, the salesperson reinforces the value of the categories and his or her observations. Then the salesperson steps in to make the sale. Personalization works much the same way on a Web site, but across a larger number of prospects and in real time.

other companies can see it? Will it be made available to government in-vestigators? What should be done if a child tries to register?

This dilemma about wanting a better experience while demanding con-trol over information translates into a market demand for you—and a set of governmental regulations created to make Web consumers more com-fortable doing business with people they cannot see. For example, the Eu-ropean Union's Data Protection Directive states that personal data can be collected only for specific and clearly defined purposes. Therefore, if you want to track what Italian visitors to your site do, you must clearly indicate this fact in your site's *privacy statement,* a prominently displayed announce-ment to visitors that explains exactly what you intend to do with data that you collect from them and what rights they retain over that information.

Over 40 countries now have privacy laws in place. The European Union's regulations on privacy are only a directive with no force of law, so each EU signatory will have its own national law based on the Directive. Because Internet privacy laws can differ significantly between countries, you must test the legality of your privacy statements, customer data collection, and data usage practices against the rules and regulations of these countries.

Thankfully, the European Union and the U.S. government have been working to reduce some of that legal unevenness. In a North Atlantic pri-vacy initiative, the two polities worked to reconcile their laws regarding the use of customer data, culminating in the Safe Harbor Agreement, which took effect in 2001 (see Table 5.4). National versions of the EU Pri-vacy Directive are mandatory for European companies. The Safe Harbor principles apply to American companies transferring data about a Euro-pean to the States for whatever purposes. For example, an American com-pany might have a branch office in France that employs a number of French employees. Before the French unit can transfer any employee records to the parent company in the States, the U.S. parent must comply with the Safe Harbor principles. Companies that do not comply would be exposed to lawsuits in Europe.[12]

No Smooth Sailing to the Safe Harbor Yet

Since the Clinton era, the U.S. government has advocated industry self-regulation, an approach that many American companies prefer to government regulation. TRUST-e and BBBonline have created nonprofit oversight programs to foster Web site reliability and, in the case of the Better Business Bureau's online ser-vice, general and kids' privacy.[13] They implement the notice, choice, and data integrity principles of Safe Harbor but do not follow the enforcement principle. Unfortunately, these voluntary programs do not always inspire

Principle	What's Required
Notice	A company must tell individuals how and why data are being collected, whom to contact if they have any questions or complaints, the types of third parties their data will be shared with, and how to limit its use and disclosure.
Choice	A company must offer individuals the chance to "opt out" of having their personal information disclosed to a third party or used for a purpose that is incompatible with the purpose for which it was originally collected or subsequently authorized by the individual. For some very personal data such as sexual habits and orientation, the principle requires that the data subject explicitly affirm ("opt in") the choice.
Onward Transfer	Companies must apply the Notice and Choice principles before providing data to third parties.
Access	Individuals must have access to personal information about them that an organization holds. They must be able to correct, amend, or delete that information where it is inaccurate.
Security	Companies creating, maintaining, using or disseminating personal information must take reasonable precautions to protect it from loss, misuse and unauthorized access, disclosure, alteration, and destruction.
Data integrity	Personal information must be relevant for the purposes for which it is to be used. A company should take reasonable steps to ensure that data are reliable for its intended use, accurate, complete, and current.
Enforcement	Companies must establish procedures to settle complaints and resolve disputes about compliance with the principles.

Table 5.4 Safe Harbor Privacy Principles

Source: Safe Harbor Privacy Principles, issued by the U.S. Department of Commerce, 21 July 2000. For current information, visit http://www.export.gov/safeharbor/.

Note: These seven Safe Harbor theses of online commerce are intended to provide a strong foundation for building consumer trust and properly treating the collection of any information about European subjects.

confidence. In several highly visible cases, companies were caught surreptitiously collecting personal data, but TRUST-e failed to revoke its certification.[14] Until these programs do more than suggest privacy platitudes, consumers will not trust them to protect privacy rights.

These instances illustrate the limitations associated with self-regulation. In fact, both U.S. and European firms have found themselves outside the law:

- According to a survey conducted by the London Chamber of Commerce, 44 percent of businesses in the United Kingdom are not executing online strategies specified by the Data Protection Act guidelines, the U.K. implementation of the EU Directive on Privacy. Forty percent surveyed did not know if they complied with the law.[15] Of the worlds' top 100 brand names, only one complies with English law on e-mail business communication.[16]
- In a spring 2001 *Computerworld* poll of 300 information technology (IT) managers and other attendees, 69 percent said that their companies do business outside the United States, but 48 percent have not yet dealt with international privacy regulations.[17] Twenty-six percent said that they simply copied data privacy policies from other businesses, a real problem if they are ever audited and if their posted policy does not reflect how your company really handles information.
- The United States might still renege on the Safe Harbor agreement, as some senators threatened to do in 2001, claiming that implementation would cost consumers—a proxy for "large contributors to their reelection campaigns"—billions of dollars. Expect this battle to continue on an industry-by-industry basis. If the United States does back out, American firms can then be sued in Europe for violating the directive's requirements whenever data is transferred because the European Union does not view the privacy afforded by the United States as "adequate" to permit transfer.

Creating a Privacy Policy for Your Company

Given the opt-out policies implemented by most U.S. companies, they now have to provide for greater privacy in their interactions with customers to comply with European laws. U.S. companies will take one of a few approaches: (1) ignore the principles altogether and stay at home, (2) do the bare minimum to get by, or (3) adhere to the spirit and the letter of the law.

Ideally, companies will move toward adopting the Safe Harbor principles for their customers everywhere, lest they end up in the untenable position of providing more privacy for their foreign customers than they do for their American compatriots—and risk being sued in Europe and elsewhere. For example, hotelier Six Continents is making personalization an intrinsic part of its global systems by centralizing the capability in the software itself. The company has been able to build in a repository of international rules that considers a customers' nationalities before offering them promotions or other services that may not be available in their own countries.

Best Practices for a Privacy Policy
The safest course of action— and the one most desirable to visitors to your sites—would be to ensure full compliance with even the strictest international electronic data privacy laws and to inform visitors and customers of your compliance with these standards. Some basic rules of thumb for maintaining goodwill in your target markets include the following steps to implement the principles of notice and choice:

- *Be upfront with your customers.* Make it clear when you are collecting data and what you will use it for. Post a comprehensive statement about your corporate privacy policy on your home page. Remind visitors about your policy whenever they disclose additional information. This low-cost disclosure presents a real opportunity to do well by being good.
- *Enable access.* Let customers see their profiles and, where possible, view the data that you have collected. Allow them to edit their profiles or even opt out of your database. Few companies do this today, largely because the most commonly used personalization and content management software do not support it (IBM and NCR have made headway on creating this next generation of software).
- *Give your customers a reason to share data.* You can overcome discomfort about disclosing personal data with incentives such as loyalty points, access to more information or personalized sites, or special discounts. Provide customers with good reasons for volunteering information.

Dealing with the Organizational Impact of Privacy
Consumer privacy has legal ramifications, too. To protect your company, you should

- *Designate someone who is responsible for privacy.* Some companies have actually created the role of a chief privacy officer,[18] while most of the firms that I interviewed have designated either a senior executive or an individual in the legal department as responsible for privacy. Over time, privacy data management will become a much more difficult problem as the volume of data and number of customer information laws increases.
- *Conduct a privacy audit both at home and abroad.* Assess how you currently collect, use, protect, and employ customer data. Document customer access to their own data and the remedies that you offer for disputes. Seek in-country legal counsel that can explain the extent of

local legislation, examine your firm's current customer data collection activities, and identify potential conflicts.

- *Create and document internal policies.* Defaulting to the most rigorous national standards, document your company's policy for dealing with customer data. Create a mechanism for monitoring compliance with the policy. Educate teams across offices about the new policies and monitor them for compliance. Where possible, develop or buy software that you can use worldwide to collect customer data, monitor its usage, and safeguard its integrity.

- *Educate your content authors.* Employees throughout your company produce information that you publish on the Web. You can ensure that this content complies with legal requirements by adding a section to your corporate style guide that discusses your privacy and other data usage policies. You can also add work-flow steps that ensure that each bit of content has passed through a legal review for a given market before being posted.

The net: The days of posting content on the Web as soon as it is written are long gone, especially for globally ambitious firms. The chief globalization officer (CGO), working with corporate legal resources, should develop and document policies for contracts, data usage, content, and any other written communication. The CGO should include these policies in the corporate legal guidelines, as well in any corporate style guides or glossaries. Chapter 7 discusses these guides in more detail.

Manage the Legality of the Content Itself

Nearly everyone is surprised by a business or social practice the first time that they visit another country: The salad comes at an unexpected time in the meal, or the service charge does or does not show up automatically on the bar bill. The same thing happens with a Web site: Information that is presented as a matter of course in your country suddenly becomes illegal in another.

If you are an American, you are likely to be surprised by strictures that prohibit you from comparing your product to a competitor's. You might find that your product claims need much more substantiation than they do in the comparatively laissez-faire United States. Regardless of where you come from, it is pretty likely that you will be taken aback by the unexpected illegality of some element of any market that you enter. Again, call in the local legal talent to help you avoid criminal content on the Web.

Case Study of a Legal Review of a Marketing Site

Consider the case of MedSupply, a fictitious firm that sells medical devices and pharmaceutical products and provides consumers with product and service information. MedSupply decided to expand its Web presence beyond the States into several promising markets in Europe and Asia. Its international market entry team worked with its globalization director to conduct a site audit of the company's informational and marketing pages. The goal was to determine the legality of both (1) its products for sale in the United Kingdom, France, Germany, and Japan and (2) how it markets and sells them.

- *MedSupply reviewed product suitability for other markets.* The team's review started with a list of products that MedSupply could sell, based on market need and suitability, regulatory issues, and patents. For example, its geriatric supplies might fill a need in Japan's aging population, but it could sacrifice patent protection in Brazil.
- *MedSupply reviewed how it marketed products.* The team studied how the company represented products at its American site, determining what kinds of claims and selling practices would be allowed in the targeted markets. MedSupply's analysts, working closely with the company's in-country counsel, found that Japan was the most restrictive of content describing products, claims, and benefits.
- *MedSupply analyzed its privacy and personalization policies.* MedSupply actively collected information about doctors at its U.S. site, using that information for follow-on marketing campaigns. While it did post a privacy policy describing how it would use this information, MedSupply's internal systems could not distinguish an American doctor from a European one, thus signaling potential problems with EU privacy regulations. As expected, when it came to privacy, the United

States was the most tolerant of MedSupply's markets in allowing the use of personal data.

Thus, MedSupply's market entry team realized that the company would have to make some tough decisions about how it represented itself worldwide. These choices boiled down to the question of whether the company should adopt a global standard for its content offerings, a good practice to follow and one discussed in more detail in Chapter 3 (the concept), Chapter 6 (the impact on internationalization), and Chapter 7 (where it figures in the translation process).

MedSupply could have settled on a country-by-country approach, tailoring its content to the laws of each market. It could also have adopted the least common denominator by using Japan's regulations as the benchmark for its international sites. Instead MedSupply chose to create two tiers of regulatory compliance:

1. *Laissez-faire* for less restrictive markets such as the United States and future targets such as Switzerland and Sweden
2. *Europeanized* for those countries following the European Commission's directives and standards

MedSupply chose this bifurcated strategy rather than deny U.S. customers what they were currently getting. The next challenge was to develop the systems that would enable this two-tiered approach, translate the content, and, importantly, to keep everything legally compliant and correctly translated as new products emerged.

Research the Laws That Protect Your Company

Thus far we have talked about protecting your customers and employees. Do not forget that the global markets that you are entering may not have the same respect for your intellectual property as your home market does. An international-savvy law firm can identify major areas of exposure, but there are two issues that most companies face:

1. *Protect your brands by registering domains in target markets.* Although the limited number of unique domain names and the phenomenon of cybersquatters buying up well-known names will make it difficult for

some companies, best marketing practices dictate that you register your names and brands with country-specific domains—such as .de in Germany and .co.uk in the United Kingdom. Consumers in countries often prefer to do business with branded, localized firms such as www.travelocity.de.

AmBev is a good example what can happen otherwise: American Beverage Corporation, a unit of the Dutch food group Royal Wessanen, is known as www.ambev.com on the Web, while the Brazilian Companhia De Bebidas Das Americas owns www.ambev.com.br. Each company has built equity in its home market around the AmBev name, but each is limited in the other's market. Make sure that getting the domain name for your brands and product in countries you intend to sell is part of your market entry strategy.

2. *Protect your intellectual property.* Check on trademarks, copyrights, and other intellectual property that your company owns but that might come under legal challenge in other markets. In the United States, first use of a trademark typically guarantees it some protection, but explicit registration is a good idea. In Europe, a single filing is adequate for all EU countries, but elsewhere you must register in each country—sometimes in person. Similarly, just as business-method patents such as Amazon's "one-click" ordering method will be disputed in the Untied States, they will face even closer scrutiny in other markets.

Don't Try This at Home without a Legal Safety Net

This chapter introduced the vicissitudes of the various legal environments on the global Web. Unless you prepare your site, corporate policies, content, and teams for the complexities of this variegated world, you might find yourself on the wrong end of a lawsuit, in arrears on taxes, or facing EU action for illegally transferred data. This chapter outlined some of the best practices employed by companies that have already gone global. The very best practice, though, is to get some market-savvy legal counsel on your team right away.

Mira's Log

Mira learned far more about the legality of international trade than she ever wanted to, but she valued this basic education in the issues and argot of the legal trade. She added a slot for legal help in the organizational chart that she had drawn. Her next job was to figure out how to pull together the content, culture, and logistics of selling internationally.

6

Building the Foundation for New Online Markets

With legal facts and market entry details in mind, Mira now turned her research to actually building Web sites with international appeal. Her first inclination was to call up some translation firms that advertised in the back of a Latin trade magazine. But first she spoke with some folks in corporate information technology (IT), chatted with the Web master, and called some of Acme's international Web site managers.

Following these conversations she realized what a tangled Web Acme had woven. Whatever showed up on the corporate Web site at corporate or at country sites in Prague or São Paulo had passed through a maddening array of authors, work flows, and technology—from outdated mainframes at Acme's corporate headquarters to PCs from offices around the world.

Regardless of where it originated, IT personnel always had to perform manual rework. In some cases that meant time-wasting file conversions and retyping. In others, the words had lost some of their effectiveness because they appeared with dates and numbers formatted for the United States rather than for Europe. As Mira learned, these issues are part of the process of internationalization.[1]

Getting Down to the Basics of Global Content

Mira realized that most non-IT executives do not know where Web content comes from or how corporate information systems work. She also found that the separation between what a company posts on its Web site and how these executives run their departments is decreasing.

If your goal, like Mira's, is to take these systems into new markets, you have to understand the purpose and scope of the Web well enough to budget staff and resources for developing your company's world-friendly Web presence.

This chapter discusses the following elements:

- *Process.* Here you will learn where content comes from and how it gets to the Web.
- *Organization.* Based on the models outlined in Chapter 3, you will see which organizational structures work best for going global.
- *Preparation.* Most content is conceived and written for a single market and typically must morph for global publication. This activity will often involve digging deep into corporate systems for transaction data that is posted on your site.
- *Internalization.* This is the work to make information appear as intended—using the correct characters for a language and making sure that everything looks right for the *locale* in which it will be seen. While many companies try to internationalize themselves, some are coming to realize that it is better and more cost-effective to outsource this activity.
- *Cost.* The preparation and internationalization can be very expensive or quite cheap, depending on your company's content authoring and IT practices. This section lays out the tariffs associated with making your content suitable.

Where Does Web Content Come From?

In the early days of the commercial Internet, the fact that you could put a product brochure up on your Web site and update it when specifications and prices changed was a quantum leap in producing and propagating timely, accurate information about your company's wares. But this old "brochureware" approach soon yielded to online businesses such as Dell and Renault that configured goods to your exact needs and desires. Information-only Web sites morphed into transactional tours de force that allowed customers to buy goods and services 24 hours a day.

As this happened, organizational charts started changing to reflect the newfound strategic nature of the Internet, and companies stopped treating their Web sites as a novelty and now viewed them as a full-fledged sales channel to generate revenue. Where the old Web was governed by getting online fast, this officially sanctioned and budgeted Web development grew up—some in marketing, others reporting into the mainstream IT group. These teams trained their own support staff, implemented systems to manage content development and publishing, and developed strict processes to ensure that only accurate information found its way to the corporate Web site.

Now that e-business has become just plain business, the supporting infrastructure has become just as intricate and distributed as your other channels. In this newly codified world, specialists from across your company create product information. Various internal workflows and systems make this content available to visitors, customers, employees, or business partners—both on the Web and through catalogs, stores, customer service representatives, and other channels.

These content publishing processes draw on many different sources of information, use formal and informal work-flow processes to keep everyone honest, and employ technology to make everything happen in a smooth, reproducible way:

- *Content and data come from every conceivable source.* In a well-ordered Web publishing process, the content authors represent many relevant groups around the company, from marketing to engineering. They will draw on a wide variety of operational databases in Oracle and DB2, Word and Excel documents, and even corporate folklore to populate the site. The bottom line: Work flows must encompass all the systems that authors and data collectors use to populate your information systems.
- *Work flows and approval processes ensure value.* Once these authors develop content, they send it on to a corporate editorial, Web marketing, or publishing group that is responsible for guaranteeing accuracy and quality. These publishing groups usually establish manual or automated work-flow processes to ensure that nothing is posted without appropriate checks and balances, and that everything is updated in a timely fashion. This corporate publishing group may be an official function, but it is frequently a virtual organization made up of points on a work-flow diagram.
- *Process and technology bring discipline to content delivery.* Once the work flow has been approved, technology groups use homegrown

or commercial systems from companies like Interwoven, Oracle, or Vignette to string it to other content on the Web site and to what visitors can access.

While not perfect, these defined processes and supporting systems brought long-needed discipline to the Web, replicating the practices in the world of the printed world by standards like ISO9002 or by edicts issued by individual governmental agencies around the world.

Going Global with These Processes
Now consider the prospect of entering international markets online or enhancing your established physical presence. If yours is like most companies, what you have done on the Web in your home market—in terms of site quality and the people and systems you use to support it—is far better than what you offer in any other market.

As companies move into international markets, many are tempted to take shortcuts around these processes and organizational best practices. Do not yield to this short-term temptation. Now that you have a stable, powerful Web presence that reaches the far corners of your home market, it is time to figure out how to take this online development rigor forward to increase the quality of your efforts worldwide. This process of improving your company's outward-facing Web operations will likely go a long way toward improving the global persona of the company at every virtual and physical touchpoint.

The net: The Web began as an experiment in marketing but evolved into a bona fide commercial channel. As it matured, so too did the processes and organizations that supported it. Apply this same discipline and organization to your international efforts. Given the widespread employment of Internet technology at companies, you can use this effort to drive greater awareness of and sensitivity toward global issues everywhere in your company.

Getting the Core Content Catalog and Applications Ready to Go Global
Remember to walk before you run: Do not try to enter every international market overnight with everything in your online satchel. Instead, take your core content catalog into new markets first, targeting the markets that make the most economic sense for your company. In the case

of a marketing initiative for a new country-language pair, you might reserve a subset of your corporate site to explain your company and its value proposition with the minimum amount of content. This limited content catalog lets you optimize the presentation, navigation, and rhetorical effectiveness of the content itself without spreading your content authors and translators too thin over too much content.

At EMC, this basic content about the company's operations and globally available products comprises roughly half of the company's 1,500-page corporate site. A "page" is what you see when you click on a Web address, and it is a commonly accepted way of measuring a site. Another measurement is megabytes of database storage, a metric used by companies that generate Web pages on demand. Eastman Chemical manages about 7,000 pages for its U.S. operation, but its international core content catalog typically employs just 50 pages describing the company and 400 pages detailing its products in a given market.

Measured either way—pages or megabytes—this is a lot of information that has to be managed and adapted for use outside the home markets of your company. As you get started, it is easier to think about accomplishing this smaller task in two or three markets than about taking your entire e-business and supporting systems into the top 15 markets in the world.

This limited approach—with its enforced commonality of basic content for the same kinds of applications in different markets—enables these companies to make their branding and the look and feel of their online presence consistent across markets. In most cases, they have hosted their international branding sites at the corporate headquarters' site that lets visitors interact in their choice of several languages (see Figure 6.1).

Besides providing a consistent brand image worldwide, this centralized approach makes better economic sense than the alternative of letting each country do its own branding effort.

Some companies that have taken this centralized approach reported that they initially had a hard time convincing local business units to give up their locally developed online presence. What overcame their objections was a combination of local involvement with the CGO, some form of service level agreement, and, most importantly, actual results. For a summary of the benefits of the organizational model, see Table 6.1.

- *The corporate site carries the brand internationally.* In this centralized model, headquarters makes the decisions, develops international sites, and maintains them all from one location. Ideally, the sites share common technology architecture, processes, and staff.

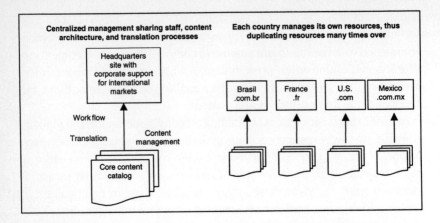

Figure 6.1 Central Corporate Branded Site Saves Money and Reinforces Consistency

Note: To manage brand and costs better, many companies host their international variants at the corporate site, which is usually reachable through some form of www.company-name.com or www.brand-name.com because the brand is where most people start their search for information about a company. By centralizing this international resource, companies maximize not only limited budgets for software such as content management systems but also the efficiency of work flow, translation, and other processes. However, this may not be the right model for employee-focused intranets, supply chains, or e-commerce sites.

In many cases, especially with American and British efforts, the international component of a site represents little more than a listing of contact information for each country where the company has a presence.

On the other hand, Brazilian oil refiner PetroBras offers its Latin American neighbors the option of Spanish and English. The Portuguese, Spanish, and English corporate pages share the same format and content, thus giving all visitors the sense that they are not missing out on anything.

- *Each country goes its own way.* When a company chooses the decentralized approach, it cedes decision making to the country offices. This model most often results from a decision at corporate headquarters not to do anything internationally, so local business units take the reins to meet their needs. Even if a firm has chosen to centralize its efforts, it will sometimes find itself fighting to keep countries from backsliding into this model if the corporate site fails—in reality or in perception—to meet the needs of a local market. Whatever the cause, these local sites tend to be off-brand and less complete in conveying critical information about a company.

Publishing Model	Quality	Time	Cost
Centralized	✔ Maximum control over branding, messaging, and design ✔ Consistent publishing of update schedules ✔ Shared process infrastructure, and tools ✘ Less tailoring of content to client or market needs—unless companies use in-country designers and marketers	✘ Increased latency due to fewer people doing the same amount of work ✘ More time as content shuttles around the world among authors, translators, and reviewers	✔ Big savings economies of scale in headcount, administrative costs, technology, training ✔ Increased ability to monitor and predict costs
Local or decentralized	✘ Less consistency in corporate branding among country sites ✘ Less consistency in managing schedules for global corporate news and products ✔ Maximum tuning of content to client or market needs	✔ Greatest responsiveness to market needs as countries devote resources to their needs ✔ More flexibility in authoring, translating, and reviewing content	✘ More expensive in maintaining duplicate organizations, technology, etc. ✘ Less ability to predict costs

Table 6.1 Publishing Centralization versus Decentralization

Note: There are pluses and minuses to each organization model, so it makes most sense to pick what is right for each application. As you recall from the discussion in Chapter 3 (see Figure 3.1), companies that let each country manage its own Web site tend to have sites that are more highly tuned to the personality and the velocity of change in that market. However, this comes at a high price: inconsistent brand and lost economies of scale, for example. Service level agreements with centrally managed or headquarters control will help most companies overcome the shortcomings of the centralized model and reap its benefits in scale and consistency.

- *Market or application needs dictate more local control.* The CGO must determine when local needs mandate less centralized activity. For example, given international variation in employment law or the issue of permanent establishment mentioned in Chapter 4, a human resources application or e-commerce site may require a local or regional solution. In most cases, though, these locally controlled applications should mimic the strategic platforms and use the corporate supporting technology. The work flow and other tactical provisions that the CGO has defined in concert with business units and geographies will also reduce complexity, cost, and duplication.

The net: The most effective way to create and manage an international brand online is by centralizing your efforts. The biggest loss will be in fine-tuning content to local needs, but you should be able to soften that blow with service level agreements combined with the strong advocacy of international representatives to your CGO. You will win big in lower costs because of more consistent branding, improved infrastructure, greater economy of scale, and the resulting lower costs. However, some applications demand local or regional control, and your policy should be flexible enough to respond to those needs.

Markets, Content, and Management Model Chosen, Is It Time to Translate?

At this point you have picked your target markets, developed your core content catalog, and perhaps determined that you will you manage international sites from your headquarters country. However, except for closely related languages and markets—such as Spanish-speaking countries in Latin America—significant technology preparation precedes translation, and some heavy-duty logistical adaptation follows it (see Figure 6.2). Without this prep work, translation will result in odd-looking passages—for example, French or Czech without their accents and diacritical marks.

Lay the Foundation for Multicultural Sites

National or cultural discrepancies in alphabets, measurements, currency, and representing dates make a basic translation difficult to achieve. Before you can even think about getting your company's message across in Japanese or Czech, you will have to make sure that your Web systems can handle the characters, serve up intelligible informational and error messages, and let them buy in kilos or pounds.

Called *internationalization,* this activity aims to eliminate any assumptions that your Web developers or system designers made about *language* or *locale.*

- On the language side, much of the content and commercial software developed for the North Atlantic zone supports only the alphanumeric

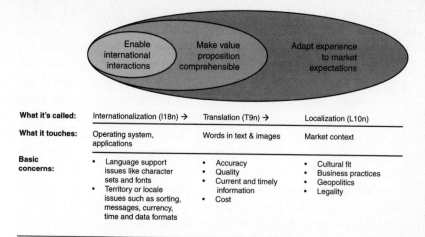

What it's called:	Internationalization (I18n) →	Translation (T9n) →	Localization (L10n)
What it touches:	Operating system, applications	Words in text & images	Market context
Basic concerns:	• Language support issues like character sets and fonts • Territory or locale issues such as sorting, messages, currency, time and data formats	• Accuracy • Quality • Current and timely information • Cost	• Cultural fit • Business practices • Geopolitics • Legality

Figure 6.2 Technical Prerequisites to Successful International Experiences

Note: Entering an international market means more than just translating words in text and graphics. For example, before you begin translating, you must be sure that the software can deal with other character sets such as that used for Japanese. Translation should not be a mechanical exercise, but should emphasize the rhetorical nature of the Web. Finally, for your tier-one markets, the site should meet the expectations of visitors from those countries, allowing them to interact with your online business on cultural and business terms that are familiar to them.

characters used in that region—and thus cannot support the ideographs of the major Asian languages.

- On the locale side, the same content and software complies with a particular country or territory's conventions for numbers, dates, currency, and other key elements of business. Done properly, internationalization will let your Web site display whichever language you choose to support and give you the means to deal with whichever logistics make sense. Internationalization enables high-quality localization, including translation, and makes it doable from a technical standpoint.

Language Support for Displaying or Printing Languages

The first task in internationalization is giving translators the characters that they need to do their job. For U.S. companies looking to Europe or South America or to their own Latino population, this means supporting the diacritical marks and special characters used just to say the words "French" or "Spanish" in those languages—*français* and *español,* respectively. Text might be legible without these special characters, but such a site would not win any awards for marketing effectiveness.

Ensuring that your corporate site can display all of the languages and currencies it needs can be tough depending on the software systems that you have developed and bought to run your business. Few developers consider or test any conditions outside their home markets when they build their first- or second-generation e-commerce systems or commercial packages. Your site may very well support only the character set for your home market, preventing you from even thinking about translating your core content into other languages. Without the character sets, the translated text would appear either without the diacritical marks that can change the meaning of a word (in Latin-based alphabets) or as placeholder system graphics (Japanese and other Asian languages). While the resulting non-accented text for French or Czech will be legible by a native speaker of those languages, your online clientele and prospects have numerous other choices for transacting in superior renditions of their language.

Basic Technology Elements for Correct Language Representation

To represent a language correctly, you need more than just the fonts sitting in Adobe's Type Manager or Word's font list. Table 6.2 lists the basic elements used to store and display a language.

Worldwide, the software industry is moving slowly toward a standard way of representing characters. Called *Unicode,* it will enable software to deal with all character sets, but even basic support is still over the horizon for many packages. Until then, most companies will tackle the character set issue in two phases:

1. *Most runes lead to Rome.* Latin-based characters based on an International Standards Organization standard (ISO8859) will suffice for European languages. This ISO convention also supports Greek and Arabic.[2] Supporting the base characters is one of the many challenges with display, storage, input, and manipulation of a writing system in other languages.
2. *They'll take a slower boat to Chinese.* Asian languages such as Japanese and Chinese require that sites and underlying applications use so-called double-byte character sets (DBCS). Many American and European software packages do not support DBCS out of the box, thus adding time and cost to any project involving Chinese, Japanese, or Korean.

Element	Major Characteristics	Examples
Language	One language can use several scripts Many languages might use the same script	• Most Western European languages use the Latin script • Japanese uses four scripts: Romaji (Latin characters), Kanji (Chinese characters), Hiragan, and Katakana.
Script	Characters such as ABC, abc, and 123 Upper- and lowercase variants Writing direction such as left-to-right Characters grouped in words Word separation such as blank spaces between these words	• Latin • Greek • Cyrillic • Hebrew • Arabic • Tamil
Character Set	The actual characters or glyphs available to a script	• Pure ASCII • ISO 8859x for languages using Latin, Cyrillic, Arabic, Hebrew, and Greek scripts • GB 2312-80 for China • Big Five for Taiwan • JIS X 0208: 1997 for Japan • KS X 1001: 1992 for Korea
Encoding Method	The number of bytes that a computer requires to store and display each character	• European languages use a single computer byte to represent each character. • Chinese, Japanese, and Korean each require two bytes per character.
Code Page	The computer's setting for a particular character set and encoding	• IBM CSDID 935 (EUC encoding, JIX X 208 character set) for Japanese • MS 932 (Shift-JIS encoding, JIX X 208 character set), also for Japanese
Font	The esthetic representation of a character set including characteristics like: • Serifs or San Serif • *Italics* or **bolding**	• Arial (sans serif) • Arial CE for central Europe • Arial Cyr for Cyrillic • Times New Roman (serif) and similar variants for other regions

Table 6.2 Elements Required for Correct Language Representation

Note: This table describes the elements required to store and display a language properly on an electronic device such as a computer or personal digital assistant. For more information, try your favorite search engine; the Web is full of techie sites bursting with more detail.

<u>Language Representation Matters for Personalization</u>   This issue
goes deeper than simply representing characters on the screen or in direct
mail promotions. Perhaps you let prospects register online for special services and then personalize interactions to their preferences—meaning
that you have to accept input from your visitors and then process and store
what they input. This requires going beyond simple content management,
deep into the database systems that underpin most modern applications.

Try to register as "Félix Nuñez" on almost any U.S. English-language
site such as Yahoo!, and the registration software probably will not recognize the second character in the first name or the middle character in the
last name, thus creating a homogenized "Felix Nunez." The result: If a customer cannot register his name the way he spells it, do not expect that your
international one-to-one marketing will succeed.

Putting the Dots in All the Right Places

As you leave the foreign airport on a shuttle bus, you wonder how long it
will take to go those 10 miles or 30 kilometers to downtown or to the city
center. You think about how far that behemoth Ford Excursion might
travel on a gallon of gas or where a liter might take that Mercedes A-class.
If the radio says that the temperature will reach 70° or 20° later today,
should you take an overcoat? In short, unless you are a frequent habitué
of transcontinental flights, you probably have to perform a little bit of mental arithmetic until you acclimate. Your lunch tab comes to 250 colones—
how much is that in your money?

Visitors from the Eighth Continent might have just stepped in from a
street where they deal regularly in kilos and meters, and they expect you
to understand these measurements. Indeed, to achieve effective translation, the translator must choose the conventions that are appropriate for a
given locale or territory (see Table 6.3).

- *Basic measures.* The bare minimum is supporting national currency
  symbols and commonly accepted formats for the date, time, or temperature. Visitors also expect information to be sorted according to local standards that might be different for that market. They also expect
  the "right" weights and measures, a problem that comes up frequently with clothing sizes around the world.

Element	Major Characteristics	Examples
Sorting	The physical order in which products, employee phone lists, or results are displayed.	• Binary sort—based on a code point value • Dictionary sort—based on language tradition • Assorted sorts for Asian languages based on radical, the total number of strokes, and pronunciation.
System messages	Visible text used by the operating system, other application software, or your Web site.	• Day names: mon or Monday • Month names: jan, January, 01
Date and time formats	How date and time are displayed	• AM/PM or 24-hour military time • Sequence: mmddyy, ddmmyy, yymmdd • Short or long: yy or yyyy • Separators: d/d/d; d.d.d.; d-d-d
Numeric formats	How large numbers or numbers with decimals are displayed	• Thousands separator: comma, dot, space • Decimal separator: comma or dot • Negative numbers: –x, x–, (x)
Currencies	How national or regional currencies are displayed	• Symbol position—before or after the amount • Debit amounts: $x, –x$, $x–, $–x, ($x) • Subunits—for example, no 1/100 yen in Japan • Rounding rules—for example, Swiss francs round to .05 increments

Table 6.3 Locale-Dependent Character Internationalization

Note: This table describes the elements required for your business to present a familiar face to international visitors, customers, partners, and employees. Any of these components can be a dead giveaway to the origin of content at your site.

- *Messages—errors and otherwise.* Because your company's software is not perfect and cannot provide for every possible choice, your visitors might see informational or error messages while perusing your site. The next level of internationalization involves taking any user-visible text in your system and placing it into message catalogs where they can be translated for your target markets.

- *General formatting problems.* The templates that direct content placement on a Web page reflect the language of the home market; however, they often have rigid definitions, meaning that a one-inch square text box designed for English will not meet the needs of many more verbose languages. For example, a German translation of your English core content could expand in volume by 20 or 30 percent, thus breaking your finely crafted design schemes. For this reason, designers should work closely with translators to ensure that the Web site designs that they use can work with different languages.

More Specific Challenges Mean "Localization"

A whole range of related business issues comes up under the rubric of *localization*—how content is interpreted in a different culture, whether it is legal, or what a culture's expectations might be. Because localization is an element of other major concerns, it is covered throughout this book in the context of other discussions:

- Chapter 3 discusses the challenges of full-context personalization that by definition cover every aspect of localization.
- Chapter 7 deals with the market-by-market translation and adaptation issues.
- Chapter 9 describes the vendor landscape for internationalization, translation, and localization.

How Native Should You Go?

Internationalization dogmatists set as their highest goal the ability to change locale during a Web interaction. In other words, someone could switch midstream from reading your site in English to ordering a product in Dutch. Laudable as this capability would be, though, it would involve an Olympian effort beyond the abilities and budgets of most practitioners.

Indeed, the cost to achieve this locale-shifting capability would be very high, and you would likely reserve it for tier-one markets. A more achievable and practicable aim would be to offer consistent information—pricing, availability, and product descriptions—regardless of the choice of language or locale. The auction site eBay delivers on this promise, providing consistent information and current bid prices whether you use English or Japanese to get there. While it does not allow a bidder to shift language and locale midstream, this synchronous access of the same items and knowledge about pricing does inspire buyer confidence.

The net: Without the proper foundation for translation and market localization, a business that aspires to work for New Yorkers, Muscovites, Paulistas, and Yokohamans will look pretty foolish with text with missing characters, badly formatted dates, incorrectly sorted lists, and incomprehensible error messages. Internationalization is a critical component that precedes your company's entry into any market, both online and in your traditional channels.

How Deep Must the Foundation Reach?

Chapter 3 introduced the ideal of globalization: full-context personalization that strives to offer visitors in your key markets the same quality of experience, taking care to cater to an individual's psychographic motivators, the business and political ecosystem in which they live, and the way that they get to the Internet. While this is a lofty goal that most companies will not realize in the near future, now is the time to start laying the foundation to support it.

What scares off most aspirants to international markets is the massive complexity of a Web site, relying as it does on an entrenched set of corporate and industry applications that lie beneath the waterline of what most visitors expect to see (see Figure 6.3). A basic corporate Web site and its derivative international sites are very complex organisms, both technically and organizationally. Removing or modifying any one part can break a lot of things: Pages might break, a transaction could fail, or visitors could see messages never intended for them.

One way to improve your chances of success is to use enterprise software that has been built for international markets. For example, Oracle's database, IBM's WebSphere application server, and the Tridion content manager have been tuned for use in major international markets. Each of these products lets your developers deal with the most common internationalization issues.

<u>Avoid the Mañana Syndrome</u>   One challenge of internationalization is to make changes within the underlying core system. Your development teams will have to work through these systems, many of which have evolved over the last few years when time to deployment was a bigger issue than quality.

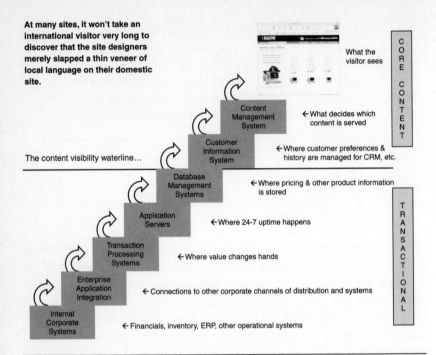

At many sites, it won't take an international visitor very long to discover that the site designers merely slapped a thin veneer of local language on their domestic site.

What the visitor sees

CORE CONTENT

Content Management System — ← What decides which content is served

Customer Information System — ← Where customer preferences & history are managed for CRM, etc.

The content visibility waterline…

Database Management Systems — ← Where pricing & other product information is stored

TRANSACTIONAL

Application Servers — ← Where 24-7 uptime happens

Transaction Processing Systems — ← Where value changes hands

Enterprise Application Integration — ← Connections to other corporate channels of distribution and systems

Internal Corporate Systems — ← Financials, inventory, ERP, other operational systems

Figure 6.3 How Content Gets to a Web Site: Impact on International Projects

Note: Though somewhat simplified, this figure still represents the depth and complexity of the technology that supplies a Web site with its content. The waterline indicates a typical assumption: that basic sites do not need much more than a simple translation of what the content management systems manage. In reality, corporate systems deeper in the technology value chain might provide information about backorders and other product availability.

Internationalization often finds it way to the bottom of many project lists. In some cases, these projects with their focus on fixing flaws in existing systems may not have much appeal to developers more accustomed to new coding projects.

Fixing underlying systems after you have built things on top of them is a sure recipe for expensive and often ugly rework—sort of the equivalent of tearing out a kitchen because the plumbing was not installed correctly. Furthermore, the notion that the Web is a stand-alone system just does not fly. While a new Web site for German might be a clean-sheet design, the reality is that it is probably tied to less pristine corporate systems that provide up-to-date information about your company's product. To make sure that your German customers do not see the plumbing, make sure that your internationalization efforts trace the path of an inquiry or a transaction throughout your system—and isolate all of the touchpoints with internal systems. You will be further ahead if your infrastructure includes globally aware and internationalized enterprise software such as Oracle's database system and IBM's WebSphere application server. Make such compliance a requirement for future enterprise software purchases.

The net: Few online businesses have the luxury of standing alone. Whatever they serve up comes from somewhere else in the company, so most internationalization projects will go far beyond and much deeper than your Web server or content management system. That means that such projects often require a high-level executive mandate to review and repair corporate systems, a budget to do so, and cross-organizational commitment to make it happen.

Should Your Company Do the Internationalization Itself?

In most cases, this is not a project that your IT developers will want to tackle on their own. Most likely, only very large companies with international development teams have the staff and internal expertise to take it on. With a defined strategic corporate platform for your Internet initiatives—content management, database, Web servers, and the supporting pieces diagrammed earlier in the chapter—your developers will have to do this only once instead of every time you tackle a new market. Companies like Autobytel and Travelocity have extended this approach to mimic a commercial software developer: After their first two or three generations of software, they began packaging their code on a regular basis, making these new versions available to their international subsidiaries, partners, and distributors as if they were Oracle or SAP. This discipline is an ideal practice to emulate for global efforts.

Two things will help get your IT group on its way to international systems:

1. *Work closely with your software suppliers.* Your technology suppliers should be able to give you a hand as well. Companies like Microsoft and Sybase build internationalization from the ground up in many of their products. They abstract messages into files that you can modify and create resource bundles from to allow international support. While this is exemplary coding hygiene, it is uncommon—especially for the

first few generations of Web software currently in use. For software vendors that you consider strategic, push for Unicode and localized product support, making such support a condition for future purchases. Until then, you will probably need their professional services to customize their software for a given market. For a content management system, this could add several hundred thousand dollars to the cost of the system.

2. *Call in the internationalization cavalry.* Large companies with experience in international markets may choose to conduct their own internationalization checkup, using so-called "spider" programs to crawl through their sites in search of offending code. Most companies, though, have little expertise in this arena. Your best bet will be to get a company such as Basis Technology, Lingoport, or Rubric to examine your site and its associated code and diagnose its readiness for global markets. Their staff and tools search for a wide range of real and potential problems, many of which even your most experienced, international-savvy developers would miss. Depending on the scale of problems identified by this checkup, you might enlist these outsourcers to fix the problem. Alternately, you can use their list of internationalization problems to direct your own developers or use an outsourcer such as Sapient or IBM Global Solutions. There are too many variables to say how much this costs, but it is most likely the quickest and most cost-effective way to internationalize your software.

Chapter 9 outlines best practices for working with third parties.

<u>Once You Choose an Internationalization Partner</u>   The typical internationalization project looks like many other software development projects: scope, diagnose, fix, review, and finish. In this list of common steps, I weave in the anonymized story of CallCentro, a company that contracted with an internationalization supplier to make a Web-based software call center product more suitable for global markets. In many ways, this product resembles the kind of systems that your company is building for customer, employee, or partner interaction, so it can be a proxy for your strategic platform.

1. *Scope out the project as you understand it.* You provide the detailed requirements to your supplier, and your supplier lays out the scope of work for an audit or assessment of your company's situation. This scope includes cost, duration, resources, requirements, and so on.

In the case of our exemplar, the project included two phases to globalize CallCentro's English-only product. The first step was to add character support for all western European languages and to localize it into Spanish. This included making the software easily localizable by moving all user-visible strings into message catalogs that could be translated without having to rebuild the software.

The second step in the project was to add full Unicode support so that it could support the needs of any language's character set. In addition, CallCentro asked for all communications within the system to be *transcoded* into Unicode, meaning that the software would store all information internally in Unicode, thus eliminating the need to do a lot of code and message conversions. For example, CallCentro wanted to be able to take in any customer e-mail, automatically identify the encoding of text that came in, convert it into Unicode, process it accordingly, and then respond using the same encoding as the original e-mail.

2. *Create a project management team.* CallCentro pulled together a small technical team to run the project, including a savvy leader to coordinate with each of the prospective and chosen partners. Most companies underestimate the time associated with managing a vendor, and some have gone so far as to commission a rotating staff that takes on the extra "burden" of dealing with the business partner. Many projects lose much time, efficiency, and quality because of poor client-side project management, so CallCentro did itself a service by dedicating resources early in the project.

3. *Conduct an audit.* This step will take much of your staff's time as a good supplier will interview your people relentlessly in order to understand how things work. The internationalization supplier will charge for that effort, and most customers figure that they get their money's worth. This audit will typically involve these interviews, software crawling of the site, and the application of large dollops of knowledge and expertise by the internationalization expert's staff.

4. *Agree on the project and a price.* The output of this phase is typically a written audit with an estimate of the work to be done. If the supplier doing the audit does not have the resources to do the implementation work itself, ask for an estimate of what such work should cost if you brought in experts. Whomever you choose to do the work, make sure that the work includes well-defined milestones; it is tough to manage big projects without clear-cut, smaller checkpoints. Price is not so simple, so we will talk about that in a moment. Because your interna-

Component	Problem
Development language	• Too many languages. Typically, multiple programming and scripting languages comprise a site, its user interface, and hooks to other systems. These systems are difficult to troubleshoot. • Perl doesn't have good internationalization support. • C++ has great support but many traps for programmers. • Java has far fewer locale limiting methods, but developers always get into trouble with encoding and locale-limiting logic. • COBOL has pointer arithmetic and data size traps. Back in the 1960s legacy languages like COBOL and FORTRAN were considered major advances in computing because they were so "English-like."
Database	Proprietary and homegrown databases are very expensive to deal with due to the lack of tools and standardized interfaces.
Application software	Many third-party software products don't support internationalization.
User interface	Complex user logic, integration, and formatting
Programmers	Most programmers don't think about international deployment, so their business logic is frequently mono-locale and mono-lingual.

Table 6.4 Typical Internationalization Pain Points

tionalization partner will not be there forever, ensure that there is sufficient provision for knowledge transfer to your developers.

5. *Start the work.* Actually, the scoping part of the project performs a lot of the work. This step is the remediation of your software and content to fix the problems. Make sure that enough review cycles are built in to make you feel comfortable with the effort. During the project, expect to see some fairly typical problems in each of the major components of your site (see Table 6.4).

6. *Keep on top of the project.* CallCentro found that it benefited from a few best practices that its internationalization vendor shared with it. The first was regular communication: On a weekly basis, the vendor's team leader met with CallCentro's IT liaison to review progress and problems. Daily communication between individual team members at CallCentro and its supplier made these weekly sessions more routine than eye-opening. The vendor put a dedicated account manager on site whom

CallCentro endowed with full company privileges. The companies also reviewed code regularly, merged code into a single code stream on a periodic basis, and used CallCentro's IT bug-tracking system to stay on top of high-priority problems. All these steps contributed to Call-Centro's peace of mind.

7. *Keep applications and knowledge current.* Make sure that your staff learns from your internationalization partners so that you become self-sufficient. Otherwise, you will have to keep bringing the outsourcer back for an expensive engagement every six months.

What Does Internationalization Cost?

What you will pay to have your code base and content internationalized will not be printed on any price sheet anywhere. What should it cost? Consultants and analysts have a pretty flip answer for such questions: "It depends." I will keep alive the tradition and note several variables that affect the price:

- *The size of the thing to be internationalized.* Some suppliers charge by lines of code only, but this is merely the starting point. If you demand a fixed price upfront, many vendors will figure the cost at US$1 per line of code, even if that line needs no work or is unused. This approach will cost you dearly, as many lines of code will not require any work at all.

- *What was used to build it.* The more languages, legacy code, and proprietary material there is, the more it will cost.

- *The amount of user interface code.* Graphical user interfaces (GUIs) are the bane of every developer's existence. While they are incredibly easy to construct, they are very difficult to debug.

- *What it touches.* Even if your site has very little user-visible code, there may be lots of work depending on the complexity of the underlying information systems and what they link to. For example, a plain branding site could be relatively simple to globalize, but an e-commerce effort might tie into an inventory control, a production system, and then a procurement system. A supply chain site could also be very straightforward until you include manufacturers and suppliers in several countries, all of a sudden raising locale-related issues such as currency. The complexity is not caused so much by the internationalization project, but rather by how global your business and its processes are. Your company is probably already doing a lot of this conversion work, but it is most likely doing it manually or with some purpose-built program somewhere deep in the bowels of your IT shop.

With all of these factors in mind, expect your vendor to estimate projects in ranges (e.g., US$100,000 to US$175,000) or "not to exceed US$150,000," though on small, easily defined jobs they may quote time and materials. The CallCentro scoping project cost US$50,000. The actual redevelopment work cost nearly US$1 million. A big part of that cost was removing American market assumptions from the software, fixing the bad programming that resulted, and laying a solid groundwork for supporting future country-language pairs.

Finally, budget for future internationalization work. If your internal processes are very complex, you should probably devote 5 to 10 percent of what you are spending on research and development for continuing internationalization work. If you are continuously doing new development, this will be a continuous process. If your development is more static, you might be able to get away with no follow-on expenditures for a year or two. And everyone acknowledges that if they had done it right the first time, it would have been less expensive than retrofitting after the fact.

How Bred-in-the-Bone Internationalization Benefits Budgets

Looking forward, your company should make international readiness a design goal not just for your company's products but also for the software applications that you use to design, manufacture, market, sell, and service them. Successful global firms have reported that the cost to internationalize systems up front typically adds about 30 percent to the cost of the project but saves them 50 percent and more over the price for doing each market individually.[3] This up-front planning involves the entire corporate infrastructure necessary to support globalization: organization, technical, cultural, financial, process, and so on.

This cost benefit comes largely from involving all your international business units in decision making and centralizing online software so that each country does not duplicate the redevelopment efforts of its colleagues in other countries. In summary,

- *The CGO makes sure that every country is heard from.* Operational groups in each country provide information on the technology and marketing needs of their countries. This data feeds the CGO, his strategy advisors, and corporate development teams with requirements for building online and related systems to meet the needs of global customers.

• *The corporate technology group sets the international development agenda.* As discussed in Chapter 3, the headquarters technology team designs and develops the online architecture, including an internationalized content management system, e-commerce platform, and supporting software applications such as personalization. This group wisely brings in outsiders to accomplish tasks beyond its core competency. Where centers of development excellence exist outside the headquarters country, the technology group subdivides projects. This is especially the case with large multinational corporations such as Siemens or IBM, but it happens even with smaller companies such as Six Continents Hotels, which develop its online applications both at its home in the United Kingdom and at a development center in the United States.

Finally, while the major expenditure for internationalization will be a one-time cost or spread over a short time frame, this project is a continuing saga. Looking forward in this dynamic environment, the technology group must establish processes to ensure that core systems, custom programming, and specialty business applications continue to be internationalized whenever they are modified. Otherwise, your international applications will gradually dry rot, exhibiting many of the ugly behaviors discussed earlier in this chapter.

Reaping the Benefits of a Sound Foundation

Lands' End calculated that its initial forays into international markets cost quite a bit more in information technology dollars than did its subsequent market entries (see Figure 6.4). When Lands' End initiated its global strategy, the company first remediated its online catalog systems to meet the needs of buyers around the world. The company attributes its heavy initial cost tab to the major software redevelopment effort required to enter its first offshore markets: the United Kingdom, Germany, and the much more difficult Japan. Then the company made incremental improvements in core software as it tackled new global markets, each one costing less than the last. With most of the heavy lifting out of the way, Lands' End predicts that the cost of entering new markets will be little more than the cost of translating words—a far more predictable project that I discuss in the next chapter—and the cost of adapting innovative applications such as its virtual model to size clothing.

Besides the inherent value of providing the infrastructure for entering

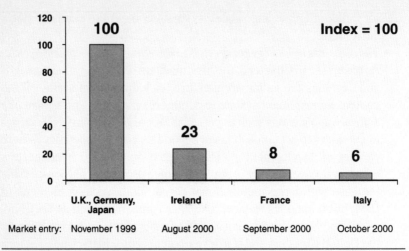

Figure 6.4 Technology Development Costs per Site at Lands' End
Source: Lands' End, 2001. Reprinted with permission.

Note: Breeding internationalization into your culture, technology, and organization can save money in the long run. Lands' End found that its entry into the United Kingdom, Germany, and Japan involved costly modifications to its base systems. Each subsequent market uncovered and fixed more obscure problems or issues deeper in the technology stack. With the hard work behind them, the company has found that more recent country debuts have been less costly and quicker to market.

new markets internationally and domestically, further benefit of this incremental approach comes from lowering the cost of Web development overall, a major expenditure at medium and large companies (see Figure 6.5). At the height of the Internet feeding frenzy in 1999, large firms in the United States spent an average of US$182,000 to develop and maintain an e-commerce site.[4] More ambitious companies laid out upwards of US$4 million on their online efforts. However, very little of this loot was spent creating international variants of the corporate sites.

Internationalization Is Basic Hygiene for International Business

Here are three things that you should internalize about internationalization:

1. *Internationalization is not an option.* Internationalization is a critical piece of the foundation for a global business. It allows the designers

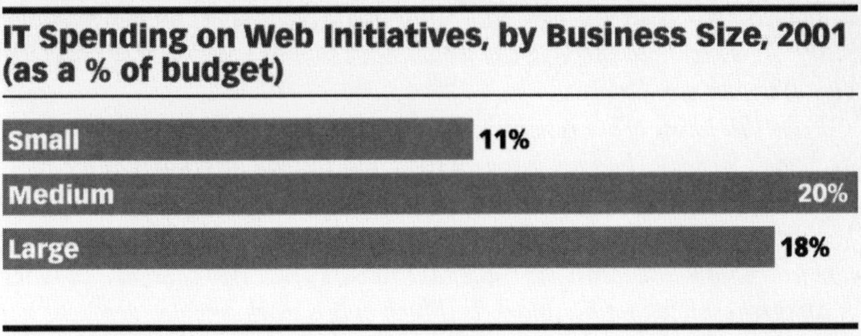

IT Spending on Web Initiatives, by Business Size, 2001 (as a % of budget)

Small	11%
Medium	20%
Large	18%

Figure 6.5 Information Technology Spending on Web Initiatives
(as % of budget)
Source: International Data Corp. (IDC), 2001. Retrieved from www.eMarketer.com.

Note: Improving the ability of online systems to support international markets up front means that more budget is available over time for other projects. This is important as your company strives to do more with less budget. Therefore, infrastructure improvements such as the internationalization bred in the bone of its signature systems means that Lands' End's efforts translate directly into bottom-line results.

of your site to create correct, credible experiences. It also provides the basis for content authors and translators to do their jobs.

2. *Internationalization is best left to experts.* If you do not have the experts in house, look to industry specialists such as Basis, LingoPort, or Rubric to do it for you. Integrators IBM Global Solutions, Sapient, and the professional services divisions of most large software companies can help as well.

3. *Adopt a commercial software approach for your corporate platform.* As your firm rolls its software out into regions and countries, think of it the same way that major vendors such as Oracle and Microsoft do. Make sure that it can support all the territories where you expect it to be used.

Mira's Log

After a long couple of days of digesting information about internationalization and the best organizational structures, Mira remembered the fateful day in college when she chose marketing over information technology as her major. This stuff was tough to slog through—boring and like an onion whose layers never seem to end. Upon more reflection, however, she realized that there were rocket scientists out there who could create great international sites and that if Acme were to succeed, she would have to make sure that she had her own Wernher von Brauns.

From this phase of her research, she understood that the compelling content at Acme's Web site does not grow on trees, but instead originates at the roots of the company's core systems—the same systems that run other parts of the business. She found that a heavy dose of internationalization was needed before translators and localizers could take Acme's great Web content and make it comprehensible in other markets. Much of this work, she decided, was not in Acme's core competency, but would require the help of outsourcers—which Mira took to calling her Blanche DuBois strategy of relying "on the kindness of strangers."[5] Her next step was to look at the translation and localization issues to understand what it would take to make Acme's content more accessible and understandable to its new target audiences.

7

Putting Your Value Proposition to Work on the Eighth Continent

With her list of target markets in hand, Mira focused on how Acme could effectively communicate its value proposition to new audiences. She looked at sites in languages that she did not understand, putting herself on the other side of the linguistic and cultural divide that defines the Web for many non-anglophone surfers. She also played around with automated translation services on the Web, frequently generating ludicrous translations; however flawed, these rough translations let her "read" sites that would otherwise be gibberish to her.

Knowing that a Web site might be the only thing that a prospective customer ever saw of Acme, Mira studied both the accuracy and the rhetorical effectiveness of the information she saw online. Whenever she looked at a translation from a rival or a supplier, she compared what she could find at corporateinformation.com with what she saw on the screen. She also looked at international marketing sites side by side, weighing what the corporate headquarters offered against what it published in other markets. She discovered that many companies had great intentions when it came to offering translated information for other markets but that they could not keep their disparate global sites synchronized with consistent, current data. That set her to looking at Acme's own processes (and sometimes lack of process) for getting information from market A to market B and from language X to language Y.

What Issues Will Keep You Awake?

This chapter discusses *translation,* the art of rendering something written in one language into a second language. Good translations communicate whatever messages were in the source document to readers of the translated text. They convey the meaning of the original author as closely as possible. Quality, cost, and timeliness underlie the basic translation issues that you will face as you take your online business and its supporting information systems into international markets.

- *Effectiveness.* Translation quality should be measured by how well it communicates your message to international customers, employees, or partners. Your job is to align your business goals for new markets with the level of translation needed to succeed in that venue. Translation often melds with *localization,* the task of translating words and transactions to local needs and of adapting the experience to the different devices and networks used in international markets.
- *Process.* Translation should be an integral part of product development, the processes that manage content flow, and your overall communication strategy. The challenge will be to achieve effective translations within the context of your established business practices, technology, and time frames. Project plans on the Web or offline rarely identify translation as a distinct component, thus leaving it out of the timeline and squeezing it in at the very end.
- *Cost.* Translation is expensive, so it would be extremely cost-prohibitive to render all the content from your corporate site in every market that you support. Quality translation has two components: the initial cost to translate and the continuing expense of keeping it current. The content catalog, an improved content architecture, and specialized tools combine to lower the cost of managing multiple international sites. Using a computer to generate translations—a process called *machine translation* (MT)—might complement your *human translation* (HT) efforts.

Business Goals Must Drive Translation Requirements

What motivates a company to do anything? Money, corporate valuation, and competitive pressures lead the list of business drivers. To succeed in wrenching international customers away from a competitor, you must offer them a powerful experience in a language that they can understand. If your goal is worldwide branding, your offerings must be rhetorically effective. If you want to support technicians in the field better, information must be accurate and current. If the customer calls up your Web site via a cell phone, you must telegraph your value in his language on a tiny screen. So let's look at what you are trying to accomplish.

- *"We want more share from international markets."* Large companies expect that an increasing part of their business both online and offline will come from outside their domestic markets. For example, Xerox launches over 60 products per year in up to 40 languages. Sabre, operator of the largest central reservations system, serves over 50,000 travel agencies around the world in a variety of languages. In financial services, brokerages like Schwab exploit new markets at home by offering information and services in Chinese and Spanish.
- *"We have to shave weeks off getting a product to our key markets."* High-tech manufacturers like Hewlett Packard and Dell find that their engineers can react faster to market opportunities, competitors' thrusts, and component improvements than can their marketing, documentation, and support teams, both domestically and internationally. Although engineering groups react quickly, translation often delays a product's debut in critical non-U.S. markets.
- *"We must improve collaboration and knowledge sharing across business units."* To make sure that it does not continuously reinvent the wheel or lose valuable knowledge, Ford translates information for dealers, service technicians, and employees around the world at its Volvo, Aston Martin, Land Rover, and Mazda subsidiaries.
- *"We have to be all over customer service."* DaimlerChrysler knows that its dealers and customers expect to receive correct information immediately so that if a customer requires service anywhere in the world, the dealer will have the right tools, equipment, knowledge, and parts to fix it. In today's global automobile business, manufacturers know that consumers do not care where the car was made—they just want it fixed. In the service sector, hoteliers like Six Continents practice personalization down to the level of language, market demographics, and individual needs.

Good Translation Conveys Your Corporate Values
The messages that you convey through the Web may be the first contact that a future cus-

tomer or business partner has with your company, brand, and products. If you successfully communicate your values to your global prospects, the Internet gives you an additional chance to enhance this relationship.

But for many companies on the Web, their message just did not make it through the medium. They publish sloppy, poorly formatted translations, in contrast to their corporate sites. Prospects that do not speak the corporation's home language are left to the mercy of the local Web presence, and if all a visitor sees of the company is what is online, you have lost him forever. Clean presentation on the Web and effective translation—linguistically sound, consistent with what you offer to your domestic customers, and culturally tailored—can mean the difference between success and disgrace in a market.

Therefore, effective translation complicates budgetary and time-to-market plans for every product launch. But translation doesn't happen overnight, and there's always some lag time before translation can produce rhetorically effective renderings. Unfortunately, translation all too often shows up at the end of a process as a necessary evil rather than as a critical component of an international debut. This end-of-the-line thinking has condemned translation to second-tier status. In today's rapid product development cycles, though, the first link of this chain should be at the very beginning of the product design cycle, when documentation and marketing plans are discussed and budgets are allocated.

Consider the difference between a rough translation and a quality rendering of the same information.

- *Rough translations may be better than nothing.* We have all seen translations that left a lot to be desired with misspellings, missing punctuation, misplaced diacritical marks, and awkward grammar. Inadequate translations affront native speakers but do, despite their flaws, convey the meaning of the source text that would otherwise be unreadable. Where will you find such rough translations?
  - At sites where the sheer quantity of information to be translated overwhelmed the company. Planners decided that everything needed to be translated, but time or budget could not get everything done to a consistently good level of quality.
  - At under-funded projects where the planners decided that conveying the *gist* would be better than nothing. Increasingly, as such companies think about offering more such background material to their customers or development partners, they might consider machine translation to perform other rough translations.

- *Quality translations make up the baseline for effective communication.* Even if your goal is just to accelerate the flow of information through your supply chain, the language should be clear and to the point. The translated information that you provide should be readily comprehensible to your international clientele: grammatically correct, spelled correctly, unambiguous, and reasonably fluent. You should budget for this base level of accuracy and marketing effectiveness at your Web site, and in supporting material such as product catalogs online and offline, technical manuals, and so on. This is also the ante for supply chain interactions such as procurement and internal applications such as human resources.

In addition, software suppliers such as AskJeeves (at its ask.com and pregunta.com sites) provide fast access to a wide range of customer service information. AskJeeves cannot answer all of the questions that are asked because there are just too many; instead, it answers only the questions that are absolutely necessary—and typically most frequently asked. For each question that they can answer online without involving a customer service representative, companies using this software—Dell and Nestlé among them—save significantly on the US$33 it costs to answer a phone call. Answering the same question online costs approximately US$1. For a large company with a high volume of customer inquiries, even a 10 percent reduction amounts to enormous savings.

Increasing the Rhetorical Effectiveness of Translation through Localization

Let's ratchet up the translation requirement to what people really expect on the Web: an experience that answers their questions, meets their needs, and keeps them coming back. While the improvement from a rough to a quality translation provides more value, it does come at a higher cost (see Table 7.1).

At the same time as they "speak" to the visitor, translations must represent your company using the language of your industry. This more powerful style of rendering raises two new requirements for the effective business translator: He or she must not only be an artist but also understand your business:

- *Portrait of the translator as artist.* The translator of Web sites or marketing materials must create a more localized translation that reflects the cultural context of the target market and the psychographic needs of the audience; rather than providing the Japanese functional equiv-

	Increasing Quality → Increasing Cost		
	Rough	**Quality**	**Localized**
WHERE	• Basic meaning or gist • Grammatically rocky and misspellings	• Complete • Correct grammar and spelling • Clear expression of ideas in source	• Culturally tuned • Not obviously a translation • Adapted metaphors • Local business practices
	• Background information such as articles, reviews, and abstracts	• Web sites • Manuals • Supply chain interactions • HR systems	• Persuasive advertising • Highly evolved Web sites • Wherever you want to "pass" as a local
PRO	• Low cost • Little time to produce • Translate what otherwise would not have been translated	• Accurate transmission of information from source language • Communicates the basic marketing message or operational procedures	• Visitors feel right at home • Interactions and transactions seem natural in that market context
CON	• Flawed grammar • Misspellings • Lack of fluency	• Higher cost to translate • More time • Increased need for staff to translate and edit	• Much higher cost • Much more time • Very skilled resources

Table 7.1 Just Good Enough or Great Translation? A Matter of Time and Money

Note: Translation spans a range of quality, from rough, quickly translated text to very polished, very local prose. It begins with very basic, rough gisting that conveys the sense of what the source text said, but with very few of the niceties of a polished communication. A quality translation adds the elegance of proper grammar, correct spelling, and even fluency of expression. Localized translations would sound to a native speaker as if they were originally created in that language.

alent of British text, the translation should "speak" to the Tokyo native. Such high-quality translations will typically be so fluent and idiomatic as to disguise the origin of the text. However, many different errors could reveal your site for the foreigner that it is—for example, lexical choices, pricing in the wrong currency, failure to reference the right delivery service for a region, or using inappropriate date formats.

• *Translators must know the territory.* Besides competence with source and target languages, companies like Sabre demand that their translators know the industry (see Table 7.2). This is especially critical as companies call upon their Web sites to support customers and resellers after the fact.

The right people . . .	Professional translators competent in both the source and target languages	Equally proficient professional translators who know your industry
using the right words . . .	Dictionaries in both the source and target languages provide guidance about meaning and usage Bilingual dictionaries show equivalent words in each language	Specialized lexicons for vertical industries (e.g., automotive or financial) or professional domains (medicine or particle physics) Corporate lexicon including product names and commonly used terms that are unique to or frequently used in your company
correctly.	Grammar—correct grammar, and the ability to deal with complex sentences, ambiguous ones like "the shooting of the hunters bothered me," or nonsense ones like "colorless green ideas sleep furiously"* Clean presentation	Your company's style, conveying its tone or attitude The language, the tone, and appropriate adaptation to culture, business practices, and market behaviors

Table 7.2 Basic Elements of a Good Translation
* Noam Chomsky, *Syntactic Structures* ('s-Gravenhage: Mouton & Co., 1957).

Note: Good translation requires a combination of the right translators, words, and grammar. You will not get that by just plopping a translator in front of a PC. Words, grammar, and context all conspire to provide meaning. Business context becomes more important—and limiting—as you work in specific industries. Tools for enhancing a translator's ability to do his job are discussed later in the chapter.

Translations should also be "localized" to your company so that the tone that you convey in your home country comes across internationally, where appropriate. For example, Lands' End tailors its catalogs to a very literate customer with an above-average income. The company strives to convey that same upmarket tone everywhere it operates. However, it comes at a cost: When Lands' End launched its French sites, it failed to "indoctrinate" its translation partner in its tone before the work started, thus spending more time in translation revision later on.

This localization must also reflect the venue or channel. Advertisements in newspapers are different from online banner advertising, and a troubleshooting chapter in a user's manual has a focus that differs from that of a FAQ page at a Web site. As you hire translators, make sure that you convey what you are trying to accomplish online and that they have demonstrable experience in that venue—online/offline, marketing/technical, consumer/supply chain, and so on.

In summary, this more evolved translation can erase physical borders, as it has at sites such as U.S.-based eBay and Hong Kong air carrier Cathay Pacific. Localized translation will become especially important as your company adapts its customer relationship management (CRM), personalization, and other marketing systems for international markets. Systems that depend on creating a deep, enduring link with prospect or customer will not work if the language gets in the way. This localized translation will touch many other systems in your business, too, as prospects become customers and their relationship with you extends beyond basic Web information to call centers, transactional systems, and brick-and-mortar establishments.

The net: Translation is an absolutely critical element of international business, but all too often it is an undervalued piece of the value chain. Having words that are merely functionally equivalent might satisfy some international prospects, but the increasing sophistication of Web markets worldwide and the many choices offered in their own countries will keep your global clientele pushing you for clear, compelling communication wherever you interact with them.

Translation for Global Firms Becomes a Process, Not an Event

The blistering pace of product innovation and Internet marketing have led to the truism that a Web site is never finished: Details about products, availability, and pricing are constantly in flux. This pace creates the demand for *timeliness*—that information you publish online is correct, current, and consistent with other sites and offline channels that you manage.

This demand for timeliness also makes yesterday's translation inaccurate. While your domestic customer can read the most up-to-date detail, the international customer must make decisions based on information that is ultimately suspect.

This all-too-frequent lack of site synchronicity highlights today's translation reality: Translation on the Web is a continuous process rather than a one-time or infrequent event. Companies will have to change their translation work flows to reflect this requirement for timeliness; in part, there has to be a process that will flag changes. For example, a change to a product specification made in the engineering group must find its way to the product marketing group. From there it goes off to brochures, TV spots, and product catalogs in each market where it is sold, thus extending the quality translation mandate well beyond the Web to every customer-facing facet of your company.

Translation work flow overlaps heavily with content management work flow. As your IT team formalizes and optimizes how corporate content moves through your organization, make sure that they include translation work flow in their mix of data, document, and other information types. That way you can bring translation into the mainstream of your operational functions and benefit from crucial development work that your company is already paying for.

The problems of translation can show up as expensive or legally disastrous errors. A faulty translation might lead to the loss of brand equity if changes do not find their way to the international sites.

Dealing with the Translation Process   To understand the difficulty of keeping multiple international sites telling the same story to your Eighth Continent customer, consider a prototypical drug company that we will call MondoPharma Ltd. Mondo has an international network of markets, laboratories, and distributors. Its Web site consists of thousands of pages, each made up of a dozen or so elements—a logo, an image, product description, clinical trial data, and so on. It changes the site daily, adding new products, modifying pricing and availability information, and publishing press releases about breaking events. Like many companies, Mondo has been most effective in keeping only its corporate site up to date with the actual state of the business—executive profiles, press releases, earning reports, product descriptions, availability, and so on.

Many firms manage consistency manually, but this approach will not work even for a single domestic site. Most are turning to content management systems from suppliers such as Interwoven, Stellent, and Vignette to manage this process for large Web sites. Now add to this simple scenario the pace of Web publishing, product innovation, and multiple international sites and the challenge of keeping your corporate story and product detail consistent becomes much more complex. The contest will only get greater as content volumes increase and customers expect to use a widening array of devices—cell phones, personal digital assistants, and televisions—to gain access to your content.

The net: Translation is a never-ending process because the source materials—content, data, images, information derived from your supply chain—are in constant flux. Reliance on manual monitoring and processes will not work for very long. Instead your global planning should include a review of the processes, technologies, and organizations that manage content inside your company and that support collaborative activities online with your business partners.

Where Effective Translation Begins

By now you should be thinking about translation as a critical new dimension to the processes that are currently in place for designing, developing, and marketing a product. From the day a project is launched, your product teams should be thinking about international markets and what it will take to succeed in those venues. Some localizers call this integrated view *transcreation*—they think of translation in the same context of creating the original content, so they produce the translated variants in step with the original. Documented work flows ensure that the critical translations of the original user's guide and Web catalog description immediately follow the source. Quality assurance and usability testing for each of the critical markets occurs early enough in the process to have some effect on its outcome.

The ideal approach stresses a concern for the international viability of your company and its goods, injecting this concern into every facet of your business. This awareness is far-reaching and starts in your current Web infrastructure and its supporting information systems. The following sections introduce the inevitable organizational debate, expand the discussion of the core content catalog, and review the technology that will be part of any translation strategy. Chapter 8 discusses the staffing and management issues that come with this model.

First: Review Your Content Management Architecture   Rushed to deployment under the mantra of "now or never" in the late 1990s, many Web sites are ill-designed and run on aging software. Functional changes to these sites will require major development and integration efforts.

Many of the companies that I have spoken to have undertaken a rigorous review of their online architectures and the systems that support it.

They are looking for things such as easier integration with other corporate systems, greater flexibility in adding new features, and the ability to respond dynamically to visitor requests through personalization. They are also bringing the Web under the umbrella of corporate reliability, availability, and scalability (RAS) goals as they integrate their Internet investments with other channels of corporate communication and commerce. Finally, they are looking at how their Web sites can morph to support any market on the planet. Let's review the major concerns that will be on the table.

1. *"We need more reliable, standards-based software."* Many early-generation Web sites were cobbled together with shareware,[1] version 1.0 commercial products, or do-it-yourself code built on top of shaky, easily corrupted file systems. Newer Web software is built on a sturdy foundation of databases such as DB2 and Oracle, on reliable application servers boasting J2EE[2] and XML[3] compliance, and with well-defined interfaces for plugging in content creation and translation tools. More importantly, many of the lower-level technology such as Microsoft and Sun operating systems and Oracle and Sybase database systems have built in the internationalization capabilities discussed in Chapter 6.

Unfortunately, as you move up the technology stack to the content management systems such as Interwoven and Vignette, they tend to be less able to deal with international users. The personalization systems do not even try, having been built mainly for the U.S. market during the heyday of the new economy.

These shortcomings show up in everyday functions. For example, in its review of content management technology, Six Continents Hotels found that its Hong Kong–based marketer could not create a promotion for a one-day event using a commercial content management system hosted in Atlanta. His one-day 8 A.M. to 8 P.M. event actually happened *yesterday* in the eyes of the Georgia-based software: The content management system was able to handle only one time zone, even in an application shared around the globe. By the time you read this, Six Continents will have chosen a software solution that works, but probably without a good deal of coding on their end.

Your software platform should be able to support critical functionality such as dynamic content generation or personalization for any market, using the same backbone technology. Otherwise, you will be doomed to reinvent the same one-to-one marketing wheel for every country that you enter.

2. ***"We have to support wireless."*** Take care that any software that your company chooses or develops does not strand your online business in the Siberia of the personal computer. Make sure that your content architecture can support wireless as well as PC-based access. Otherwise, you will have to create a costly duplicate of your content architecture.

In a typical application of wireless support, Travelocity wanted to let its members check the weather at their destination, schedule flights, book hotels and car rentals, and modify existing reservations—regardless of whether they were using a PC or a cell phone. The company created a software application that transacts with the Sabre central reservation system for the actual bookings but is smart enough to format the information differently for the needs of a PC, a cell phone, or another Internet connection. Its biggest challenge with wireless adaptation is stripping down the interaction to the barest detail to fit the small screen of a cell phone. This minimalist approach has the added effect of limiting the number of words that must be translated.

3. ***"We have too many tools—we've got to limit what we use."*** During the dot.com boom, anxious companies used whatever tools let them build sites fast—but often with little concern about future enhancements, integration with other systems, access by other tools, or standardized formats. While doing routine software audits, some IT departments have discovered that their developers have been using 30 different content creation tools to manage content. This smorgasbord of technology incurs heavy costs in training, software acquisition, time to market, and translation, and for each localization project, the source content must be converted into a form that a translator can edit and then converted back to the original file format before it can be posted.

If you expect to keep your international sites consistent, this costly, time-consuming cycle must end. Over the last three years, many of the early Web tool companies have yielded to open standards such as XML and Java, both of which address the problems of integration and file formats. On the translation front, newer aids from companies such as Atril, Lionbridge, and Trados employ variants of XML to ease the exchange of information between competing products. This drive toward fewer tools, combined with more centralized management of corporate content, will make translation and market adaptation more cost-effective, thus improving the return on investment for these projects.

4. *"We need to standardize the format of our documents and data."* As companies increase the flow of information around the world, they invariably increase the number of file and data formats that they are forced to manage, thus increasing the need for content creation tools, conversions, integration, and the other problems mentioned earlier. In response, many firms are moving to more regimented document types (often called DTDs[4]) for both free-form text files and structured data such as part numbers stored in database systems like Oracle and DB2. Using these templates, authors fill in descriptive fields, called "tags," that are later used to sort, query, and manipulate the content that the author writes or that a data entry clerk inputs. Used consistently, this allows companies to remove much of the inconsistency in format and structure, thus enabling a greater sharing of information.

At very large global companies such as GM, well-defined structures and processes are critical as data flows between divisions, from manufacturing to customer service, and from owner's manuals to the Web. It becomes even more important as the company works with its supply chain of original equipment manufacturers (OEMs) that provide core components to GM's manufacturing units. Without a consistent way of representing product information, every communication with a supplier would require translation between document formats—even before you could translate between languages for a part coming from Getrag in Germany. Having consistent documents and data considerably lessens the burden of translation on developers and translators alike, thus cutting costs.

5. *"We need to document and standardize our content processes."* Employees and business partners from all over the world contribute content to your online business and other parts of your company. Unfortunately, as the Web evolved in most companies, there was little established work flow to manage the creation, modification, sharing, and deletion of these contributions. As part of their content management initiatives, many companies are just now creating work-flow standards, establishing permissions and security, and defining roles associated with distributed authoring. Well-defined and documented processes will lower the cost and decrease the elapsed times of translation projects, especially as you extend your systems internationally, work with your supply chain, and employ outside translation bureaus.

Translation Ping-Pong—A Worst Practice to Avoid

Many companies exhibit the following pathology when it comes to translation work flow.

- You specify which content you need translated. Working with your IT group, you define the components that you need to create the master copy for globalization. The IT group packages site components such as files and databases and transmits them to your translation partner. Given the size of these files and typical firewall restrictions, this process is time-consuming and prone to error.
- Next, you tell your translation outsourcer that you are ready. Your translation partner decides on tools and translators, converts your files into formats that they can work with, and then divvies up the work. A quality assurance group performs static QA tasks such as proofreading and notifies the translator of any visible errors. Once the translator is done, the translation company converts the document back into the original format and sends it back to you.
- Then your Web team puts the translated files on a staging server, finding out that the static QA tests failed to capture some problems with interactions with the Web server, did not fit in the modified templates, or just plain did not show up as specified. So the whole translation process is repeated until the content loads properly. At this point, it is ready for review by the in-country specialists who will vet it for local accuracy and approachability. If it does not meet those criteria, it heads back into the translation loop.
- By this point, critical days or weeks may have passed, thus delaying a product launch or making a call center answer inquiries that could have been fielded by a FAQ posting.

This flawed excuse for a work flow results in a much longer time to produce translations for critical markets, thus increasing the cost and decreasing the likelihood of meeting go-to-market schedules.

---

6. *"We need to educate our authors and translators."* To ensure consistency across business units and among individuals, companies should create style guides and glossaries to guide their content creators and translators. A style guide describes the company's general style of expression and specifies corporate conventions for grammar, punctuation, and word usage, and might even include boilerplate language for corporate policies. Glossaries are guides to the use of corporate and industry terms. Broadly defined, these glossaries form the basis for managing terminology and associated knowledge (see Table 7.3). Very large companies

Elements	Corporate Directive	Market Guidance
Writing style	Corporate writing style, often based on Strunk & White, Associated Press, or *New York Times* recommendations, including active vs. passive voice, tense, person, and grade level of writing	Similar guidance for each national market
Words	Approved terms, idioms, and jargon, referencing glossaries	Country/language variants of the glossary
Images	Approved logos, icons, and graphics, sometimes incorporating a corporate photo and image library	The same library, but with market-specific cautions about the use of certain of the images
Formats	Text format, layout, and font rules	The same rules, but adapted to language and market needs
Colors	The corporate color palette for everything from Web sites to corporate helicopters	The same palette, but with an understanding that certain colors might not play well in certain markets
Processes	Basic spell checking, grammar review, editorial checks, and other work flow	The same, integrated as appropriate with corporate standards

Table 7.3 Guidance to Authors and Translators

Note: Style guides document the agreement that your company has on how it will express itself. The corporate style guide lays out the basic rules, while country-specific guides or section describe how these rules must be adapted for each market. This table lists some of the major elements that should be included in a style guide. Several sites on the Web offer guidance about colors, fonts, and other multicultural design issues on the Web. See sites such as www.webofculture.com, www.geomarkets.com, and www.idiominc.com/worldwise for information about local cultural issues and taboos.

such as GE or Siemens that have many different business units will likely generate not only corporate guides but business-unit guides as well. To be most effective, style guides and glossaries need to be available in both the source and target languages.

High-tech companies such as Cisco, IBM, Microsoft, Oracle, Sun, and Xerox have adopted aggressive terminology management strategies. While none are willing to share monetary results, a 2001 survey by the Localisation Industry Standards Association (LISA) showed that 90 percent

Action	Corporate Benefit	International Benefit
Standardize platforms	• Stable platforms • Easier integration • Economies of scale in purchase, training, and management	• Consistency in look and feel • Common functions across markets • Leverage centralized investment
Limit tools	• Lower software licensing fees • Less training • XML consistency • Easier application integration	• Decreased file format conversions • Lower costs • Less time to translate • XML-based information sharing
Use document templates	• Consistent format and structure • Easier information sharing with partners and supply chain • Easier sharing with other information applications	• Less conversion headache • Easier translation of supply chain data and information
Document processes	• Well-defined roles and responsibilities • More able to gauge the impact of changes to content and data	• Lower cost • Lower elapsed time of projects
Guide authors and translators	• More consistent source documents • Less subjective creations	• More consistency in translations • Better translations

Table 7.4 Benefits of Globalizing Your Content Architecture

Note: Translation is not something that should occur in isolation. You will benefit both on the corporate side and in your international markets from a methodical review of how content is created, managed, presented, and kept current.

of the respondents that use terminology management can point to quality improvements; 72 percent saw increased productivity; and 62 percent saw cost savings.[5] These improvements come from the higher quality and consistency of the original documents, resulting in faster translation turnaround times and lower costs (see Table 7.4).

Experienced firms acknowledge that although guides are difficult to produce, they are becoming an absolutely essential way for transnational companies to communicate both with their customers and with their widely dispersed business units. And as mergers and acquisitions continue to turn more and more companies into businesses without borders, these guides to effective communication will become even more critical. Several companies have also found that these style and terminology guides are useful in their global knowledge management projects. Finally, creating and revising the guides and glossaries provide an opportunity for companies to test the work-flow processes and content management technology that form the foundation of the company's online presence.

Second: Consolidate Whatever Looks Reproducible

The most revisited discussion in e-business globalization is whether you should centralize efforts around your corporate site or let your country units manage their own markets' sites. One of the likely outcomes from the review of how your company manages data, documents, and other content will be that you should centralize your technology investment, focusing on the creation of the most reliable platform for your business applications, whether online or offline. Content, on the other hand, will come from around the company and from throughout your supply chain.

For most firms pursuing a global marketing presence and striving to represent its brand consistently, this move toward consolidating technology at corporate or regional headquarters will have one of a few different manifestations.

- *Centralize everything.* Ducati has a unit that services its online presence in international markets, employing a team of six full-time editors who produce about 70 percent of the company's content in-house; the rest comes from contributing editors. Ducati manages its sites for Italy, the United States, Germany, and Japan using the same software in Bologna. Of course, the company relies on its national affiliates for localized sales and event information.
- *Centralize the really hard stuff.* Six Continents centralized its content management, CRM, and personalization technology in Atlanta but relies on local market resources for translation services and on regional managers to approve the translations. Individual hotels can edit entries at the corporate site as well as create and link their own marketing sites.
- *Centralize selectively.* EMC produces core content for each of its international sites but allows countries where the company has a large physical and business presence to contribute as much information to their national sites as they would like. Smaller markets with fewer resources rely on the corporate offices for everything, providing the U.S.- and France-based centers with local information.

Third: Translate Only What Matters

Working with corporate and local market specialists, you should determine exactly what people are looking for at your international sites. You cannot afford to make much of your content available in very many markets, in part because translation and continuing updates cost you by the word. Besides cost, there is a direct, inextricable relationship between the quantity of content that you translate and its quality. Early movers have found that thoroughly localizing complex Web sites that host enormous amounts of content and interactivity is very difficult. This realization has led these companies to limit the content to a nucleus of essential facts, called the content catalog.

This benchmark also helps the company's global planners because they can accurately estimate the cost of setting up and managing a national site. Using the content catalog allows EMC to calculate its return on investment (ROI) accurately in each market. Planners can also point to the power of translated material in increasing traffic to the site or converting more lookers to buyers. Like most international leaders, EMC will not divulge the financial benefits of its translation and localization investments, but the company does say that it is the only way to make sure that customers get the EMC message quickly enough—so much so that during the slowdown that started in 2000, globalization remained one of the company's priorities.

For more complex transactional sites, such as Eastman Chemical's e-commerce activities, creating a content catalog can be a much more difficult task. The chemical manufacturer found that its legacy transaction and product catalog system could not support languages other than English or locales other than the United States. Combined with the older systems' inflexibility, this shortcoming led Eastman to revamp its content and transaction architecture. Besides gaining the ability to support its international markets, the company found that its new systems gave it greater flexibility in managing new products and improved its ability to integrate its corporate systems with companies that it acquired.

As Eastman discovered, the content catalog boosts the corporate mission by improving the quality of information systems in general (see Figure 7.1). This online nucleus maps to a corporate best practice for content management in general.

Finally, as part of your work in developing a content catalog and a corporate style guide, you should clean up the source content. Translation companies such as Architext have developed a service offering that reviews your content for unnecessary text before translation. Eliminating repetitive text, verbosity, multiple synonyms, and market-specific graphics will save on translation costs.

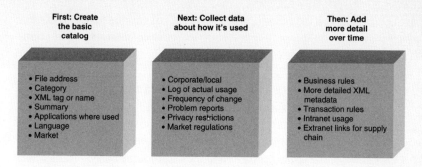

First: Create the basic catalog
- File address
- Category
- XML tag or name
- Summary
- Applications where used
- Language
- Market

Next: Collect data about how it's used
- Corporate/local
- Log of actual usage
- Frequency of change
- Problem reports
- Privacy restrictions
- Market regulations

Then: Add more detail over time
- Business rules
- More detailed XML metadata
- Transaction rules
- Intranet usage
- Extranet links for supply chain

Figure 7.1 Content Catalog Will Improve Corporate Content Management

Note: The content catalog also captures information that is critical to enterprise-wide content management. Data about the data—called *metadata*—tells you how and where content is used, thus improving your ability to forecast the effect of any changes. Tied into a translation scheme, content creators and translators will have much greater insight into the information that they touch. XML tags provide guidance to software tools and systems about how they should manipulate and display the content items that the tags describe.

Fourth: Aggressively Use Cross-Language Tool Technology

How well translators render information into another language and how quickly they can do it and at the least possible cost will all factor into the complex calculus that accompanies every discussion about the return on your globalization investment. With that in mind, your company should either complement its revivified content architecture with tools that optimize the translation process or insist that your external translation partners use them. These aids will increase the productivity of international teams by letting them reuse previous translations and monitor rules that let them know what has to be translated.

The most basic cross-language technology lets you reuse previously translated work such as corporate backgrounders and product descriptions for your key markets. However, that is when the really pernicious part of your international foray begins to unfold: The source content and data are in constant flux as companies and products evolve.

Keeping the data consistent can be an expensive Sisyphean task. Rather than retranslating each and every word in a document whenever anything happens, however, you should have to translate only the changed part of the text—and keep the previously translated material that did not change. Even phrases from older translations and preapproved text such as legal boilerplate and corporate messages could be reused in new documents. This capability is called *translation memory* and is frequently packaged as part of a *translation workbench,* which consists of various productivity enhancers such as online dictionary support, cost calculators, word counters, and lightweight work flow.

- *A translator's memory.* In its simplest form, a translator records his work in a file or database. When performing future translations, he might search the database for matches with his previous renderings of the same words, phrases, sentences, or even concepts.
- *Computer-aided translation memory.* Computer-based translation memory from suppliers such as Atril and Trados records segment pairs—a source-language segment such as an English sentence or phrase plus a target-language segment (the equivalent German sentence or phrase)—in the database. Whenever the software sees an identical source language segment occur in a subsequent translation, it suggests the previously translated segment as the basis for the new translation. The translator can then approve the suggestion as is, use the suggested translation with minor editing, or reject the suggested translation outright.

Most translation memory tools also support *fuzzy matching* for less exact correspondences. For example, the new source text might include a request like "send 5 fireplace pokers by March 1," but the tool will recognize the very similar "send 4 fireplace pokers by April 10" and suggest that as a match to the translator, making the appropriate changes in quantity and date.

Two words of caution:

1. *Insist that translators use tools with standardized interfaces.* Through the late 1990s, these memories were proprietary, with each software supplier creating its own format for the stored translations. However, LISA and a standards definition group called OSCAR have developed the XML-based Translation Memory eXchange (TMX), a specification for tools to share translation memories. OSCAR[6] has also been working on standards for parsing sentences. This capability, called "segmentation," provides a consistent way to specify where and how a sentence can be subdivided (e.g., at the prepositional phrase, clause, or syntagmatic level). Without such agreement, TMX memories are difficult to share because one tool might partition text at the sentence level while another divvies its up by the phrase. You should specify that translators should use TMX-compliant tools.

2. *Retain ownership of your translation memory.* If you're using an external firm, make sure that it is clear that your company owns the translation memory that results from their work and that your ownership will survive any termination of your business relationship. If the translation vendor owns the memory, your switching costs will rise astronomically. Translation memory is a critical business asset that will save you enormous amounts of money over each translation. Make it the supporting technology for your international glossaries and terminology management.

Fifth: Automate "Impossible" Tasks, Such as Monitoring Every Change

In an earlier chapter I outlined why the growing volume of content and its increasing volatility demanded an organizational solution—service level agreements—to ensure brand and product consistency across markets. However, most companies address this issue with cumbersome manual processes or expensive purpose-built software solutions, neither of which solves the problem for long. These ad hoc approaches work for small amounts of volatile content shared between two or three markets, but they collapse with larger volumes of information spanning multiple country-language pairs. The best solution will be to have software constantly monitor for any change to internationally shared content and automatically trigger translation and localization operations.

Let us consider MondoPharma, a hypothetical U.K.-based pharmaceutical giant that had undertaken a full Web site review to remedy the instability of its first-generation online offerings. One of the study team's conclusions was that content supporting the brand and global products needed to be shared across the company. The team had a few requirements for brand elements and globally distributed products:

- Every product with worldwide distribution—such as its MonProxen (naproxen) pain reliever—had to be translated for every market where Mondo had a sales office. Each translation had to be exact (i.e., semantically and legally identical) because Mondo's lawyers—and local regulators—insisted that these descriptions were the legal and scientific description of the company's formulations.
- Each translation had to be localized. Mondo distributed the product in a different form for each market. Distribution in Canada might be through federal clinics, through HMOs in the United States, and through charitable nongovernment organization (NGO) channels in Africa. In each case, Mondo's marketers had to adapt product discus-

sions, usage information, and other details to satisfy those market distinctions.

- Each time there was a change, these content adaptations had to occur within the 24-hours mandated by the service level agreement between Mondo's headquarters in the United Kingdom and its individual country units.

To date, Mondo has relied on a manual process to make sure that its marketing teams translated and adapted the information for different markets. The company's study found, though, that updates frequently slipped through the cracks of its ad hoc work-flow process. To prevent this, the planners wanted to have software constantly troll the source databases for any changes in globally shared content. If the software noticed a change, a *rule server* would initiate a localization work flow for the changed content, thus assuring that it would be updated for the target market (see Figure 7.2).

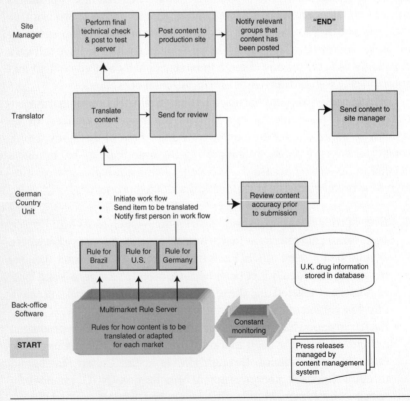

Figure 7.2 Automating the Translation Process

Unfortunately, Mondo's planners found that no products in the marketplace met these requirements in full, especially for the integrated rule server. However, they did see how their content management software would evolve over the coming years to help them out.

- For the near term, they would employ specialized globalization management servers (GMS) from suppliers such as Idiom, Uniscape, and Global Sight to help content management systems keep multiple international sites synchronized. They do so by allowing developers to define the rules for how international sites should respond to changes to their source content, automatically monitoring those sources for changes, and then initiating the work-flow process to make sure that those changes are executed. At first glance expensive, these solutions actually avoid the expense of purpose-built code.
- In the longer term, Mondo would rely on the content management systems themselves to internationalize themselves and to add their own global rule servers, likely by acquiring the GMS companies.

Looking forward, as your information technology colleagues automate the content update task, they should apply strict international buying criteria to their purchases of the enterprise software—databases, content management, application servers, and ERP systems—that figure in most content architectures (see Table 7.5). Other things to look for to increase

	Prerequisite	
Data Transparency	**Localizable**	**Rule Server**
A system allows end-to-end support for any of the scripts, character sets, and encoding discussed in Chapter 6. Ideally, someone anywhere on the planet can input his name, have it stored, managed, and otherwise pass through the system without any corruption or loss of information.	A system can manage all aspects of data processing such as displaying error messages in the local language and presenting prices or calculations in local currency. Ideally, developers can flag individual pieces of content or whole classes for use in specific locales using XML tags.	A company can define content rules to specify adaptations and usage for each market where that content is used. The software automatically executes these rules whenever changes are made, thus enforcing consistency and correctness across all sites.

Table 7.5 International Buying Criteria for Enterprise Software

automation and efficiency are localized interfaces (i.e., development tools in German, Japanese, Portuguese, and so on) so that you are not limited to anglophone developers and open product interfaces that allow third-party products to plug in as needed. Meanwhile, push hard on your enterprise software providers to make international market support a key feature in future releases.

Using a global Rule server, Mondo could specify rules laying out exactly which content should be used in which market and how they would be described. Mondo's developers would create a work-flow process so that the company could grab information from different labs around the world, from its distributors, from field trials, and so on, and then adapt that content for any market. Mondo realized a much tighter level of control over Mondo's global brand, but with the ability to have each location incorporate local content as appropriate.

Why Is the Computer Unable to Do All This Translation?

Computer-generated translation—often called machine translation (MT)—figures prominently in military intelligence and science fiction. Simply stated, a computer translates text from one language into another at lightning-fast speeds. Depending on the power of the software, its ability to learn, and the use of specialized dictionaries, computer-generated translations have approached high levels of accuracy—better than simple gisting, but nowhere near the level of an accomplished or even pedestrian human translator. Suppliers of MT include IBM, Bowne Global Solutions, and Systran. Each supplier claims that its accuracy reaches up into the ninety percents for different kinds of content.

Where Machine Translation Has Been Successful—And Not
Given the massive amount of information that companies would like to share among its employees, with business partners, and with its consumers, many have studied how they might employ computer-generated translation engines in their businesses. Their uses range from rough translation to prepopulating translation memory to allowing development teams to collaborate (see Table 7.6). Two immediate applications are product catalogs and e-mail:

- *Translating product catalogs.* Telecommunications gear supplier Lucent and aerospace manufacturer Rockwell International have long

Role	Function
Translate articles for background information	Provide a rough translation of information that might otherwise never be translated due to cost, time, or resource constraints.
Rapid population of translation memory	Quickly load vast amounts of supporting content into translation memory. This capability—combined with an industry and corporate lexicon—would give human translators more pretranslated words and expressions to validate against their own translations.
Linguistic analysis	Score the linguistic difficulty of source content, helping both content authors and translators forecast the cost and complexity of translation.
Collaboration	Support multinational development and marketing teams. IT staff further upstream in the site development process might not be able to communicate effectively. MT-enabled e-mail could improve the collaboration among these nonlinguist developers.
Development aid	As a way to bootstrap development. HTML, Java, and interface developers must test their applications, layouts, and templates for common localization problems such as language character expansion and basic look and feel. Provide reasonable facsimile of corporate content in target language rather than printer's Greek ("Ipso Iorum . . .").

Table 7.6 Where Machine Translation Can Add Value

Note: Although machine translation is not ready to create compelling sales pitches or translate best-selling novels, it can perform several important supporting roles as companies move into markets. These useful functions range from translating materials that otherwise will never get translated down to helping multinational development teams communicate. Expect this technology to improve over the coming decade as linguistic technology improves and as more potent computers provide the platform at lower prices.

used machine translation for translating product catalogs. Lucent first loaded telecom industry lexicons and Lucent glossaries into the MT engine that it bought, then translated enormous numbers of documents that were then picked apart by a company expert. The human made changes to the lexicons and then reran the translations, getting a more accurate rendering each time. By the end of this process, Lucent had achieved a result closer to quality translation than to rough renderings. This level is adequate for the many small changes to telecom product specifications. This combination of MT with postprocessing by company experts is the best approach to improving MT quality.

- *Dealing with e-mail.* Some firms are looking to MT to deal with the massive flood of e-mails both inside and outside companies. Germany conglomerate Siemens has been using machine translation to provide gisting for internal e-mail. Network gear manufacturer Cisco has been working with MT companies like Systran to add automatic translation to its call center products.

Other companies are experimenting with MT to respond to inquiries in the same language as the incoming e-mail, typically not a strong point for many companies responding to questions from the Eighth Continent. In 2001, only 8.9 percent of the companies surveyed by Australian MT supplier WorldLingo[7] responded correctly and in the same language as WorldLingo's e-mails. While WorldLingo does have a vested interest in companies using more MT solutions, the results indicate that over 90 percent of the companies that invite contact with their online prospects simply cannot respond. MT could be part of the solution to that shallow promise.

In venues requiring marketing rhetoric or exact instructions, other companies have found less benefit in MT. For example, General Motors experimented with a prototype authoring environment using MT, translation memory, and tight process control with its translation partners. It ultimately decided that the benefits of MT implementation did not justify the upfront investment.

Should You Use Machine Translation?

Does it make sense for your company to use MT online or for your customer service group to supplement its human translations (see Figure 7.3)? If you do not use machine translation at all, you can expect to lose some customers who want more information and will go to your competitors to find it. If you rely on more ambitious prospects to seek out and use a free MT offering at Google or freetranslate.com to translate your site, you are giving up a lot of control over your branding and message to an unaffiliated source. If do you choose to offer it at your site, make sure that visitors understand that what they are seeing is a gisted translation made available for their convenience. You might add an industry-specific lexicon and perhaps postprocessing, but each additional step costs more money.

Marching Orders from This Chapter

You should undertake these three tasks next:

1. *Announce that quality translation is not an option.* Even though many of your potential customers and partners may speak your language,

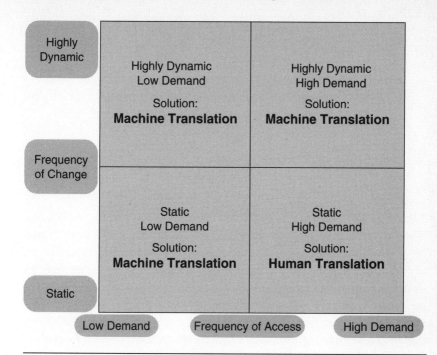

Figure 7.3 Decision Matrix for Machine versus Human Translation
Source: SDL, presentation at LISA conference, August 2001.

Note: This matrix from a presentation by an MT supplier compares machines with human translation on two axes: frequency of change and frequency of access. For fast-changing content that otherwise would not get translated, machine translation wins in most cases.

many do not. By not offering them the choice of interacting in their language, you are putting your company into a net deficit position relative to their needs. Creating a core content catalog for your company and using it as the vehicle to enter new markets will bound both the cost and the required resources.

2. *Revisit your content architecture.* The rapid development of corporate Web sites in the mid to late 1990s resulted in unstable software, cobbled-together work flows, and too many tools and file formats. Newer, more stable technology, key standards, and better understanding of how distributed authoring works are a few of the benefits that will result from a systematic review of your online business. In the course of this review, it will be easy to see where and how translation fits into the overall mix.

3. *Insert translation into the heart of your business.* Viewing translation and adaptation as an afterthought or a necessary evil will not win you any international marketing awards. As you build out your global

business, include translation as an early step in product development. Support it through mainstream content management, good translators, documented processes, feedback, translation workbench, monitoring, and the automated business rules in global resource servers to keep international sites provisioned with only correct, current, and consistent information.

Mira's Log

Mira began to understand that Acme was unlikely to become an international superstar unless it paid more attention—and devoted more of its budget—to localized translation. But she also learned that translation at the end of product development was a sure-fire way to increase the cost and probably delay the project. She determined that translation and localization had to be an intrinsic part of Acme's business planning and product development. That meant making sure that her colleagues in IT, engineering, marketing, sales, and other operational groups around the company also understood—and did something about—the scope and depth of the requirement.

8

Organizing to Serve the Eighth Continent

With the heavy-duty globalization tasks laid out in some detail, Mira now turned her attention to the question of how Acme could deliver on the flexible organizational model that she had laid out. From her audit of Acme's international sites, she knew that the company already dedicated a lot of money and staff to projecting its brand in every market where it did business, but these efforts were often off-brand and out of sync with the corporate pitch. She decided that these variably branded Web sites would be a good test bed for the new organization and its outsourcing partners, the work flows these teams would establish, and the technology that they would build and buy.

By consolidating Acme's international branding presence and more efficiently applying staff around the world, she hoped to formalize the more flexible global organization that she envisioned as CGO. She would unite these resources—from corporate, transnational business units, regional headquarters in Europe and Asia, and individual countries—to meet the company's online needs across the full range of Internet, intranet, and extranet applications, however they evolved. And she intended to be more cost-efficient than followers of today's shotgun approach.

Practical Organizational Issues That the CGO Will Face

This chapter discusses the nitty-gritty of the flexible, multinational organization that a CGO will put together to maximize the use of resources. Major issues include:

- *Alignment with corporate plans.* Many of the business plans for globalization that I have read lay out a project schedule that simply states "Add support for France and Germany in the second quarter; Brazil and Japan in the third quarter," and so on. However, the plans specifying enhancements to the domestic market are far more detailed, outlining exactly which technology and marketing resources will be required at each step. A successful entry into international markets or an Intranet requires that same level of planning detail, especially as it relates to who is going to do the work.

- *The right skills.* Most companies lack the right mix of skills and geographic location of those competencies to support international markets. The combination of budget realities and job market availability will keep most from hiring the necessary people, so practical CGOs will evaluate the inventory of internal talent around the globe, add them to their virtual team, and fill gaps with outsourcers. As discussed in Chapter 3, no single model works for establishing roles and organizational structures. The CGO must apply these resources at hand on a case-by-case basis to structure the teams that make most sense. This impermanence is critical because available resources are always in flux. As Chapter 9 discusses, you will likely use outsourcers to manage and execute some of these functions.

- *Short-term success.* In order to make globalization a mainstream, company-wide concern, the CGO should undertake a showcase project to demonstrate its value. Corralling international branding would be a good first effort because it is a high-profile part of the business. Improving the consistency in international brand management is a visible, enlightening exercise for marketing units around the company.

- *Cost.* This all costs a lot of money, and it has to show some value. Chapter 10 will also talk about measuring the returns on these investments.

CGO Enunciates the Vision

As part of his global leadership, the CGO must clearly articulate the vision, objectives, and benefits of global business to the entire company. In most cases, even with top management's full-fledged endorsement, that means showing results. One way to show some results in the near term is to get branding under control and use that success as a springboard for broader efforts to get the various global online activities integrated into the corporate mainstream. In your company, it may make more sense to get the supply chain or employee Intranet under more systematic management and control first, but I will use the branding effort for this case study.

A Showcase Project to Demonstrate Some Progress and Benefit

Given how dysfunctional many online branding efforts beyond the headquarters country are, this is a visible blemish on the online escutcheons of most firms. Combined with the real need for on-brand messaging, this is a good place to start: The before and after pictures will be obvious to all, and the future vision will be easier to illustrate. Phase 1 is very straightforward.

1. *Inventory assets.* This first step is mainly grunt work, finding all the branded sites that your company has in place in different markets and capturing information about site ownership, the technology used to deploy it, the staff that was involved, and any other resources that keep it running. You will need a precise picture of your current assets and capabilities in order to determine the extent to which they can be leveraged to clean up international branding.
2. *Link to corporate branded site.* With this information in hand, the next step is to have your corporate developers create a new home page with an international directory. Cross-link all of your international sites to this drop-down menu, allowing viewers all over the world to access your company, thus creating a universal entry point. Individual country URLs continue to work, but the dot.com site is country-agnostic, navigating any visitor to the language and country that they need. This is the most common approach of the largest companies in the top Internet economies that I have reviewed.

Remember that this is just the first step toward global brand consistency. Behind that drop-down menu, the individual country sites will continue to look as balkanized as they did before. But two things will have changed: (1) The branded dot.com site points visitors to a place where they can get the information they need, and (2) the individual country sites can direct visitors to a more corporate view. Alternately, when visitors pass from a country site to the corporate site, they can use the directory to find information about another market.

Executing this approach will cost you very little. You can conduct the inventory via e-mail, telephone, and shared workgroups on your Intranet, storing the results in a network-accessible Excel spreadsheet. Then your technical teams at corporate will build a new home page, linking in sites from around the world to the drop-down menu. Each country unit in turn will add a link on their home page to tie back to the corporate site.

The second phase of this international branding-consistency project is to proceed from the mishmash of sites behind a common international interface to a more coherent representation of the company (see Figure 8.1). In this second phase, the CGO will work with countries, regions, and multinational business units to unify the branded look and feel, establish consistency through the core content catalog, and provide the same levels of service and reliability in different markets. This "later" phase in Figure 8.1 is a more evolved corporate branding site where the same front door offers a choice of different market sites to visitors but provides an on-brand experience regardless of where the visitor strays.

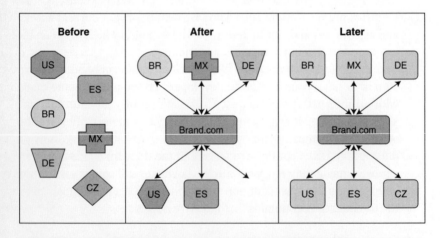

Figure 8.1 Consolidate International Branding Sites

Note: This figure represents the gradual unification of brand under the corporate dot.com site. The "before" phase shows what many companies have today: disconnected international sites with different levels of information, off-brand messaging, and a different look and feel. The "after" view links those disparate sites—warts and all—to a drop-down country choice menu on the dot.com corporate site. The more evolved "later" stage unifies brand presentation, look and feel, navigation, and core content.

The net: Globalization is a big issue that touches every part of the company. To gain credibility, the CGO should launch a well-defined project to show a near-term benefit and demonstrate how he or she will tackle the bigger issues. A great candidate is the first phase of an effort to consolidate international branding. Success here will be seen as a solid step in making international support part of the mainstream business.

Applying This Model More Broadly

Many firms figure that they are finished once they have country-specific sites and a common interface. But there will not be many visitors if they do not know that your site exists. Furthermore, prospect interest will fade quickly if a given site is unbearably slow, if it presents information that is inaccurate or outdated, or if it is visibly inferior to other corporate sites at the visitor's fingertips. The CGO must identify staff to help create the right experience. Companies typically undertake these five steps:

1. *Find the people to do it.* Globalization requires a lot of skills: Traditional Internet competencies such as authoring, engineering, quality assurance, marketing, and project management top the list, but you will have to supplement those talents with business, internationalization, localization, and translation expertise. You will find some of these people around your company, but you may have to dig deeper, hire, and bring in contractors for many of the more esoteric tasks such as internationalization.
2. *Specify the technology and tools.* A common task such as establishing a consistent global brand image has the same requirements worldwide, so the technology should be the same: content management, maybe a database, some personalization, reliable application servers, work flow, and a limited set of tools. The hardware and software capable of delivering multiple local sites should enable consistent, 24-hour-a-day performance and service levels across all target countries.
3. *Define the content.* As discussed in earlier chapters, the core content catalog is key to conveying the same message in each new market. Defining the content catalog is a communal effort involving everyone from product designers to lawyers, but implementation falls on the

shoulders of the small online content groups that many companies have evolved over the last several years.

4. *Design a corporate presentation model.* Here you will establish the corporate look and feel, including the esthetics of user experience, usability engineering, site design, color palettes, and other elements. This work is frequently done by marketers and brand managers. They will need to reach out to both digital branding professional, localization specialists, and their branding and marketing associates in the different geographies.

5. *Develop the information architecture.* The concept of *information architecture* is relatively new and involves a deeper, more involved analysis of how someone navigates his way through the depth and breadth of your site. Typically, this architecture involves creating a planning "war room" where the practitioners post diagrams of each page or function, and where a visitor might branch from each of those points. These techno-savvy designers usually carry the title of information architect and work with any of these three groups—technology, content, or marketing—rather than in a separate organization.

Find the People to Go Global

If you staff these functions improperly, any part of this organization could become a bottleneck. As content volumes and visitor demands increase, a bigger group will be required to grow or risk becoming ineffective. To make sure that everyone knows who does what and in what time frame:

- *Assign responsibility for each undertaking.* Organizing and supporting e-business globalization requires dedicated senior leadership. You should identify a top manager to head up the entire effort. This person should have a profound understanding of your company's business, Internet strategy, and globalization objectives. For example, Cemex has set up cross-region teams that it calls e-Groups to implement its strategy for the global Internet. These groups report to a process owner—let's call this area specialist a *group director*—who in turn is sponsored by the CGO. Patronage and support go up and down the hierarchy.

- *Assess the skills that each group needs.* Use the talent that you have on hand from corporate, transnational business units, regions, and individual countries. Some companies have implemented a skills certification program both to ensure that only qualified people are involved and to train those who need it.

- *Flesh out missing skills with contractors.* You probably do not have all the resources to deal with the business, language, culture, and technology issues of every target country. Using outside contractors for internationalization, localization, and translation is a good idea, but they will not help you very much on aligning these efforts with your business goals. See Chapter 9 for more on this point.

Equipping Staff for Their International Mission

Globalization cannot happen in isolation. Because it affects every functional area of your company, the CGO should drive every department to review its operations, identify overlap, and make adjustments where necessary. The CGO must also make sure that the whole company is responding—for example, order administration, shipping, invoicing, and customer call centers. This should be a bidirectional effort. Any new or modified product lines, adjusted pricing, or changes to local distribution and support that you make to support new markets must be reflected online.

The CGO must ensure that the online globalization work becomes a coherent and integral part of the company's overall strategy. Information must constantly flow between the Internet and the globalization-related activities occurring elsewhere in the company. The CGO will also have to see that employees get trained in a few key areas:

- *Global awareness.* Long accustomed to single-market activity, many of your most expert employees have never had to think about cross-cultural marketing, code pages, export restrictions, or any of the other arcana discussed in earlier chapters. If your company has an education or training department, consider having them put together presentations based on each of the chapters in this book.
- *Best practices.* Your company probably already has a policies and procedures manual that describes basic corporate policies. Revise these guides to reflect the growing globalization of your company. Your company may also have a style guide, glossaries, legal guidelines, and other manuals discussed in Chapter 7. You should complement these corporate resources with additional material to deal with global audiences.
- *Education on cross-cultural interaction.* As a result of the work flow that drives the core content catalog, it is likely that many of your employees may be working directly with foreign nations for the first time

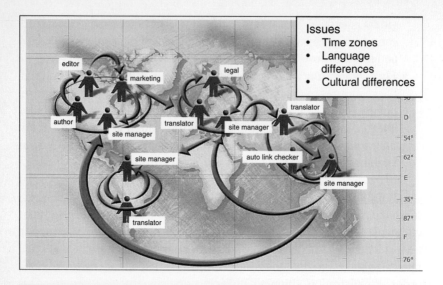

Figure 8.2 Worldwide Work Flow Spurs Need for Training

Note: Cross-cultural interaction results from the flow of information through the content catalog and the work flow that supports it.

(see Figure 8.2). Everyday activities such as e-mail and common job functions such as collaboration may be radically different from culture to culture. The bottom line: Budget for the necessary training in cross-cultural communication and collaboration.

This is the flip side of the issue raised in Chapter 3 in the discussion of full-context personalization: Just as the audience is different, so too are your in-country staff members. They have different individual motivators, value systems, ways of doing work, and expectations about how things should be done:

- *Individuals respond in their own way.* They often have very different protocols for online interactions. Flip expressions and irony are often lost within a country, and very regularly across languages and borders. Different countries have varying degrees of tolerance for sexual and racial expressions and anecdotes.

  The CGO's team should provide guidance on how to communicate with coworkers around the world. Some companies have adopted the six-hats method whereby the speaker prefaces his remarks or e-mail with the color hat indicating his attitude.[1] For example, a white hat signifies facts, figures, information needs, and gaps, while a black hat symbolizes judgment and caution. Other companies encourage employees to use explicit call outs or emoticons, while Lands' End includes a translation by a native speaker in many e-mail communications with its Asian employees.

- *Companies work differently, too.* Understanding that there are major differences in how companies work can surprise people even at the highest levels of a company. Difficulties can arise on any front, from managerial behavior to notions of what size of a staff is required. For example, when General Motors and Fiat announced that they would jointly develop and market products, marketing vice presidents from both sides gathered to discuss how the teams would work together. Fiat's representative said that "GM's head of public relations tells us that they have about 600 people working PR. Well, once we finally included all of our secretaries and delivery people, we came up with a padded total of 50 on our side. In reality, we've only got five, maybe six for the whole world."[2]

Getting to Know the Local Talent and Empowering Local Organizations   Most people like to do business with others whom they know and trust—and greater confidence comes from a personal meeting than from voicemail or e-mail interactions. Therefore, a good practice is for the CGO to make an international tour to meet the people with whom he will be working. Conversely, the CGO should make a point of meeting any international employees who are visiting headquarters.

Hoover's globalization advocate, headquartered in the United Kingdom, notes that very frequent face time at headquarters is critical. Twice-yearly visits to Hoover's Texas base of operations have made him someone whom people expect to see and are not surprised to hear from. This familiarity holds people accountable for promises and action items that they have taken.

As the CGO heads out to meet the people in the field, he or she should use this opportunity to assess the regions and the countries. As he builds out his virtual teams, he has no alternative but to evaluate the resources that the company already has in place, match them up against needs, and make the necessary decisions. If the CGO makes an honest evaluation of each overseas office's capabilities and staffing, he may have to get rid of some staffers. However, he must comply with the local employment laws, deal with the possibility of resentment, and patch any holes that layoffs might create in the oral tradition of local work flow.

<u>Identifying Staff for Globalization Efforts</u>   In the following sections
I propose an organizational staffing for a company intent on globalizing its
online presence and providing support for other units of the company. The
roles that I describe might not match up with the way you do things inside
your company or with your particular needs. However inappropriate these
particular titles and job descriptions, the goal is to get your company thinking about the following:

- *Functions.* The globalization teams deal with essential operations inside your company. They could act in a similar fashion to cross-
  functional teams already in place. For example, they might model
  themselves after your product teams, which act as a conduit for information, management, recommendations, and problem resolution between your company's suppliers and management.
- *Composition.* The exact number of resources and employees that your
  company needs will depend on many variables, including the ultimate
  size and complexity of your company's globalization effort, the
  amount of content, corporate structure, the tools utilized to develop
  and maintain the sites, and the extent to which the sites are managed
  centrally, locally, or regionally.
- *Responsibilities and titles.* These titles represent tasks that need to be
  performed (see Figure 8.3).

If yours is like most companies, your staff often takes on other responsibilities or wears multiple hats. As the globalization initiative grows within
your company, so too will the responsibilities for all positions, both official
and unofficial. One thing that often stands in the way of globalization success is that international responsibilities are unofficially assigned. Because
these undocumented new tasks are not listed on performance evaluations,
they drop to the bottom of the employee's priority list. One way to safeguard against this common problem is to create official positions responsibilities, thus ensuring that employees are evaluated for all the jobs for
which they are responsible. However, recognizing that the budget may not
be there today, the CGO should make every effort to ensure that all employees have ample opportunity to complete their official and critical globalization tasks. As soon as business and budgets allow, the company should
establish roles and responsibilities on the principle of "one job, one person."

<u>Working with the Group Directors</u>   Each of these teams needs a
chief who reports directly to the CGO. Depending on the size of your com-

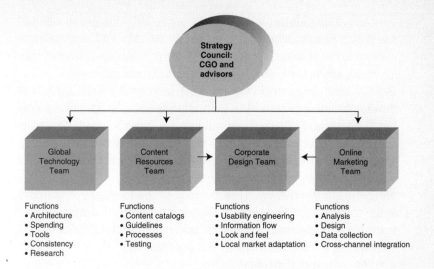

Figure 8.3 Major Functional Areas

Note: Working with executive and other management advisors around the company, the CGO defines the corporate strategy for globalization. SWAT teams focused on the major functional areas employ the same virtual model, drawing on resources from inside the company as well as from contractors.

pany, these leaders will likely be senior managers running multiple projects. These group directors are responsible for managing the team, its planning, its budget, and its deliverables. They will also coordinate the team's activities with other groups inside and outside the company. The following sections discuss their duties in more detail.

Global Technology Team

This group has one basic mission: to optimize the use of Internet technology to meet corporate needs wherever they are, integrating it as much as possible with existing investments and practices.

- *Revise corporate architectures.* This team will work with other groups to develop and revise corporate architectures to meet the international market needs for language, currency, and common business practices and formats discussed in Chapter 6. It will identify interactions and dependencies.
- *Consolidate technology spending.* It will centralize investment wher-

ever something looks shared and reproducible. This group will find the things that it makes no sense to pay for over and over again in every market. It will consolidate corporate purchasing, training, management, and other typically duplicated functions and costs.

- *Develop tools for content creators.* This squad will select, apply, and develop technology resources for market specialists, translators, content authors, and others. They will bring in cross-language tool technology that increase the productivity of content creators and translators, improve work flow, and ensure that only current content is published at your international sites.
- *Maintain site consistency.* This group is at the forefront of the challenge to keep your site vibrant. Working with the content resources team, this group ensures that your international sites continue to offer current, correct, and consistent information to their visitors, regardless of where they come from.
- *Research new technologies.* These developers will constantly scan the Internet horizon to see what's happening next. They will stay on top of advances in core technologies such as content management, database, application servers, and personalization. They will also evaluate capabilities, capacity, and viability of these systems to meet international market needs.

Staffing for the Global Technology Team

Because it will leverage corporate systems and expertise, the global technology team usually makes its home wherever your company builds its major systems. At more globally evolved companies, this is not a separate organization but rather a nonnegotiable requirement for all corporate development activity. For example, as it designs its next-generation Internet architecture, Six Continents has made global deployment a key design goal. Regardless of how evolved your thinking is, however, you do need to provision for the following activities.

- *The group director.* One person must have clear oversight for the intersection of international technical needs with other corporate systems. Having someone in this role should limit—if not eliminate— any redundancies in the system, such as the independent sales sites in Germany that duplicate the regional offering in Belgium. The group director may also work to set up technical development centers wherever your company has big concentrations of developers or wherever personnel costs might be lower.

- *Other managers.* Development leaders at the business unit, regional, and national level will be pulled into this virtual organization. Whatever online activity they are developing should be pulled under the bigger tent of the global technology group.
- *Architects.* Globalization offers your best and brightest engineers a chance to add some impressive words to their résumés by applying their RAS[3] mantra to more complex multinational systems. For example, security will be an increasing concern as your sites break down the walls between Web, intranet, and extranet. These architects will have to assess the vulnerability of newly exposed systems, plan for offsite backup, and deal with issues such as denial-of-service attacks against revenue-producing systems.
- *Developers worldwide.* Your best and brightest developers will also find major new projects to work on, at both the system and tool level. For example, developers at a European airline created a "toolbox" to let Web content authors do more publishing themselves. This kit allowed less savvy or understaffed local offices to add content and even additional pages to the corporate site, giving them the ability to plug in local advertising banners and customer responses and to tailor the level of interactivity to local telecom performance.

Once you move beyond the centralized branding activity outlined earlier to procurement and employee-focused systems, you will find that it makes sense to host some of these systems locally. This means having a local-country infrastructure to support market interactivity with local customers or visitors with whom you want to interact. Ideally, the local or regional units will be able to take advantage of core technology built by the global technology team, adapting it to their market requirements. For example, if they want to service customers in China, you must supply them with the technology and people necessary to support a Chinese-speaking population.

Content Resources Team

Content creation is a widely dispersed, highly variable function. Its volume and volatility increase daily, raising new demands for companies to manage better the data and other information that describe their offerings and value propositions. Many firms have implemented systematic work flows on top of the document, database, and content management systems discussed in Chapter 7. The next step is for the content resources team to extend the reach of these technologies to create a foundation and support more discipline for international sites and content. This is critical to ensuring that translation and localization are correct and timely.

- *Develop content catalogs.* This content repository, first discussed in Chapter 3, outlines the core set of information and basic information types that must be translated and adapted for each market where the company sells its wares. In close consultation with sales and marketing groups around the company, the content resources team will create the first such catalog aimed at basic market entry and branding. Subsequently defined catalogs will provide more specialized information sets for supply chains, employee intranets, procurement systems, and other critical business functions.
- *Provide guidelines.* The content resources group will create physical deliverables such as style guides and translation glossaries. It will also use cross-language tools and work with partners to develop a company-wide translation memory to facilitate consistent adaptation of content for each market and to set standards for the appropriate use of bandwidth-hogging features streaming video and audio. As it develops work-flow processes, it will also build in steps to ensure the proper and legal use of capabilities such as personalization.
- *Clarify processes.* This team will define processes to build integrity and editorial discipline into the creation, update, management, and translation of content. It will specify work flows that will involve all concerned groups in iterative review processes to guarantee content correctness, cross-market consistency, timeliness, and legal compliance. At many companies, this group is also responsible for managing the review server that stages all content in context so that in-country reviewers and other specialists can appraise sites before they go live.
- *Test and vet the tools.* Testing both off-the-shelf products and software developed by the technology team, the content resources group will validate that the content creation and translation tools work as advertised and comply with the work flows and other procedures that they have set up.

Staffing for the Content Resources Team   Because content is generated in every nook and cranny of your company, the content resources team will span the globe. Content contributors in product management, marketing, sales, and other operational groups will be involved as well, using the tools and processes defined by this team to do their jobs. Two strategic functions are critical to designing and building a robust international presence:

1. *Content architect.* This individual is responsible for defining the content catalogs that meet both domestic and international needs. He or she will work closely with marketing and other groups to create the catalogs that meet their needs in different markets and will also consult with local market teams and professional translators to tune the catalog to each market.
2. *Information architect.* This person designs the flow of control through a site, determining interactions and navigation. He or she is typically quite versed in *usability engineering,* a field that has gained new prominence in the era of hyperlinked Web sites that behave like randomly firing synapses. Consultations with specialists for each target market will be critical to ensure that the flow is correct, that site elements work with different languages, that visitor expectations are met, and that no cultural sensibilities are offended. The information architect will also work with user experience and usability engineers to ensure that every visitor in each market leaves with the best possible impression of the site, the company, and the offer.

After these two architects define the structure of the site, the tactical and operational staff comes into play:

• *The group director.* The worldwide site director, typically at corporate, carries overall accountability for deploying global Web sites. He or she oversees the design of site content and navigation architecture and also manages the corporate editorial process, creating, editing, and reviewing all content that is modified or created in domestic and local markets. The group director is also responsible for managing contracts with localization and translation partners to make sure that the content "sings" for each intended audience.
• *Corporate Web master.* This is the operational keeper and publisher of the core content catalogs—the basic information that you offer in every market. The Web master is responsible for the day-to-day management of any visitor-facing content. Working with the technology team, he or she monitors the traffic to and performance at the corporate branded sites. Working with market intelligence analysts, the

Web master cross-tabulates site performance with the real-life network connectivity of the various markets that the company targets.

- *Regional and local Web masters.* These people manage the day-to-day approval and posting of content to localized Web sites. Whether the site is centralized at corporate or locally hosted, they are responsible for making sure that it looks and reads right for in-country users. Beyond the core content catalog, they review and approve all content that is to appear on a local site or on sites within the region, and they manage the translation process in the country. They work with the work-flow mavens to make sure that all local content has been approved prior to publishing and that all content updates, deactivations, and deletions occur in a timely and error-free manner. Working with local content contributors, they enforce the corporate communications policy and editorial guidelines. They also keep their fingers on the pulse of site traffic, reporting usage statistics to their online marketing colleagues.

- *Multicultural site managers.* Other than managing the domestic ethnic variants of a company's online presence, these Web masters perform the same duties that a local Web master does. They are responsible for making sure that the site continues to meet the needs of the ethnic community being addressed. Like the Web master, they keep tabs on what is happening at the Latino or Turkish site, but they do so with the added responsibility of aligning it with the "dominant" American or German culture while keeping it linguistically and culturally tuned to the expatriate Mexican or Turk mindset.

Coercing Content Creators around the Company
Most content is created around the company in response to product or company needs, repurposed or adapted to other uses, and translated as needed. In this distributed authoring environment, anybody can be a content creator. Regardless of where they are located, these authors—many of whose primary jobs do not involve international markets—need two things to cooperate: (1) tools and processes that are simple to use and (2) incentives to cooperate.

Over time, you can make compliance with corporate style guides part of everyone's job, but until then you may have to get creative in cajoling these authors into cooperating. You might include global job responsibilities in their job descriptions and ensure that managers assess employees on their ability to meet global as well as local requirements. The upside of compliance for your company comes in the form of lower costs for translations resulting from less purple prose, use of standard terminology, and other simplifying techniques discussed in Chapter 7. Until "global" is part of everyone's vocabulary, bonuses for compliance and contests might be one way to get everyone on the same page.

Online Marketing Team

The online marketing team draws on resources and disciplines from across the company, ranging from established Web teams working with personalization technology to the direct marketing group doing mailings to the crew responsible for enterprise-wide customer relationship management (CRM). The online marketing team will

- *Analyze customer behaviors and market potential.* What motivates buyers in international markets will likely vary from what drives them in your home country (see Chapter 3). This team will work with corporate resources and local knowledge to assess each country-language pair as a new market with its own revenue potential, business rules, government regulations, consumer preferences, and cultural behavior.
- *Design campaigns and sites that meet these expectations.* Basing their efforts on the needs of individual markets, the online marketing team will identify campaign resources and content assets that can be reused as-is, others that need just to be translated or localized before being reused, and what must be built from scratch.
- *Comply with privacy and other regulations. Permission marketing* and privacy regulations that vary by country bring a new complexity to marketing. This group will work with the global technology team to develop cross-market technology that will allow personalization within the context of any given country's regulations (see Chapter 5). For example, hospitality companies such as Six Continents and manufacturers such as Renault now build their online systems to international specifications, allowing in-country marketing units to tailor offers to the specific requirements of their markets.
- *Improve the collection and application of data.* As they improve back-end systems to meet national regulations regarding the use of data, the online marketing group will work with other organizations throughout the company to enrich the quality and usefulness of the data that they do collect and manage. Starting with their in-house customer

information and data warehouse expertise, they will bring in out-sourcers such as Vality, Innovative Solutions, and Requisite to clean up their data collection and management systems.

This effort will involve a complete internationalization of everything from registration systems to databases to campaign management. Otherwise, they will continue to address Félix Nuñez as Felix Nunez, belying the hard work that you did to create a site culturally and linguistically tuned to the U.S. Latino market. Unlike the semiannual direct mail campaign of the past, however, you now might misspell his name and otherwise undermine the relationship anytime you e-mail him or he logs in to your Web site.

- *Integrate with other corporate activities.* Remember that the Web is just one part of the marketing equation. Customers around the world increasingly expect that whatever you learn about them or tell them via one channel will be the same in another. The online marketing team will figure out how to make this capability—already available for your domestic customers—flow through your enterprise worldwide and tie in CRM systems, enterprise resource planning (ERP) systems for your supply chain, and employee e-mail.

Improving Market Intelligence
Knowing what is going on in your target countries is critical to executing the right marketing programs. The reliability of this market intelligence will be highest when your sources are in-country or have strong local ties. They should also have a proven, professional level of market expertise, perhaps using focus groups and usability studies to understand how discrete markets differ from each other.

To illustrate where your company excels and where it requires improvement, benchmark yourself against your top rivals and best-of online companies. One high-tech company chose its two biggest markets, Germany and China, in which it would judge its offering against its five rivals. A market intelligence team compared three sites for each company: (1) the globally branded U.S. site, which in all five cases pointed to other countries; (2) the German site that was accessible from the U.S. site; and (3) the Chinese site that was linked to the U.S. site. The team's analysts assessed the high-tech company and its rivals on the basis of five simple questions that you might ask about your own site (see Table 8.1).

Staffing for the Online Marketing Team
This work will touch many parts of the company, so the team will draw its resources from marketing teams at corporate, in business units, in regions, and in individual countries.

Question	Expectation	Best Practice
Can you locate the local Web site doing a keyword search on a local search engine?	Most people use search engines to find you.* Prospects should be able to find your site using the most popular search engines. For Germany, the teams chose Yahoo! Germany. For China, they used both Yahoo! China and Sohu. Sites like www.searchenginecolossus.com list search engines by country.	For each country where you expect to do business or offer a localized Web presence, find the most popular search engines and register your site with them.
From the globally branded U.S. Web page, could a user easily navigate to the target market and then back again to the U.S.?	For this particular company, many of its international prospects speak English, so the online marketers expect visitors to bounce back and forth to the U.S. site for more information.	This is a question of well-designed navigation. Make the links between sites visible and obvious. Test the navigation schemes with nonemployees.
Do the navigation bars and subject headings use local languages?	If you offer separate sites or pages for international visitors, most will expect to be able to navigate around the site in their own language.	This issue goes beyond simple translation to internationalization. Many sites go halfway: while they translate the text, they don't invest in adapting the text embedded in images, buttons, and other navigational elements.
Do the local Web sites have the same look and feel as the global U.S. Web site?	As a visitor navigates from the U.S. to other market sites, he expects to see some consistency in branding, messaging, and content.	With the content and information architects, the marketing team should ensure that the experience, the look and feel, and the content itself retain corporate identity globally.
How deeply have they translated or localized the non-U.S. sites?	If they see the availability of a site in their own languages advertised on the global home page, most visitors will expect more than just a welcome.	For your initial entry into a market, use the local language translation of the core content catalog to provide crucial information about your company and its offerings. For more evolved sites, work with the local marketing team to offer content from deeper in the site—which sometimes will mean using machine translation technology.

Table 8.1 Competitive Analysis and Benchmarking

*According to a June 2000 Forrester Research study, 81% of respondents use a search engine to find a site.

- *The group director.* The online marketing director manages online promotional activities such as advertising on various media, campaigns, and integration with other marketing channels. He also consults with the content team to identify the appropriate global and local content for international Web sites and with the technology group to ensure cross-market support for permission for marketing activities. His team is responsible for measurement initiatives and keeping current on regulatory issues such as privacy laws that affect marketing programs.
- *Local marketing teams.* In-country expertise is a critical success factor. Local teams provide the understanding of the needs and expectations of your prospective customers in those markets. For example, Hoover's globalization advocate argued that you need people who watch local television and regularly talk to taxi drivers to achieve the intimacy that will come through as native and natural in a market. Lands' End's Japanese director pushed to add petite sizes of clothing to the company's product mix.

  They will be your local eyes and ears, working with national news and information media to spot market trends before your competitors. These local teams will vet the translations of corporate content for local suitability and also suggest locally produced campaigns that might have globally or regionally relevant content. They will oversee the use of corporate measurement tools. They will also work with the global technology and online content teams to adapt corporate style guides, glossaries, and localization packages to local market needs.
- *Ethnic marketing specialists.* These marketing experts will help you mine the rich multicultural opportunities in countries with large ethnic minorities. Since the release of year 2000 census data in the United States, the number of resources available to help American firms market to ethnic groups has increased tremendously, ranging from industry sources such as the Cable Television Advertising Bureau[4] to objective research from companies such as Cheskin Research. Similar activity is heating up outside the United States, especially in Canada, where agencies are paying more attention to nonanglophone populations.[5]
- *Marketing technology specialists.* As online marketing campaigns morph into cross-channel phenomena, you will need to draw on experts around the company to share and apply knowledge and best practices. These professionals work in other marketing departments or in the technical organizations supporting them on projects such as customer information systems, data warehousing, business intelligence, market

intelligence, and customer relationship management. Rather than reinventing the wheel, the online marketing team will lean on these known resources to improve the professionalism and efficacy of their international efforts.

- *User experience experts.* Creating a compelling experience for visitors to your company has long been the holy grail of online business. Designers accustomed to working on paper and other static media will not cut it on the more dynamic Web, so you will have to locate staff who can work with your information and content architects to create engaging experiences. They must also be sensitive enough to local market telecommunications realities to know when to pull back on the more interactive elements, thus meaning that they will work very closely with national and regional marketing managers to get the lay of the land.

What Will This Effort Cost?

As Lands' End's experience documented for its technology build-out, your first international version will carry the highest price tag. The same applies to content, design, and marketing issues as well before costs start dropping for new markets. Why? Because if your online efforts have monogamously courted a single market to date, the chances are that none of these elements have been prepped for the broader needs of international markets. Once you've made the upfront investment in systems and people, your cost per market entry should begin to drop as you understand your core systems and processes better and begin to take advantage of economies of scale and share resources, staff, technology, and algorithms across markets. Staffing costs are hard to break out for technology and content redevelopment, while the loaded cost of the human resources suggested in this chapter will be easier to pinpoint.

<u>Bundled Staff, Technology, and Content Expenses</u> If you design and scale your back-office systems and infrastructure properly, your initial investment should be able to support several new sites. The best time to do this is when you are designing your corporate Internet architectures. You will be able to recoup these costs over a broader range of market instances than if you did it on an on-off basis (see Table 8.2).

Investment	Type	Cost US$	Vendors
Content management software (CMS)	Software license fee (initial cost; annual maintenance not included)	250,000	Documentum, Interwoven, Microsoft, Oracle, Tridion, Vignette
Professional services	• Implementation (3 developers for 8 weeks at US$15,000 per day) • Training (two-day training course for 3 at US$1,000 per student)	180,000 30,000	Software professional services groups plus integrators like Accenture, IBM Global Services, and Sapient
Knowledge engineering	Controlled vocabulary and content hierarchy (50,000 pages)	200,000	Vality, Requisite, Saqqara
	Basic content management:	633,000	
Technology, process, and content review	Analyzing infrastructure for internationalization and other issues discussed in Chapter 6; actual work to fix things would cost more	50,000	Internationalization experts such as Basis, Lingoport, and Uniscape
Glossary	Extracting terms from corporate sites, documentation, and other sources to create a bilingual glossary of 1,000 words	3,000	Localization and translation suppliers such as Bowne, Lionbridge, Rubric, Architext, and others (see www.lisa.org)
Terminology management	Additional work in knowledge engineering dor one language to clean up terms, identify synonyms, establish equivalent terms, and characterize attributes	15,000	Localization and translation suppliers; cost assumes that supplier will work on the glossary, style guide, and actual translations
Translation style guide	Enhancement of single-market corporate authoring style guide for translators developing content for other markets; for one language	1,000	Localization and translation suppliers.

Table 8.2 Basic Costs for Internationalized Content Management Infrastructure
Source: Content management, implementation, and knowledge engineering costs are from John Dalton and Harley Manning, "Managing Content Hypergrowth," Forrester Research, January 2001. Other costs are from suppliers of those technologies and services.

Note: This table represents the estimated 2001 costs of a basic content management system, first implemented for a single market, then internationalized for multiple markets. Everything below the basic content management line remains in limbo until you can factor in the cost to translate, develop terminology management practices, and so on. These issues are presented in Chapter 9.

Investment	Type	Cost US$	Vendors
Translation	One-time translation of core content catalog of 100 pages, assuming 250 words per page and a loaded cost of US$0.45 per word	11,250	Localization and translation suppliers; The loaded cost includes the 10–15% project management fees that these providers charge
Synchronization software and/or implementation services	Software to ensure content and message consistency between the headquarters' site and one international market site	50,000 to 250,000	Globalization management solutions from companies like Idiom and Uniscape, or services from CMS suppliers
	Cost for first international market exclusive of basic content management system, implementation services, and major internationalization work	130,000 to 380,000	Each additional market will cost much less because of the sunk cost in the content management software

Table 8.2 *continued*

- *Infrastructure enhancement.* If your site is going to address distant customers, your current server and supporting infrastructure may be too remote for acceptable performance. You may also have to invest in RAS technologies such as load balancing, traffic monitoring, security, encryption, and backup. Of course, each of these additions involves more technical staff and even call center resources to handle more time zones.
- *Back-end technology fixes.* The cost of internationalizing back-office technology such as databases and ERP systems varies based on the nature and functionality of your site, the complexity of its architecture, the number and type of technologies used, the volume of dynamically generated content, the need for interfacing with enterprise applications, and so on. Certain programs may have to be replaced or entirely rewritten to handle Asian double-byte character data properly. Each of these activities costs money and is best managed by using commercial software that can handle these international demands.

You should also factor in indirect costs. For example, internationalization may delay or even bring your update cycles to a screeching halt. You need ongoing help from the technology group to identify affected components. You will probably also involve the authors of the original content to assist translators as needed.

- *Content development.* Translation and localization costs are directly proportional to volume. The more words you have, the higher the bill. Furthermore, some languages cost more than others to translate. Finally, this is a recurring cost; as Chapter 7 outlined, online content changes constantly.

  Most companies will not do translation in-house but instead work closely with translation firms and manage the process internally. Although tempting, entrusting your translation to the lowest bidder is a recipe for market failure. Chapter 9 discusses the vendor landscape and other issues in more detail.

Loaded Staffing Costs   Marketing and design costs vary by how aggressively you use this online channel. In many cases, you will find that you are already paying too much in individual markets for ineffective campaigns, off-brand messaging, and duplicated effort on both marketing and design. By setting up organizations as suggested in this chapter, you should be able to start consolidating some of that investment and getting a better return on what you pay out.

Don't panic! Most of these people are probably already at work inside your company. In fact, if yours is like most companies, you may find that different groups in the same countries may be funding individual teams that look a lot like what you should have as part of an enterprise-wide globalization support team. Bring those people into the organizational fold first.

Globalization Requires Dedicated Resources

As you lay out the organizational structure and budget for your globalization projects, keep the following in mind:

- *Globalization needs a budget.* Whether you pursue 10 countries simultaneously or pick just one for starters, globalization requires more than part-time resources and leftover budgets. Although you will leverage your existing site, be prepared for recurring costs, both direct and indirect.
- *Commit for the long term.* You should not go through the trouble of launching your business in another country unless you plan to sustain and grow it there. Duplicating—even partially—this constant update

work for every country version is at the center of your globalization commitment and is also your biggest challenge.

- *Someone has to own globalization.* Whether you call this person the globalization czar, vice president of international e-commerce, or CGO, you need someone who is responsible for these activities. Otherwise, you will end up with chaos, duplicated effort, or both.
- *Start out with a showcase project.* Nothing is more convincing than a successful project. The CGO should pick a well-defined, easily circumscribed project to showcase what can—and should—be done with resources at hand.
- *Enlist employees for key functions.* If you look inside your own company, you will probably find that various groups around the world are already doing a lot of the technology, content, design, and marketing work that you will need. Before bringing in outsiders, troll the employee lists for resources that you can redeploy. By labeling this activity "knowledge management," you may be able to co-opt additional corporate resources that are already trying to improve the sharing of information and expertise inside your company.

Mira's Log

Recently elevated to the post of chief globalization officer, Mira was one of the first to hold this title. She set off on the requisite whirlwind tour of her new dominions, using both electronic and kerosene-fueled means to visit with her global staff. Anxious to get projects underway, she aimed to enlist the best marketers, developers, designers, and system architects into her group. She encouraged the group directors to put their thoughts regarding market support in the form of service level agreements and began thinking about how to deal with conflict resolution when the long knives inevitably left their scabbards.

Meanwhile, she hurried to put together a budget, mapping market opportunities and benefits against expected costs. But there was one more cost element that she had to investigate: the outsourcers who would perform a lot of the work. She now turned her attention to the vendor community, hoping that they would not have what one colleague called "eyes as wide as checkbooks."

9

Outsourcing Work to Fellow Travelers

After reviewing Acme's operational needs for going global and evaluating the corporate resources that were available to her, Mira decided that she would have to look outside the company for assistance. Her globalization resource shortfalls ranged from Acme's strategic planning to specialty marketing to system development and integration to daily translation.

With these necessities in mind, she began researching the outsourcing alternatives and quickly realized that there was no one-stop consulting or integration shop for going global—although many of the companies she contacted claimed to be such. She found that even traditional system integrators and consulting organizations such as IBM, Cap Gemini, and Accenture frequently outsourced many of the global bits such as internationalization and localization. As she and her team evaluated the offerings and developed shortlists of suppliers to contact, they also reviewed Acme's operational procedures and began to assemble metrics for measuring the performance and effectiveness of their ultimate suppliers.

Selecting Partners to Help during the Journey

As Mira discovered, you must carefully choose among many firms for each of the functions within globalization. Her major concerns include the following:

- *Doing the work in house or using outsourcers—but more likely both.* As Mira learned, this is one of the most fundamental decisions that the modern corporation must make, not only for globalization but for just about every other major corporate project. Do you have a better chance of meeting your goals with your own resources or by engaging the services of a specialist? You need to strategize as to what is best for you to do yourself versus outsourcing based on variables such as competencies you have in house and in different geographies, competing projects drawing upon the same resources, and time-to-market considerations.

- *Picking your partners.* The CGO and his lieutenants in operational organizations (the global directors) will have to review your company's operational needs, determine whether they have the required resources, and see where outsourcers might help. Because globalization will touch every part of your company, the global directors might find, as Mira did, that they need to engage multiple providers.

- *Teaching your suppliers how to work with you.* Developing and managing good relationships with your globalization suppliers is critical. Successful companies will identify their best practices and processes, document them, educate outsourcers, and hold everyone to this regimen. Capturing these practices and formalizing them is one of the responsibilities of the group directors who head up technology, marketing, and content services.

- *Managing cost and process—and measuring quality.* What should you expect to pay for globalization work? Most of the heavy technology lifting will be in adding international capabilities to your corporate infrastructure and base systems such as inventory and personalization. Once this work is done as discussed in Chapters 6 and 7, the most visible new cost will be in localization and translation—two tasks that you will deal with up front and as a continuing cost in your globalization budget.

Insourcing or Outsourcing? The Eternal Question

The breadth and depth of a globalization project—even if it touches only a few countries or a couple of domestic ethnic markets—mean outsourcing some part of the project for most companies (see Figure 6.3). Except for all but the largest multinational firms, few companies will find the internal resources and competencies to adapt their message and offering to the different behaviors, devices, and geopolitical realities of other markets (see Figure 9.1).

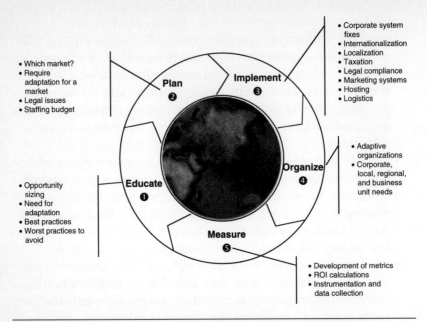

- Which market?
- Require adaptation for a market
- Legal issues
- Staffing budget

- Corporate system fixes
- Internationalization
- Localization
- Taxation
- Legal compliance
- Marketing systems
- Hosting
- Logistics

- Adaptive organizations
- Corporate, local, regional, and business unit needs

- Opportunity sizing
- Need for adaptation
- Best practices
- Worst practices to avoid

- Development of metrics
- ROI calculations
- Instrumentation and data collection

Figure 9.1 Resources Required at Different Phases of Globalization

Note: This figure represents the critical functions involved in globalization, mapped against the phases discussed in this book. From the educational and consultative planning phases all the way through measurement, most firms will need some outside help. However, as your company acquires more globalization expertise—both through experience and knowledge transfer from your development and marketing partners—you may bring some of these functions back into the company.

The question that the CGO will ask is whether your company can meet the ambitious goals laid out in Chapter 2 (e.g., time to market, effective global brand management, service level agreements, legal and regulatory compliance, improved supply chain, and cost targets) better with outsourcers or with your own resources. The CGO will have to balance into this equation other factors such as the opportunity cost of redirecting internal staff to globalization projects, available budget, and competitors' plans.

As with so many of the decisions on the very active landscape of the Eighth Continent, none of these choices can be static; the need for outsourcers will ebb and flow. For example, as Lands' End found, earlier projects took more time and cost more money, but subsequent projects happened more quickly and cost less. Besides improving internal systems and processes with each new market, your company will also benefit from hands-on experience and should expect significant knowledge transfer from your outsourcers, a requirement that you should write into every contract.

1. *Education.* With "bad" globalization (i.e., the homogenization of world business and culture) hogging the news, expect to see some resistance that you could overcome with market research at places such as eMarketer and Nua. Such outside sources will help you establish the size of the international opportunity and begin to outline the benefits of targeted global initiatives.

2. *Planning.* Look to outsiders to help you with a wide range of business, organizational, marketing, and technical issues. For companies that internalize the global opportunity into their corporate planning, this upfront planning will be a one-time activity that jumpstarts the globalization effort. The net result of this planning work will be a multiyear or multimarket plan driven by variables such as market revenue growth and business commitments to geographies.

3. *Implementation.* Most likely you lack the resources in-house to deal with the full range of internationalization, localization, translation, and local market personalization projects outlined in Chapters 6 and 7. The first few markets that you enter will cause the most problems, but as early movers have found, each successive market is easier and cheaper.

4. *Organization.* The ideal global corporation should be adaptive and flexible in its approach to each opportunity, leading to a healthy mix of corporate, business unit, regional, and local participation, as well as outsourcers to fill in the gaps and even to lead whole parts of the project. In all cases, however, the CGO and operational group directors must keep employees and outsourcers in line.

5. *Measurement.* Some companies have done well in their domestic markets but failed internationally because they did not meet expectations that might not have made sense in foreign markets. Each global effort needs metrics at every step of the way, and some of your current consultants and technology suppliers will be able to help you define and measure those business performance yardsticks.

Picking suppliers for each of these areas is no different from any other big project (see Figure 9.2). If you have the resources in-house and they are available, use them. Otherwise, consider using external globalization services to meet your corporate goals.

Strategic Consulting before Undertaking Global Initiatives The
CGO, strategy advisors, and group directors should generate a detailed project plan on how the company's global aspirations align with corporate

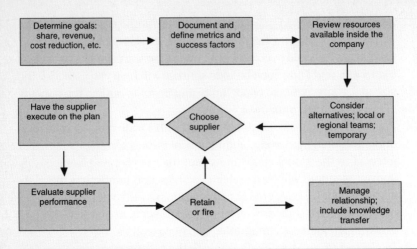

Figure 9.2 Decision Matrix and Life Cycle for Outsourcing

Note: This figure outlines a typical decision matrix for determining whether an outsourcer will help and how to manage the relationship over time. Bringing some of the expertise into your company through knowledge transfer is important as you fold global and ethnic markets into your corporate planning process.

strategy. That means a choice of market or internal application decision and the systematic analysis of what is needed in each case. Your CGO may choose to conduct an assessment or audit for all Internet-related activities, but this could be a multiyear effort that never ends.

Your strategy helpers should document the results of their analysis. They should include (1) a discussion of market opportunities suited to your business, (2) a detailed methodology for entering new markets or for extending existing systems, and (3) a road map with prioritization of what to do. This last point is important: Your strategy partners should recognize that you cannot do everything at once, so they should give you some guidance on what you absolutely must do today and what can wait until tomorrow. This document will become the holy book for all globalization activities. Critical points to cover include the following:

- *Extending Internet initiatives to embrace global business.* This business-based strategy for the next few years describes expansion into new markets or extending your company's offerings in countries where it already operates. The document should explore the same market conditions that push employee-focused intranets or supply chains over consumer-facing Web sites in all markets. Look to Accenture, Cap Gemini, IBM Global, and KPMG to provide boardroom-level advice on global market opportunities and integration with mainstream corporate initiatives. Smaller and regional integrators such as Agency.com, Sapient, and Common Sense Advisory may be able to lend a hand in online projects such as global branding and new market strategy.

- *Establishing globalization criteria and metrics.* In this exercise, you and your strategy partners determine the best global markets for Web, intranet, and extranet investment. In each case, your favorite strategy consultants should be able to help. The discipline and rigor that they bring to market analysis, segmentation, and return on investment (ROI) calculations should be useful to the CGO in laying out a plan.
- *Reviewing your multicultural strategy.* Too many companies ignore the ethnic opportunity in their backyards. For this kind of assistance, look to in-country marketing firms that understand both the national market and the ethnic opportunity. International pacts such as NAFTA and multinational entities such as the European Union will drive more immigration, and thus more ethnic opportunities. Ask your current strategic advisors for recommendations; they might already have an agreement with an ethnic marketing agency.
- *Determining your legal compliance.* Get legal advice for all of your international initiatives. Staying within the bounds of many different legal systems will be a big challenge in the best of conditions, so avoid being on the wrong side of an international suit or, worse yet, being tried for e-commerce fraud or data privacy violations in absentia.

Finally, whichever vendor you choose, make sure that their expertise matches both your level of strategic need and that of the people in your company with whom they will interact. This was an issue at consultancies where the candidate drought of 1998 to 2000 caused them to promote rapidly within their ranks, sometimes turning a research associate with no business experience into an "expert."

<u>Online Marketing</u> For international branding and messaging projects, the tasks quickly become more tactical and operational. Your online marketing group director will work with a variety of suppliers to develop a marketing plan with detailed requirements for each country. Topics will include the following:

- *Marketing goals and measurement criteria.* You may have your own goals, but your Agency of Record (AOR) working with local and regional resources will help you better understand what is required for each market. If your regular marketing partners have no suggestions for in-country agencies that might be able to help you set realistic goals, check the local trade rags and your favorite search engines. Your online marketing team will also work with local and regional agencies to ensure that your global Web sites accurately reflect your brand. Firms such as Global Reach, GlobalWorks, and Business to Business Marketing are just a few of the many companies that specialize in this kind of marketing assistance.

- *Competitive analysis.* You might consider engaging a third party to manage the kind of competitive analysis outlined in Chapter 8 or to conduct in-country focus groups to determine the effectiveness of your site and messaging. Site comparisons can be conducted by anyone who is Internet-savvy and plugged into the target culture, so you might turn to business school students at a nearby university. Alternately, you may choose to engage a usability expert such as Human-Logic to analyze the navigation, branding, technical competence, and usability of your offer and compare it to your chief competitors.

  Regardless of which option you choose, the one absolute requirement is that the reviewers be native-language speakers who are familiar with the everyday culture and business practices of your targets. Ideally, they would also be familiar with the industry sector. Focus groups are a different story, requiring a strong methodology and a local presence. Ask your local subsidiaries, distributors, or usability specialists for advice on local talent to help on this front.

- *Driving traffic to your international sites.* Now that you have built a site, you will need to determine the most effective channels for marketing and promotion in your target countries, register with the most popular search engines, advertise in other media such as television and print, and develop creative cross-channel advertising. Look to local research for the most popular search engines. In its U.S. research, Forrester found that 81 percent of its respondents used search engines to find a site, more than links from other sites (59%) and word-of-mouth (56%).[1]

  Given the dynamic nature of the Web, registration with a good search engine will serve you well in most markets. Many firms will help you register with all of the "right" search engines. For example, Wyoming-based Arial Global Reach and Madrid's Global Communications are two small Web marketing firms that will help your online marketing team select the keywords likely to get picked up, determine which search engines matter for your target markets, register with them, and monitor your performance. A search on Google (or your favorite search engine) for "marketing," "international," and "search engine" will pick up many more for your intended markets.

- *Measuring results.* Recall that the online usage data for international marketing is there for the taking, but few companies have done a good job of instrumenting, collecting, and analyzing the data. Your company probably already has a relationship with business intelligence, data analysis, and data warehousing companies that can help with both software and professional services. Some data-savvy partners are Business Objects and Cognos for business intelligence and analysis and NCR Teradata for its large-scale data warehouse. Take pains, though, to ensure that your partners' software and service offerings meet your international analytical needs. They need to support all of the capabilities discussed in Chapters 6 and 7.

Technology Readiness Assessment   The technology team must dig deep into the operational infrastructure of your company, and they are accustomed to calling in helpers for everything from database design to hosting private networks. The technology group director will bring in people to

- *Evaluate and fix infrastructure.* To meet the high-reliability, cross-border needs of global branding and commerce activities, the technology team will crawl over every square meter of its technology pyramid to find security flaws, breaking points, and other potential hot spots. Their evaluation of content management systems, databases, and transaction processing systems will most likely involve the professional services arms of their software suppliers such as Computer Associates to deal with new security and backup concerns, and large-scale integrators such as IBM and Cap Gemini.
- *Review internal processes.* The technology team may turn to process efficiency experts to analyze and monitor things such as content work flow and recommend ways to improve controls, reduce costs, and speed up turnaround time for your globalization efforts. They might also recommend improved processes for language translation and site localization. You will probably be able to find such specialists at your usual system integration shop.
- *Support international logistics.* As you saw in Chapters 3, 4, and 5, doing business around the globe is more than just a linguistic exercise. Besides geopolitical factors such as product legality, taxation, and pri-

vacy, you also face the commercial logistics of order processing, payment, shipping, security, fraud, tracking, and returns. An established industry of suppliers specializes in these capabilities, and companies such as UPS and DHL also have facilities around the world, demonstrable expertise in transporting everything from mail to heavy equipment, regional logistics centers that can act as your warehouses, and even payment services such as collect billing and export documentation. As you consider these vendors, look for functions that you would like to outsource, such as manufacturing, fulfillment, order processing, status checking, and inventory management. Going global, you will also need to consider specialized solutions from firms like Vastera and ClearCross to deal with issues such as shipper and carrier integration, bills of lading, and landed cost.

- *Improve data quality.* Good data drive so much of the Web's activity, but too much polluted data are there as well. Outsourcers can help on both the input and output side. For example, internationalization partners such as Basis and LingoPort can help with recoding, as outlined in Chapter 6. Firms such as Vality, Innovative Solutions, and Requisite will help clean up your data systems and content flows. You may also need help with *geocoding* data (i.e., adding latitude and longitude and any pertinent geographic information), changing address layouts in databases for different international markets, and validating postal codes and place names. Firms such as Geoscape can help.

Information Architecture and Esthetic Design Work   Your content resources and corporate design teams will work on your information architecture, calling in outside help from usability engineering to improve information flows, navigation, look and feel, and adaptations to local market needs. The biggest projects will be the following:

- *Reviewing and improving your information architecture.* External design firms at both the corporate and local levels can recommend design and navigation standards that allow for global, regional, and country views of information. Their work will extend to template designs that expand and contract to deal with long-word languages such as German.
- *User experience engineering.* User experience experts can work with in-country focus groups to meet the usability and navigability expectations of different markets. To test site usability and the quality of the user experience, they will ask in-market subjects to work on typical

tasks using localized Web sites. These specialists will also conduct walk-throughs and feature analyses of sites as they determine the best way to lead a subject to the desired goal. Finally, they will interview users about their likes and dislikes and observe them using the site in real work.[2] Mindshare leaders for analysis and research of user experience are the Nielsen Norman Group and Human Factors International.

The net: Going global means finding the right suppliers to help you develop your corporate strategy, define the right marketing approach, improve your Web design and usability competencies, and update your technology infrastructure. I have yet to see a company that can do all of this on its own.

Working with Globalization Suppliers

That was a quick trip through some familiar terrain. You may already know the names of some of your prospective infrastructure suppliers, marketing partners, and law firms. Now you know that you have to supplement these resources with international help. Let's move on to some terra incognita. The biggest new requirement for many companies will be in managing localization and translation efforts conducted by third parties.

The first thing that you will realize is that no translation or localization bureau "does it all." For example, Hewlett Packard uses three different translation firms just for its DeskJet printer division, and Sabre relies on the services of five different companies. They need so many because your company's translation and localization needs differ by audience. For example, consider the case of the Corvette sports car. General Motors sells this car in the United States, Canada, Mexico, and Europe. Information about the Corvette and its components moves up and down a fairly complex value chain, and many of the same details need to be conveyed to multiple audiences with widely varying expectations:

- *Owners.* The owner's manual for the Corvette provides information about how to use the car's features, including specifications, tolerances, and service requirements.
- *Aficionados and prospects.* The Web site is marketing-driven, trying to convince people to buy the car. But parts of the online forum for the

Corvette may be directed at shareholders, employees, and even government regulators.

- *Engineers and procurement specialists.* All members of the global supply chain—Krupp Bilstein for the gas-filled shock absorbers, Getrag for the transmission, and Michelin for the tires—share the goal of ensuring that GM's manufacturing units have up-to-date specifications for the parts they contribute.

Each of these venues and audiences involves a different style, but all of them require some deep knowledge of the product and its constituent parts. Because few individuals are equipped to translate documents for these different audiences at the required level of rhetorical effectiveness in these quantities, most companies find that they need more than a single translation firm. While you should always be selective in choosing firms, you must realize that one size doesn't fit all. As much as you can, centralize your online translation work with a handful of vendors and backups.

- *The quality of the translation.* Whichever firm you bring in, make sure that their translation staff can handle the work: Online marketing and microfiche parts catalogs are two very different beasts. While you may choose to engage your established offline collateral translation partners for Web translation, make sure that they can handle the tone and lexicon of the online target audience. In either case, translators must be familiar with your industry sector.
- *Speed and quantity.* The Corvette is just one product offered in many markets by GM, and its informational visage varies by audience. For example, the service manual itself is thousands of pages long. The combinatorial complexity of information about a single car offered to multiple audiences in different countries is one thing, but remember that this carmaker offers dozens of other products around the world. Add in time-to-market concerns, and no single supplier could hope to satisfy GM's translation needs even for just this one car. As product development cycles compress in the automotive and other manufacturing businesses, speed becomes even more critical.
- *Cost.* Rationalizing supplier networks down to just enough vendors, controlling internal processes and work flows, and improving vendor management are all critical elements. Negotiate for better rates, shorter turnaround times, or better project management. Some large

users of translation services also give vendors a small test project to evaluate how well they do.

In the following sections I discuss the terrain of the vendor offerings in the translation and localization space, outline some major cost-cutting opportunities around centralized procurement, and describe several best practices for working with your suppliers.

Exploring the Globalization Supplier Landscape

There are no big, absolutely safe, "nobody ever got fired for buying IBM" vendors in the translation and localization space. Most are small players, and there are a few medium-sized enterprises. The translation industry thinks of itself in functional terms, splitting the market in to *multilanguage* and *single-language vendors* (MLVs and SLVs). The biggest differences between the two are in scale (large vs. small), in the number of languages that each handles (many vs. one), and in where the work gets done. This last point is key: Whether you use an MLV or SLV, it still takes just as many steps to translate something from one language to another. An MLV takes on the project management tasks that an SLV usually leaves with the customer. Table 9.1 lists the typical steps in a translation work flow.

Multilanguage Vendors

MLVs are larger multinational translation vendors such as Berlitz, Bowne Global, or Lionbridge. They directly employ a wider variety of skill sets than do smaller SLVs, thus offering publishing, site engineering, localization, and even testing in addition to translation services. These MLVs break the translation job into smaller processes and functions that they can automate or scale to meet demand. All things being equal, MLVs are likely to have more resources at their disposal for executing projects, both online and off.

Pro: MLVs are the closest the industry gets to one-stop shopping. For example, they might offer a variety of European or Asian languages plus engineering, publishing, and testing services to create an effective Web presence in a given market. Their scale lets you have a single point of contact for managing all translation and localization services, including contracts and scheduling as well as any problems. You should note that MLVs frequently use SLVs as subcontractors and as shock absorbers when their work load gets too high.

Con: MLVs also tend to be more expensive and less responsive than are their smaller single-language brethren. Added services such as extensive

Translation Process Step	Manual	Automated
Create the original content	NA	NA
Determine whether that content should be translated	1	0
Send the document to the translator	1	1
Translate the document	6	2
Send the document file for conversion	1	0
Code the new content into test site	1	0
Conduct quality assurance tests in context	1	1
Send review comments through reviewing cycle	1	0
Make any required changes to translation	1	1
Move the content to production	0.5	0
Notify everyone of the changes	0.5	0
Total business days to post content	14	5

Table 9.1 Centralized Translation Work-Flow Duration in Business Days

Note: Regardless of whether you use a multilanguage or single-language vendor to do your translations, each performs the same functions in the same order. The biggest difference is that MLVs do more of the project management. The "manual" and "automated" columns represent one way to shorten the translation cycle—by using automated technology such as the translation workbenches, work-flow, and global resource servers discussed in Chapter 7. Larger suppliers are more likely to use this set of tools than smaller ones, thus resulting in quicker turnarounds for translation.

project management mean that you will pay more—up to 20 percent over the cost of the translation alone. As a consequence of their assembly line model of translation, MLVs employ specialists, thus involving more people and steps in a project—and accounting for their higher project management fees.

Single-Language Vendors   SLVs are smaller, in-country vendors of translation services specializing in a single language, market, or vertical industry. They tend to have expertise in a particular industry or subject matter. Check your local yellow pages for translators and interpreters. You can also check with your national association of translators (see www.fit-ift.org for links to such organizations in different countries).

Pro: With less overhead, these smaller organizations tend to be less expensive than MLVs. SLVs are usually cheaper in the near term because their project management costs are lower. SLVs also tend to be more responsive because they have fewer people between the client and the translator.

Con: SLVs have a more difficult time taking on multiple large translation projects and have less capacity to scale to meet increased demands, so your project could find itself at the back of a queue. The disadvantage is that your company will be responsible for project management and other tasks such as pre- and postprocessing of documents.

Hybrids

There are also a handful of hybrid translation service providers. These service providers may provide translation for several languages, but they specialize in a particular field. For example, ForeignExchange is a small MLV that specializes in "compliance translation" based on stringent industry regulations in pharmaceuticals, medical devices, and financial services. This cross between servicing several languages simultaneously while still specializing in particular verticals is an attractive option.

Involve your international staff and look beyond your corporate backyard for solutions—for example, European suppliers such as Logos (Italy) and Moravia (Czech Republic), South American firms such as Rosario Traducciones (Argentina) and 2TR Souções Globais (Brazil), and Asian organizations such as 8th Network (China) and EWGate (Singapore) offer quality services for translation and localization.

Application Service Providers (ASPs) and Translation Marketplaces

The Internet has enabled automated environments for aggregating translator supply and service demand, much like the exchanges set up by the automotive, steel, and chemical industries—and unfortunately as profitable as most of them. Examples of this approach are Trados.net, and Uniscape.

Centralizing Translation Purchases—An Underpracticed Best Practice

Most companies have taken a wildly decentralized approach to translation, so it is not unusual for them to spend US$2 million per year on translation projects in US$50,000 increments. Accounts payable departments pay invoices without scrutinizing the practices, and no purchasing managers discuss their translation needs with any others, so economies of purchasing scale are lost. This is the case especially in large, decentralized businesses in which a company might work with a large number of translation firms around the world. The CGO and his content resources group director can do a lot to clean up processes and save money by

- *Appointing an owner.* Put someone in place in the purchasing department who either understands the translation business or can be taught. Announce that no purchase orders for translation will be paid without a PO number issued by this manager. Use analytical tools to find out how much you are spending on translation and where.
- *Pooling translation budgets.* By pooling the money that you spend on translation into a single budget monitored by the translation purchasing manager, you can negotiate preferred pricing better than what your individual groups are now being quoted. Establish long-term relationships with language service providers; this approach can also lead to better translations. Experience has shown that as your suppliers become more accustomed to your terminology, industry position, and stylistic preferences, review cycles are fewer and shorter, thus reducing cost and speeding turnarounds.
- *Writing master contracts.* Annual pricing and volume agreement enables you to reduce the administrative effort involved in multiple contract negotiations. It also provides a way to compare apples to apples; for example, some vendors include editing tasks under the heading of "translation," while others do not. Standardized contracts and well-defined terms will eliminate that problem.

Only by exposing all translation relationships to centralized accounts payable scrutiny and management will you begin to see the scale of your investment. By reducing the number of vendors, you can expect savings from reduced administrative efforts and a more homogenous process. However, to avoid bottlenecks, you might want to consider creating a regional overseer for translation budgets. For example, you could appoint a single point of contact for a set of related markets such as German-speaking Germany, Austria, and Switzerland; another for Spanish markets; and still another for anglophone Commonwealth countries.

Managing Relationships with Vendors

Besides centralizing procurement, explore other well-established ways to improve quality, shorten turnaround time, and lower costs:

1. *Set performance goals.* Just as the CGO has established service level agreements (SLAs) with the various geographies and business units, encourage your translation and localization vendors to set SLAs for your company. These agreements should specify quality control metrics such as review, edit, and approval cycles. SLAs should also describe testing and reporting procedures so that everyone is clear on responsibility.

2. *Insist on knowledge transfer.* I cannot emphasize this point enough. Your translation vendors may be the linguistic experts in your field, so your staff could very possibly learn something from them. Build some provision for knowledge transfer into your contracts. Most importantly, make sure that you own the translation memory that results from your translations.

3. *Improve the process.* The *kaizen* notion of continuous improvement applies here as well. To build long-term, effective relationships with your partners, document and monitor translation projects. By monitoring performance, you ensure that translation quality will improve.

4. *Communicate regularly and early.* Educate your vendors in how you work, bringing them into projects as early in the product development or marketing process as possible. Have your vendor's manager communicate regularly with your lead on the project to build a close working relationship.

Equip your translators of choice with clear contact information for your company and appropriate reference materials, including those shown in Table 9.2. In addition, the localization kit should contain an inventory of the tools required to translate or localize content (see Table 9.3).

Component	Purpose
Content catalog	Detailed description of the content that must be available in every market where your company does business. This should include file names and locations for all such content.
Glossaries and lexicons	The list of terms, product names, and other specialized words unique to your company or your industry. These glossaries and lexicons are the basis for your firm's terminology management.
Style or corporate standards guides	A document describing your company's general style of expression and conventions for grammar, punctuation, and word usage. The style guide often includes boilerplate language for corporate policies.
Translation memory	A database of previous translations which allows you to translate only the changed part of a text. The translation memory can include set phrases and preapproved text such as legal boilerplate.
Other references	Background information such as brochures and annual reports.

Table 9.2 Reference Material

Component	Purpose
Content creation tools	You should make sure that your supplier has access to both the tools used to create the original content and whatever products would be used to develop content in the target language. Ideally, as discussed in Chapter 7, your company has rationalized its investment in content creation tools so that you're using the same limited set of products everywhere in the company.
Conversion utilities	However, if the original and target content tools are different, your vendors will need a product to convert the file formats.
Translation workbenches	Translation workbenches such as those introduced in Chapter 7 improve translation quality and the translator's productivity. All include some form of translation memory; make sure that your company contractually owns the translation memory used for your projects.
Corporate work flow and content management	If your company uses a commercial or homegrown content management system, your vendor will need access to the content stores, scripts, personalization technology, and other programming that runs the system.
Synchronization software	If your content architecture includes global Rule servers like those described in Chapter 7, you may need to work with your vendor to give them access to these technologies.
Project work flows	This tool box should also contain templates for communicating the completion of tasks, any problems, or the need for more information. If you're using a content management system or commercial work-flow package, you can program these functions right into the system.

Table 9.3 Tool Box

How Much Should You Expect to Pay for Translation?

This question is not as simple as it sounds. If you call up a translation bureau, you will find prices in the range of US$.20–.35 per word, so your invoice will include a calculation something like this:

Price = (number of words) × (price per word)

However, this formula does not factor in mandatory project management fees of 10–20%, assuming that it is a one-time simple translation. It also leaves out other variables such as different file types, file conversions, and per-hour costs for pre- and postengineering tasks such as file conversions and running tools on files. Make sure that your translation partner is technically able to deal with content stored in databases such as DB2, Oracle, and SQL Server. These systems are the preferred storage repositories for data such as pricing and product descriptions that are assembled on the fly by content management systems. Because databases include more structure than simpler flat files (e.g., the HTML files that you see referenced on Web pages) and require specialized interfaces, not every translation firm can work with them.

Because of these variables, your actual invoice will look more like Table 9.4, in which the final fully loaded price per word (including project management) will work out to be in the range of US$.40.

Other variables, such as language complexity (Spanish is cheaper than Japanese), project complexity (a specialist bills higher than more pedestrian translators do), and turnaround time (tomorrow costs more than

Item	Word Count	Cost/Word	Extended Cost
Word file translation			
RTF file translation			
Excel spreadsheet translation			
DB2 customer record translation			
PDF file translation			
Preengineering (hourly charge)			
Postengineering			
Graphic processing			
Glossary definition			
Project management (percentage of translation)			
Total			

Table 9.4 Worksheet for Variables in Translation Pricing

next Thursday), can run up the bill significantly. On the positive side, you may get a discount for the bigger volumes that result from centralized purchasing and master contracts. Increased automation can remove significant cost and time from the process.

Finally, remember that an active company keeps information in play, constantly changing it to meet new needs. This means that the words that you had translated yesterday may already be outdated today. To avoid paying repeatedly for the same translations, make sure to use translation memory. That way, you pay only for translating the changed words, plus some project management fee. How much you actually save depends on all the variables in Table 9.4. Let's consider a simple case in which a branding site has about 100 pages in its core content catalog, each with about 250 words. Assume that this changes about 10 percent a year. Therefore, you should be able to budget for market entry and updates using the following formulas for each country/language pair:

New market entry cost = (100 pages × 250 words) × (loaded cost per word)

Market maintenance = [(100 pages × 250 words) × .10] × (loaded cost per word)

The net: Translation costs are predictable within some rough guidelines. Do not mistake the simple cost quoted by some vendors as the final cost to you. Instead, include the project management fees that you will pay directly to your supplier or indirectly in the form of having your staff do the work.

Measuring the Quality of Translation and Localization

Longtime global practitioners recommend having objective standards for quality in place before you hire outside help. That way, any firm that you engage will know what you expect from them and how you will measure their performance. During and after projects, these benchmarks will let you find areas for improvement, remedy problems, deal with conflicts, and manage the day-to-day issues that arise in any job. The data that you collect over time will be useful in negotiating contracts and rates with your suppliers. These proactive metrics fall into four general categories:

1. *Your corporate standards.* Make sure that your suppliers work within the framework laid out in your company's localization kit (i.e., the style guide, glossaries, and processes that define how your technology, marketing, and content teams do their jobs). In addition, make it easy for both internal content creators and your outsourcers to suggest updates to the glossaries and lexicons. Companies that use several translation firms report that having all of their suppliers comply with a consistent set of standards provides a much fairer basis for judging vendor performance than do simple subjective assessments.
2. *Translator and localizer association benchmarks.* Most translators and translation firms belong to national, regional, or professional groups, many of which are in turn affiliated with the International Federation of Translators. Some of these associations, such as the American Translators' Association and National Association of Judiciary Interpreters and Translators, offer accreditation programs to their members. For a list of major translator associations in all major markets, see the Translator's Home Companion. For leading localizers, see LISA's Web site.
3. *Vertical industry metrics.* Following the lead of collaborative commerce pioneers such as RosettaNet[3] that are pushing standardization across the IT industry's global supply chain, industry groups such as the Society of Automotive Engineers (SAE) are promulgating standards for translation and standard terminology in their own industries. The SAE's J2450 Quality Metric for Language Translation of Service Information is a framework for evaluating various categories of errors in a way that lets users objectively score a translated document's quality.

   This evaluation process results in a single number that can be monitored over time for each vendor, or even for individual translators. The automakers using the J2450 method report that they have seen the error count come down over time, and they could even judge from the numbers which of their translators were using the company-provided glossaries—and which were not. GM specifies J2450[4] in its contracts, using an anonymous assessor to score translations based on quality objectives that evaluate variables such as product type, audience, frequency of update, and paper or Web delivery. Rather than score every translation, GM calculates a sample size that results in an acceptable probability of catching errors. Over 18 months this approach has allowed the company to decrease turnaround time, reduce translation errors, and shrink costs.

4. *The smell test.* Chapter 7 laid out an ambitious goal for translation, but one that is critical for marketing sites: the notion that online sites should strike the emotional chords that cause people to act. For less marketing-centric projects such as user manuals or employee guides, communicative effectiveness is essential: Did the information allow the reader to accomplish a task? At this point, you need human judges to determine whether the translation worked for the target audience. Here you should look to in-country staff to either review or—preferably—get some independent assessment of how well the translation worked. Local marketing agencies, focus groups, or even friends of your national staffs can help on this front.

The net: By setting standards for translation and localization quality and contractually insisting that suppliers meet these criteria, you provide an objective basis for evaluating performance, improving quality, and reducing turnaround times due to bad translation efforts, all of which will lead to lower cost.

Recapping the Outsourcing Question: No One Goes It Alone

Lacking the requisite skill sets, many firms look outside for help.

- *Outsource wherever you lack resources or bandwidth.* Some decisions are easy: If you lack the skills to internationalize your content architecture or the marketing muscle to create local campaigns, bring in outsourcers. But you should also consider third parties if the opportunity cost of learning, executing, and maintaining the global initiative disrupts or derails other mainstream corporate projects. This is not an all-or-nothing exercise; your options range from selectively using contractors to fill gaps in your skills coverage to vending out individual site development to outsourcing large strategic chunks of your initiative.
- *Help your suppliers work with you better.* Regular communication, agreed-upon metrics, and formalized packages such as a localization kit will make it much easier for your suppliers to do what you require of them.

- *Manage translation cost and process.* Most companies approach translation inefficiently. Avoid being in this low-achiever crowd by taking positive steps to control costs. Centralized procurement, account monitoring, and master contracts are a few of the ways to bring down the cost of global markets.
- *Measure quality.* Develop objective standards for quality translations and localization. Use these metrics to measure the performance of your suppliers, to find opportunities for improvement, and to manage expectations otherwise.

Mira's Log

Mira now had many of the pieces of the globalization puzzle laid out on her desk and covering her wall. She understood the range of issues that she had to tackle as CGO; incidentally, she still wore the title of chief marketing officer, too. She knew that the small, elite internal team that she had cobbled together from corporate, regional, local, and business unit globalization projects would take her a long way, especially in conjunction with the outside marketers, developers, designers, and others she planned to bring into the fold.

One last thing was on her list: measurement. Early in the project she had considered the seven most effective reasons for globalization. As she prepared for her next meeting with the board, she began to calculate what return Acme could expect from its investment in global marketing and its other strategic online projects.

10

Measuring the Return on Global Investment

Mira now had to demonstrate some hard numbers and returns if she hoped to get the support that she needed to carry out Acme's ambitious plans for international dominance in its field. She consulted her strategy advisors, soliciting the views of other executives from corporate, business units, regions, and individual country units. Mira worked closely with her marketing team to quantify the effectiveness of their online promotional activities and determine how their campaigns reinforced Acme's brand and sales activities in other channels. After conferring with her strategy council, she had a much better sense of what Acme's return on globalization would be. She began to design her presentation on what would compel the board to loosen its tight grip on the budgetary purse strings.

Answering the "What Do Global Markets Buy Us?" Question

This chapter brings together many of the issues from earlier chapters as it provides some answers to the question that every C-level executive worries about: What will we make by investing in this project? That is, what will be the return?

- *Return on investment (ROI).* When stock prices were in the stratosphere, few companies cared about what any new online initiative cost. But when the bubble burst, many executives found that the basics had not changed: Their shareholders wanted any investment to

make money, reduce costs, or show some other demonstrable benefit that would move the stock. All of a sudden, ROI was back on the
front burner.

This chapter discusses a more holistic ROI model, which I call *360-degree ROI* to capture the broader range of economic benefits that
companies should expect from their investments—including increases
in sales and share, the goodwill benefits of better branding, and better customer retention and satisfaction resulting from improved customer service.

- *How companies measure it.* In Chapter 2 I presented seven effective arguments for going global. In this chapter I present sample measurements that cover the strategic, tactical, and operational terrain. However, in the course of measurement, you might find that you have not
done a very good job of instrumenting your online marketing and
other Internet processes, so you will have to invest in staff and technology to collect the data that makes their case.

- *Why you should spend time on ROI.* During up economies there is a
rush to execute every plan on the table, but in bad times funds and
support run dry. Adopting a measurement model that maps globalization benefits against corporate goals provides some ammunition
for future budget debates. And as so many companies found during
the recent economic downturns, taking the time to document all the
returns—especially cost reductions and other bottom-line benefits—
means the difference between a continuing budget and cancellation.

As I suggested in earlier chapters, you should avail yourself of professional assistance on these issues. Your CFO will be able to give you some
clear advice in this area and suggest how you might be able to apply some
of the lessons learned by other companies.

Adopting a 360-Degree View of ROI for Globalization Projects

You need to broaden your ROI analysis from simple cost-basis calculations
to the more complete range of things that matter around your company—
greater sales, more satisfied customers, better branding, reduced costs,
and however else you measure your success and that of your business
units. This 360-degree view of ROI will be a new experience for many com-

panies that have yet to introduce any rigor into their analysis of online investments. And there are still a lot of firms in that camp. Through mid-2000, when companies started having second thoughts about the Internet, traditional concerns such as calculating the profit or yield on their online investments typically fell on deaf ears.

As you calculate the financial viability of their domestic online efforts, you cannot avoid reexamining your assumptions and plans for Germany, Japan, Brazil, and other critical Net economies. Some boards will halt their global projects in anticipation of more globally visible failures.

Heeding the lessons from others is a good step in the right direction, but that does not mean that you should take an all-or-nothing approach to global e-business initiatives. Rather, you should apply the same business metrics to international expansion that you would for domestic markets, aligning your globalization plans with your corporate goals and using agreed-upon measures to prove success. These metrics go beyond simple cost/benefit analysis, capturing instead economic benefits that range across branding, customer satisfaction, internal efficiencies, knowledge management, and other initiatives aimed at making your company more efficient. This more complete analysis captures a broader, more compelling range of metrics than does cost/benefit alone.

- Acquisition is often the quickest way into a market. To jumpstart its efforts in Europe, Amazon bought Bookpages and ABC Telebuch—U.K. and German online booksellers, respectively—as it grew business from a mere 4 percent of U.S. sales in 1998 to 22 percent in 2000 and took on competitors such as Germany's Bertelsmann and France's fnac.com. In Asia, GM bought Korean manufacturer Daewoo to gain a foothold in the Asian car market and will extend online efforts such as SGM BuyPower to appeal to online buyers in Asia.
- Throughout 1999 Cemex took both an acquisitional and an internal growth path to meeting its international goals, but since then the company has been using the Web also to deepen its relationships with customers, improve efficiency, streamline internal processes, and cut transaction costs. Cemex views the Internet as a way of greatly increasing its flexibility to adapt to customer requirements and environments across its entire customer and supplier value chain.

<u>What Is ROI?</u>   ROI means return on investment—for many, it is how much profit or cost savings results from what you spend on a project. Many ROI analyses stop at the very quantifiable numbers of expenses against profits or cost reductions. However, for a lot of investments that

simple equation is not enough. Say that your business has as its immediate objective getting market revenue share, building infrastructure for customer service improvements, or even positioning itself for sale. In these cases, a simple profit or return measuring only immediate profit or cost saving will not give an accurate 360-degree picture of your business goals, so financial experts may talk about the broader economic benefit that you expect to achieve from your investment. In this case, they would be talking about the economic benefit from your global operations.

Building a Business Case for Return on Globalization   How should you go about building a business case for globalization?

1. *Describe the expected pot of gold or the thorn.* The typical business case begins with a definition and SWOT (strengths, weaknesses, opportunities, and threats) analysis of the business opportunity, need, threat, or problem. It could be of the form discussed in Chapters 1 and 2—that international markets are growing, competitors are moving in quickly, or that domestic growth is slowing and future shareholder value depends on new market penetration. Work with the appropriate business unit, region, or country manager to validate the opportunity.

2. *Propose a solution.* Be specific about what you intend to do. For example, Chapter 8 suggested a quick-hit project to unify branding sites. Provide enough information that less Internet-savvy reviewers will understand what you are planning to do. Due diligence mandates that you suggest alternatives. Think through the options that are available and lay out a rich portrait of your solution against a range of options, including strawmen and even valid alternatives, as well as your rationale for discarding these options. Again, make sure that you consult local and regional specialists to focus on a solution that meets their needs, too.

3. *Estimate the cost.* As you saw in the translation discussion in Chapter 7, entering a market is a process, not a one-time event. In the case of an online marketing initiative, factor in the whole life-cycle cost of entering and maintaining a competitive presence in a market. Be encyclopedic in your life-cycle cost estimations.

4. *Describe expected benefits.* In the cost-benefit analysis for a localized marketing site, you might discuss the benefit of increased share, a decrease in abandoned transactions, the lower cost of servicing customers in their own language, and the likelihood of improved brand or unaided brand awareness. These improvements cover the full 360-degree range of benefits discussed throughout this book (see Figure 10.1).

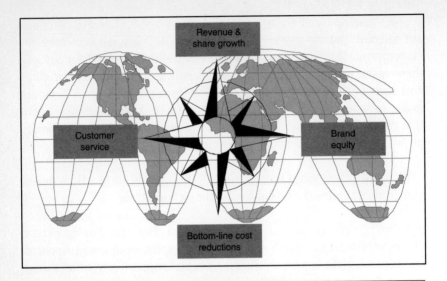

Figure 10.1 Compass Points for 360-Degree ROI

5. *Document your 360-degree ROI analysis.* This is where you lay out the indirect and direct ROI projections that you will use to measure the success of your project on a continuous basis. Include your assumptions, thought processes, and any constraints or other details that you included in your calculus—for example, market intelligence that says your major rival will do the same thing in six months. If the numbers do not work in your favor now, run some scenarios to see when they might. For example, hotelier Six Continents twice rejected a proposal for a comprehensive customer relationship management system in the span of six years but finally decided that the timing was right on the third attempt.

   If you are establishing success metrics for a global initiative, make sure that you are familiar with the goals of other regions such as Asia Pacific, Middle East, Africa, Latin America, and North America. Map your metrics to all regions, not just to those of your corporate headquarters region. Consult with project stakeholders across the globe to define what would make the project for their patch.

6. *Describe the risks.* Globalization is not a stroll in the park, so be realistic about what can go wrong. For example, political risks could make your plans for an in-country distributor seem foolish.

7. *Propose a schedule.* Finally, lay out a right-to-left schedule for each market, putting forward a time frame for the whole project and specific deliv-

erables. Make sure that you consult with the resource providers both inside and outside the company so that you factor in actual resource availability. The schedule should also include an accountant's look ahead to major issues such as break-even and projected after-tax profitability.

8. *Develop an internal marketing plan.* As a final step in the business case for any project, lay out an internal public relations and communications campaign that you will use to publicize positive returns both to management and to the rest of the company. The simple branding consolidation project presented in Chapter 8 could serve as a model. Post before and after images, a description of the goals, and names of representative team members at the corporate intranet site.

Calculating ROI on a Simple Cost Basis
As input to your business case you can sketch out a very simple ROI on the back of an envelope, assuming that you have a rough idea of the costs and expected returns. This *cost basis* is probably the most commonly used form of calculation, and it is useful for first approximations on market entry. However, it falls short for calculating returns on typical projects requiring continuing translation, enhancements, and synchronization, especially on long-running projects such as a marketing site in another country. Let's consider the benefit of both marketing and basic online selling sites.

- *Cost basis calculation.* Using this simple accounting model, the economic benefit of an uncomplicated marketing or branding site is simply the income expected from the activity minus the cost to develop. You can derive a quick take on profit from the following formula, although its value in convincing your Board will be limited.

    gROI = income - cost to develop

    If you apply this formula to your online commerce efforts, you will get a number, but you cannot easily quantify the income from a branding site. For nonrevenue sites, you have to consider other factors, such as the value of your brand or the increased productivity of employees, two of the many metrics outlined later in the chapter.

- *Ongoing cost calculation.* Keeping your online efforts competitive involves enhancing them and keeping information accurate, current, and consistent with sites that you offer in other markets.

    gROI = income - (cost to develop + cost to maintain)

Remember that the cost of maintaining a site never goes away. For example, in its calculations of the cost to enter a market, EMC figures out what it costs to translate the core content catalog introduced in Chapter 3. Furthermore, it assumes a monthly rate of change on that content as well as expected changes in what makes up that catalog. Factoring these modifications into the cost to translate, EMC then budgets a quarterly amount to maintain and update the content for each market.

Of course, other kinds of applications will have different benefit schemes. For example, you would measure your supply chain's benefit in terms of profit and inventory or asset turnovers.

- *Factoring in other variables for ROI calculations.* The problem with the cost basis approach—even in its more evolved form—is that it does not account for broader economic factors such as risk, actual losses, and the cost of capital. Economists have proposed more thorough formulas,[1] such as

gROI = income - costs - expected loss - (cost of equity × economic capital)

This model factors in all costs and losses but suffers from the same problem as the cost-basis model: It does not capture the continuing cost of maintenance. The following model adds that element:

gROI = income - cost to develop - cost to maintain - expected loss - (cost of equity × economic capital)

Losses include explicit fraud and customer default, the cost of dealing with shipping errors, and promotional tricks such as free or reduced cost shipping. Less easily quantified variables include the loss of more profitable customers over time, the cost of providing service, the effect on profitability of tactics such as upselling, and integration with other distribution channels.

What Should You Measure? And How Often?

Modern corporations evaluate ROI on a regular basis, changing their method of analysis over time. Periodic review of the economic benefits of your globalization efforts is an excellent practice that you should build into your planning cycle (see Figure 10.2).

As they incorporate the global Web into their everyday business planning, these companies are seeing immediate benefits and gaining actionable insight into their business cycles and manufacturing processes. Common among online leaders is the alignment of global efforts with corporate strategies, buttressed by tactical and operational benefits.

360-Degree Strategic Returns on Globalization Investment Topping most companies' lists of drivers for globalization is customer satisfaction; keeping consumers or corporate buyers coming back to purchase from your company is what drives top-line benefits such as increased revenue and share. You can consider strategic benefits such as increased customer retention and satisfaction, raising the lifetime value of a customer, global branding, new market development, and cross-channel integration. The next two sections lay out the tactical and operational upside.

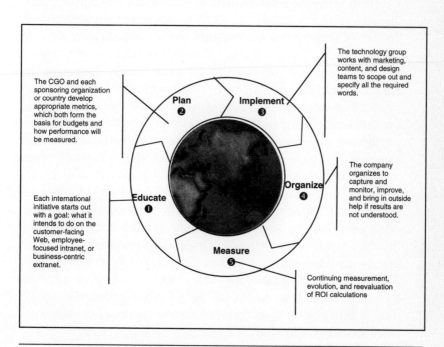

Figure 10.2 Global ROI Analysis Becomes Part of Your Corporate Planning

Note: ROI analysis will never stop. You should plug germane ROI metrics into service level agreements, making your home-country, regional, and business units demonstrate how they are earning their keep.

- *Increased customer retention and satisfaction.* The conventional wisdom is that it costs five to ten times as much to acquire a new customer as it does to retain an existing one. Statistics show that U.S. companies lose on average half their customers in five years,[2] and the percentage is likely to be higher online, where switching costs are typically lower than in brick-and-mortar establishments. Studies have shown that even a 5 percent reduction in customer attrition can increase profits by 25 percent or more.

  Using the Web to improve customer relationships on the business side, U.S. computer maker Dell has created thousands of customized homepages so that its best customers can have direct access to corporate-specified personal computers, negotiated discounts, promotional items, and records of orders and payments. The company's goals are to reduce defections to other providers and to create long-lasting relationships.

- *Raising the lifetime value of a customer.* Sales and marketing teams want to increase the net profit that their customers generate over their lifetimes as buyers, mainly through bigger and more frequent orders. To make this happen for international audiences, companies strive to improve site stickiness—that is, a customer's tendency to stay at your store or site and buy from you. Companies such as Six Continents Hotels, Embraer, Sony, and GE have done this by adapting the offers to buyers' own languages and buying motivations—thereby increasing the likelihood of purchase—by using a variety of systems such as personalization, data warehouses, and clickstream data (i.e., information collected during the course of a customer's visit by monitoring their viewing and navigation choices).

- *Branding.* Your company has spent a long time and a lot of money developing its brand in its domestic market to evoke a quality, long-term relationship, but it probably has not done as much online or internationally. By extending the reach of the goodwill associated with their brands, companies hope to vault to the front of the buying decision. While it is difficult to associate dollar values with brand recognition, they should at least be stated as recognizable assets that will increase as a result of globalization. Agencies such as DSS and Brand Institute Inc. specialize in this kind of exploratory marketing research.

- *New market development.* Returns on new ethnic and regional opportunities drive the investment strategy of some companies. For example, India—which has the largest economy and population in South Asia—can offer its goods, services, and point of view to other countries in the region. Communications-endowed gateways such as New Delhi, Mumbai, and Chennai can become "cyber Spartas," city-states that tie the subcontinent to its online trading partners in Malaysia, Singapore, Japan, and the United Arab Emirates, thus increasing the ability of companies to enlarge their overall revenue.

- *Integrating multiple channels.* EMC uses the Internet to increase its ties to customers in other distribution channels, viewing the Net as one more weapon in its marketing arsenal.

<u>Tactical Measures in Support of Global Strategies</u> To support these global corporate goals, the CGO will reach out to experienced ROI teams, including the CFO and financial analysts, to bring them into the core globalization team both to define the metrics and to measure them over time. These specialists will study international online business processes and work to improve metrics such as the following:

- *Lead generation.* Renault built out e-commerce sites in France, Germany, and the United Kingdom to provide its dealers with more leads more effectively. To qualify the leads and measure their effectiveness, Renault integrated these efforts with its enterprise information systems and databases.
- *Look-to-buy conversions.* Analysts estimate that buyers are three to four times more likely to buy if addressed in their own language. The likelihood of converting a looker to a buyer increases if the offers make local sense, can be purchased with local currency, and meet other cultural and business yardsticks. What works on your domestic site may not succeed internationally, so consider the value of your up-selling and cross-selling algorithms to local customers before making any offers. Make sure that you measure the results, taking advantage of A-B splits (i.e., several control groups receiving different offers to see which really resonates in a given market).
- *Customer support efficiency.* One way to support customer satisfaction goals is to improve the availability of in-language help. For example, Eastman maintains country and regional call centers to facilitate localized support, and Gateway advertises special toll-free phone numbers for its Spanish-speaking customers.

<u>Operational Benefits to Further ROI</u> The companies that collect and analyze such customer and sales data often use the information for market trend analysis and corporate decision making as well. They can also use

these data to document cost savings from their globalization efforts. Of course, these benefits are available if each business unit or country knows what others are doing. This is one of the collateral benefits of the flexible organizational model headed up by the corporate CGO drawing on the advice and insights of fellow executives in transnational business units, regions, and countries.

- *Lower costs.* State Street Bank has long used revenue generation and risk reduction to convince its budget committee to free up funds, but the Internet has allowed them to add in expense reduction and avoidance. For example, the company hired a fair number of people through the Internet, finding that its indirect savings from recruiting fees more than paid for some of their Web expenditures. Most costs savings, though, are especially evident in global customer support initiatives; as Chapter 2 noted, it costs only one dollar to handle a customer inquiry through FAQs or online services such as AskJeeves versus US$33.00 for each call handled by a customer service rep.
- *Share costs.* Autobytel's U.K. affiliate saved money by borrowing brand positioning and collateral from Australia, a compatible market, thus saving on development costs and getting to market much faster. When the company's globalization advocate discovered Autobytel developers in four countries working on a CRM module, he gathered everyone together, found that all were still in the initial discovery phase, and managed to pull together the specifications and business requirements from each country into one design. The savings in both money and time to market will more than pay for the project.
- *Promote new services more cost-effectively.* Airlines such as United and Cathay Pacific have found that they can promote new service offerings over the Web more quickly and efficiently than they can with the traditional combination of advertising and big customer briefings.

Instrumenting the Effort: Continuous Measurement and Feedback

The last few sections described strategic, tactical, and operational benefits that feed a 360-degree ROI model. These improvements do not come without a cost. Companies must actively and explicitly monitor applications, capture data, analyze them, feed them back into the systems that run the business, and measure the differences. Otherwise, there would be no data to prove the benefit. of course, this instrumentation of business applications, use of one-to-one marketing techniques, and feedback loops all must be conducted within the bounds of the national laws discussed in Chapter 5.

How do companies create such a continuous measurement and feedback process? Eastman started out with very clear business goals for its globalization efforts, as well as with a detailed analysis of what each step of the journey required. The planners knew that it was important to set some measurable goals, to track them diligently, and to communicate results to peers and executives. They started by monitoring overall site traffic growth on a monthly basis, determining the most frequently visited areas of the site. They also measured basic criteria for online commerce, including the last time the customer placed an order, the number of registrations at each location, the number of orders created, the amount of revenue generated through the Web channel, and the geographic mix of orders and revenue. At the end of each day, they know where its business is coming from that day, and they are beginning to understand where it might come from tomorrow.

As the company prepares more of its national and regional sites for more detailed data collection, they plan to analyze the surfing habits of users: which pages they visit most often and least often, and which unlocalized (i.e., English-language pages from corporate) pages are most frequently visited.

Before the sale, in-country marketing agencies can help you determine whether existing metrics make sense for a market or whether you need to come up with new ones. During and after the sale, monitoring the site for customer activities is the first step in feeding ROI analysis with useful data (see Figure 10.3 and Table 10.1). Regardless of the phase and depth of data, detailed analysis and feedback of your marketing campaigns is the most critical part of the process; otherwise, you will never benefit from the wonderful data available to you through your online channels.

Globalization—Treat It as You Would Any Business Issue

Many companies complicate matters by treating globalization as a special issue unlike any other. It is not. Successful globalization means making basic business decisions, just as you would for any other market. The com-

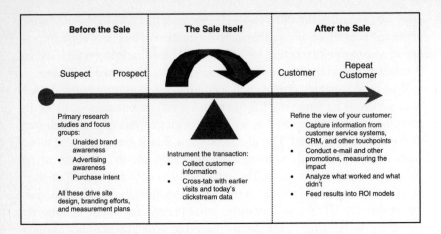

Figure 10.3 Monitoring Interactions and Feeding Results into ROI Models

Note: Focus groups, data warehousing, and business analytics are key elements of successful ROI; without them, you will know neither what you should measure nor how successful your efforts were. For those who do not have a data analysis or mining team at their companies, a whole industry of companies can help. For clarity, this figure represents only the visible marketing part of an ROI model, leaving out a lot of the underpinnings and connectivity with other corporate systems.

panies profiled in this book considered each opportunity on the Eighth Continent. They determined what it would take to achieve the required revenue or customer satisfaction impact in those markets. Then they performed a hard ROI analysis on whether it was worth the investment. In summary, they all found that three imperatives led to international marketing success:

1. *Apply rigorous standards to planning, design, implementation, and deployment.* Just being accessible to the Eighth Continent was not enough. To succeed in any online market—domestic or international—they found that they had to tune their value proposition and offerings to the needs and desires of their target audiences. That meant providing the same quality of customer interaction in each international market as they provided in their home markets. Their online success required educating their boards of directors, senior management, and fellow employees to the opportunity and challenges. In many cases it meant reaching deep into the technology infrastructure to enable corporate systems to meet the needs of international customers. It often meant reaching outside the company to collaborate with experts in areas where they lacked competence.

Category	Capability	How It's Used
Registration	Single point of registration	Identifies unique visitors for subsequent analysis
	Maintain single session	Enables visitors to pop in and out of a site without reregistering each time, thus flagging it as the single visit that the visitor thinks he's making
	Ability to track customer return visits	Provides input to customer loyalty campaigns and algorithms
Individual User	Query and modify profiles	Lets visitors see and modify his profile, and also satisfies E.U. data privacy requirements laws
	Track responses to ads, promotions, e-mails, etc.	Provides feedback on the efficacy of measured programs
	Ability to capture and extrapolate user intelligence	Follows click-through path and allows pages to be customized based on user preferences
	Set permissions (e.g., for fee vs. for free data) by specific criterion	Enables the site to screen certain information from nonpaying or unregistered guests
Integration	Integrate profile data with content management system	Lets sites personalize or dynamically serve content in response to user actions.
	Link traffic and transaction histories with profiles	Enables analysis of usage patterns by individuals
	Sort or select individual customers, groups, or other demographics	Enables marketing or e-mail campaigns to individuals or cohorts with specific buying patterns
	Export data to other systems	Enables integration of Web profiles for use in direct mail, telemarketing, and other marketing applications

Table 10.1 Basic Technology Support for Marketing Metrics

Note: Collection tools will work with personalization, marketing tools, content management, and other technologies to offer the visitor a more cohesive experience. They help to gather information that is useful in crafting campaigns and measuring effectiveness over time.

2. *Develop reliable infrastructure and organizations.* Each of these successful companies found that customers in their markets expected much of them, especially round-the-clock support, high performance, and a lifelong dedication to their market. After all, consumers and business purchasers alike could easily click their way to local or regional alternatives. These buyer expectations meant a long-term commitment in finding the staff, building the systems for interacting with and managing relationships with customers 24 hours a day, and developing the budget to justify things running year after year. It also meant a constant effort to keep international markets integrated with mainstream corporate development and initiatives.

3. *Set metrics for their return on investment.* Each of these companies measured the full 360-degree circle of ROI, broadening their analyses from simple cost-basis ROI to other economic benefits that drive growth and profitability. They aligned their metrics with mainstream corporate goals such as greater sales, more satisfied customers, better branding, and reduced costs. They found the need to revisit their business cases, paying close attention to market changes as well as geopolitical events. Periodically they had to reposition their globalization initiatives to match their companies' changes in strategy. They even had to have the courage to pull the plug on some of their favorite investments on the Eighth Continent.

Mira's Log

Mira now felt comfortable enough to approach the board again. She worked with her ROI advisory team of the CFO, a crack financial analyst, business unit managers, and country directors to write the business case for her ambitious international marketing plans. She focused first on marketing efforts, on supporting systems, and on some internally focused operations that would enhance Acme's efficiency and productivity. Her last task before heading in was to summarize all that she had learned in her short tenure as CGO. She rehearsed her first words to the meeting: "Global markets represent a big opportunity for Acme. But given the competing needs for resources at Acme, we must be realistic. I've prepared a business case for each of the leading international economies, evaluating its prospects against the board's top three spending priorities for this year. Some of these markets will make the ROI cut. Others won't. Let's get started."

WEB SITE ADDRESSES

This list provides the corporate home page, usually in English, of companies and organizations mentioned in this book. For international variants, look for a pull-down menu on the home page for these companies.

2TR Soluções Globais	www.2tr.com.br
8th Network	www.8thnetwork.com
Accenture	www.accenture.com
Adobe	www.adobe.com
AltaVista	www.altavista.com
Amazon	www.amazon.com
American Airlines	www.aa.com
American Translators' Association	www.atanet.org
Apple	www.apple.com
Architext	www.architext-usa.com
Arial Global Reach	www.arialglobalreach.com
AskJeeves	www.askjeeves.com
Atril	www.atril.com
Autobytel	www.autobytel.com
Baker-McKenzie	www.bakernet.com
Barf	www.iran-export.com/exporter/ company/PAXAN/
Barnes & Noble	www.bn.com
Basis Technologies	www.basistech.com
Berlitz	www.berlitzglobalnet.com
Bertelsmann	www.bertelsmann.com
Better Business Bureau Online	www.bbbonline.org
BigMachines.com	www.bigmachines.com
BMW	www.bmw.com
BOL	www.bol.com
Boo.com	www.boo.com
Borders	www.borders.com
Bowne Global Solutions	www.bowneglobal.com
Brand Institute Inc.	www.brandinstitute.com
Bureau of Export Assistance (U.S. Department of Commerce)	www.bxa.doc.gov

Business Objects	www.businessobjects.com
Business to Business Marketing	www.worldwide-business.com
Cap Gemini Ernst Young	www.cgey.com
Capital One	www.capitaloneenespanol.com
Cathay Pacific	www.cathaypacific.com
Cemex	www.cemex.com
Chase	www.bancochase.com
Cheskin Research	www.cheskin.com
Cisco	www.cisco.com
Citicorp	www.citicorp.com
ClearCross	www.clearcross.com
Clifford Chance	www.cliffordchance.com
Coca-Cola	www.cocacola.com
Cognos	www.cognos.com
Common Sense Advisory, Inc.	www.commonsenseadvisory.com
Computer Associates	www.ca.com
Covisint	www.covisint.com
CyberAtlas	www.cyberatlas.com
DaimlerChrysler	www.daimlerchrysler.com
Dell	www.dell.com
DHL	www.dhl.com
Documentum	www.documentum.com
DSS Research	www.dssresearch.com
Ducati	www.ducati.com
Eastman Chemical	www.eastman.com
eBay	www.ebay.com
eMarketer	www.emarketer.com
Embraer	www.embraer.com
Empirica	www.empirica.de
EMC	www.emc.com
EWGate Pte Ltd.	www.ewgate.com
Expedia	www.expedia.com
Faegre & Benson	www.faegre.com
FashionMall.com	www.fashionmall.com
FedEx	www.fedex.com
Fiat	www.fiat.com
Fingerhut	www.fingerhut.com
FNAC	www.fnac.com
Ford	www.ford.com

Foreign Exchange Translations	www.fxtrans.com
Forrester Research	www.forrester.com
Free Translate	www.freetranslation.com
Fried Frank Harris Shriver	www.friedfrank.com
Gartner	www.gartner.com
Gateway	www.gateway.com
General Electric	www.ge.com
General Motors	www.gm.com
GeoMarkets	www.geomarkets.com
Geoscape	www.geoscape.com
Global Communications	www.globalcomspain.com
Global Reach	www.glreach.com
Global Sight	www.globalsight.com
Global Works	www.globalworks.com
Google	www.google.com
Hewlett Packard	www.hp.com
Hoover's	www.hoovers.com
Human Factors International	www.humanfactors.com
HumanLogic	www.humanlogic.com
IBM	www.ibm.com
IDC	www.idc.com
Idiom Technologies	www.idiominc.com
Inktomi	www.inktomi.com
Innovative Solutions	www.innovativesystems.net
International Chamber of Commerce	www.iccwbo.org
International Federation of Translators	www.fit-ift.org
International Monetary Fund (IMF)	www.imf.org
International Standards Organization (ISO)	www.iso.org
Interwoven	www.interwoven.com
Ipsos-Reid	www.angusreid.com
Jupiter Media Metrix	www.jup.com
KPMG	www.kpmg.com
Lands' End	www.landsend.com
LastMinute	www.lastminute.com
LastMinuteTravel	www.lastminutetravel.com
Levi	www.levi.com

LingoPort	www.lingoport.com
Linklaters	www.linklaters.com
Lionbridge	www.lionbridge.com
LISA (Localisation Industry Standards Association)	www.lisa.org
Logos	www.logos.net
London Chamber of Commerce	www.londonchamber.co.uk
McDonald's	www.mcdonalds.com
McNees Wallace & Nurick	www.mwn.com
Microsoft	www.microsoft.com
Moravia	www.moravia-it.com
Morrison & Foerster	www.mofo.com
National Association of Judiciary Interpreters and Translators	www.najit.org
National Retail Federation	www.nrf.com
NCR Teradata	www.ncr.com/products/software/teradata.htm
Nielsen Norman Group	www.nngroup.com
NUA	www.nua.ie
OECD (Organisation for Economic Co-operation and Development)	www.oecd.org
Olswang	www.olswang.com
Oracle	www.oracle.com
Perkins Coie	www.perkinscoie.com
PetroBras	www.petrobras.com
Pew Research Center	www.people-press.org
Piper Marbury Rudnick & Wolfe	www.piperrudnick.com
Prestige International	www.prestigein.com
Procter & Gamble	www.pg.com
Renault	www.renault.com
Requisite	www.requisite.com
Rosario Traducciones	www.rosariotrad.com.ar
RosettaNet	www.rosettanet.org
Royal Dutch Shell	www.shell.com
Rubric	www.rubric.com
Sabre	www.sabre.com

SAE	www.sae.org
SAP	www.sap.com
Sapient	www.sapient.com
Schneider Electric	www.schneider-electric.com
Schwab	www.schwab.com
Sears	www.sears.com/todoparati/ main_home.jsp
Sidley Austin Brown & Wood	www.sidley.com
Siemens	www.siemens.com
Six Continents	www.6c.com
Society of Automotive Engineers	www.sae.org
Starbucks	www.starbucks.com
State Farm	www.statefarm.com/esp
State Street Global Advisors	www.statestreet.com
Stellent	www.stellent.com
Sun	www.sun.com
Systran	www.systran.fr
Toshiba	www.toshiba.com
Toyota	www.toyota.com
Trados	www.trados.com
Translator's Home Companion	www.rahul.net/lai/companion.html
Travelocity	www.travelocity.com
Tridion	www.tridion.com
Trust-E	www.truste.org
Uniscape	www.uniscape.com
United Airlines	www.ual.com
UPS	www.ups.com
Vality	www.vality.com
Vastera	www.vastera.com
Venable	www.venable.com
Vignette	www.vignette.com
Watson, Farley & Williams	www.wfw.com
WorldLingo	www.worldlingo.com
World Trade Organization (WTO)	www.wto.int
Xerox	www.xerox.com

NOTES

Notes to the Introduction

1. Donald A. DePalma, "Software Sans Frontières," Forrester Research, May 1996.
2. Various sources including Cheskin, Forrester, Jupiter, and Pew Research Center.
3. Cheskin Research, "The Digital World of the US Hispanic II," January 2001.
4. Sources: University of Georgia; Standard & Poor's DRI, "The Hispanic Consumer Market in 1997 and Forecasts to 2010"; Nacza Saatchi & Saatchi November 1999 report on Latin American Internet use; and Pew Research Center.

Notes to Chapter 1

1. Sources: Various reports from eMarketer and its eStats database, Gartner Group, IDC, and Forrester Research.
2. Sources: Various reports from eMarketer, NUA, and IDC.
3. Sources: Various reports from NUA.
4. Sources: Various reports from Jupiter Media Metrix.
5. Sources: eMarketer, Gartner, IDC, and Forrester.
6. Sources: eMarketer, Forrester, Gartner, and Jupiter Media Metrix.
7. "We're the reason world economy is floundering," Boston.com, 12 July 2001.
8. Source: Inktomi, early 2000 study.
9. Source: Accenture, 2001.
10. Ipsos-Reid's study, "The Face of the Web II," December 2000 at eMarketer, 17 May 2001.
11. Donald A. DePalma, "Strategies for Global Sites," Forrester Research, May 1998.

12. LISA/Geomarkets/SMP Technology Globalization Survey, November 2001.

13. Sources: Forrester, Jupiter.

14. Paul Sonderegger, "The Global User Experience," Forrester Research, March 2001.

15. At the time of publication, the fate of Fingerhut, a unit of Federated Department Stores, was up in the air. Fingerhut was very successful in its Internet channel, and its officers had been planning to expand its Web presence over its traditional print catalogs. However, the parent company chose to focus on its upscale department stores, Macy's and Bloomingdale's, rather than on Fingerhut.

16. Eric Schmitt, "The Multilingual Site Blueprint," Forrester Research, June 2000.

17. While surveys show that 80% or more of the largest European companies offer content in other languages, the number drops for smaller firms. As part of its eWorld 2001 survey, IDC studied 1,643 businesses with Web sites in North America and 4,877 in Western Europe. Only 14.9% of the North American companies offered content for other countries or regions, while 44.1% of the European companies did so. Of the 1,527 Asia-Pacific and 1,100 Latin American companies surveyed, 44.6% and 35%, respectively, offered such content.

18. Japanese and Korean companies often give their international subsidiaries autonomy to do what is right for their market, often with no connection to what is hosted in Yokohama or Seoul. Latin American firms, dealing with smaller online populations in their home markets, have been less aggressive in creating non-Spanish or non-Portuguese international sites.

19. A.S. expands to akciová společnost, the Czech equivalent of the German Aktiengesellschaft (AG), the American corporation (Inc.), or British limited company (Ltd.).

Notes to Chapter 2

1. Ernst & Young Shareholders' Guide, reported in *Computerworld ROI*, July/August 2001.

2. Source: *Internet Week* survey about global e-business strategies (19 March 2001).

3. "The Asian American Business Explosion," *Business Week,* 31 May 2001.

4. Source: U.K. National Statistics (www.statistics.gov.uk).

5. Sources: Competitive Media Reports and Greenfield Online Brand DNA.

6. Matt Hamblen, "Shell Protects Brand via Net," Computerworld, 10 January 2000.

7. Source: AskJeeves.

8. Frederick Reichheld and Thomas Teal, *The Loyalty Effect: The Hidden Force behind Growth, Profits, and Lasting Value* (Cambridge, MA: Harvard Business School Publishing, 1996).

9. Source: Prestige International, September 2001.

10. Source: DaimlerChrysler press release, 20 December 2000.

11. Sources: Ducati.com and Ducati corporate reports; *Motorcyclist* magazine, June 2001; *New York Times,* 18 April 2001.

Notes to Chapter 3

1. In his book *The Rise and Fall of the Great Powers* (New York: Random House, 1987), Paul Kennedy uses the term *polycratic chaos* to describe the strategic failures of the Axis powers in World War II. Germany and Japan failed to assess their theatre battle plans and to allocate resources accordingly, thus depriving them of the opportunity to create a "grand strategy" for their war efforts. His description of their failure sounded too much like this multinational company not to mention its failure in these terms.

2. "Let's Get Back to Basics, Folks!" *Business Week e.biz,* 29 October 2001.

3. Jakob Nielsen, "The Top Five Mistakes of E-commerce Design," *Red Herring,* November 1999.

4. Barf is a major brand of household goods in Iran. The company that produces Barf is the Paxan Corporation of Tehran, Iran. In English, "barf" is a colloquial synonym for emesis.

5. For more information about Astérix, see www.asterix.tm.fr/france/index.asp?f=1.

6. The Japanese word *kaizen* means gradual, orderly, continuous improvement. According to Masaaki Imai, who popularized the term in his book *Kaizen, the Key to Japan's Competitive Success* (New York: McGraw-

Hill, 1986), this business strategy requires that everyone in an organization collaborate to make improvements without large capital investments.

Notes to Chapter 4

1. You can find a short description of the Quebec Bill 101 (1974) and its implications at www.aq.qc.ca/English/qsignlaw.htm and the Charter of Rights and Freedoms (1981) at http://lois.justice.gc.ca/en/charter/.

2. The International Retail Forum (IRF) promotes the free exchange of information among national retail trade associations around the world. Membership is open to all national retail associations outside the United States. You can find information about current members at the National Retail Federation's Web site.

3. "Italian coffee connoisseurs believe the expansion of the US coffee chain Starbucks into Italy may appeal to the younger generation; however, its older generation may not be as responsive to the relaxed coffee atmosphere Starbucks is known to represent. . . . According to the president of the Italian Coffee Committee, Starbucks could lead some Italians to quit drinking coffee standing up in bars in favor of sitting down and savoring their beverage." The National Italian-American Federation online (www.niaf.org), September 2001.

4. The Organisation for Economic Co-operation and Development (OECD) characterizes itself as "an international organisation helping governments tackle the economic, social, and governance challenges of a globalised economy." Its 30 member countries are Australia, Austria, Belgium, Canada, Czech Republic, Denmark, Finland, France, Germany, Greece, Hungary, Iceland, Ireland, Italy, Japan, Korea, Luxembourg, Mexico, Netherlands, New Zealand, Norway, Poland, Portugal, Slovak Republic, Spain, Sweden, Switzerland, Turkey, United Kingdom, and the United States.

5. Donald A. DePalma, "City States Will Drive Internet Commerce in South America," *Forrester Research,* February 1999.

6. Donald A. DePalma, "Multicultural Marketing," *Target Marketing,* December 2000.

7. Source: Statistical Research, Inc., "Internet Usage Online Security and Privacy," 11 June 2001, via eMarketer.

8. Michelle Delio, "A Chinese Call to Hack U.S.," *Wired News,* 11 April 2001.

9. These are just a few of the many payment issues that face interna-

tional retailers and manufacturers. For a good overview of the topic, see Martin Nemzow's article, "Juggling Global Monetary Complexities," *Multilingual Computing,* January/February 2001.

10. Source: "Electronic Commerce General Population Survey" from Empirica, a German communications and technology research consultancy.

11. SWIFT is a format for transmitting and verifying financial transactions. CDA manages disbursement of funds via PC to initiate wires from checking account to a supplier.

12. Source: Jupiter Media Metrix, "B2C Electronic Commerce Transportation and Shipping Polls and Surveys," 12 June 2001.

Notes to Chapter 5

1. Using Google, my search for Internet-aware, globally capable law firms replicated what a potential client would consider. The firm had to have (1) a reasonable presence on the Net, (2) expertise with Internet law as demonstrated by information posted at their site, (3) an international presence, and (4) a willingness to respond to my online inquiries. Several firms made it through these filters, including Baker-Mckenzie, Clifford Chance, Faegre & Benson, Fried Frank Harris Shriver & Jacobson, Linklaters, McNees Wallace & Nurick, Morrison & Foerster, Olswang, Perkins Coie, Piper Marbury Rudnick & Wolfe, Sidley, Venable, and Watson, Farley & Williams. Most provide only English-language information at their sites.

2. The Rome II agreement is now being drafted to update the E.U. law (*New York Times,* 27 June 2001).

3. According to a *New York Times* article (21 June 2001), U.S. Courts have become the arbiters of global right and wrong as non-Americans have taken to suing in American courts because they do not have the right to sue in their own countries. Legal experts feel that America is exporting its legal framework much as Britain did in the nineteenth century. However, European regulators are now starting to apply their laws to U.S. companies—witness the 2001 objections to the proposed GE-Honeywell merger.

4. "Global E-Commerce Conduct Code Discussed," Reuters, 23 April 2001.

5. The WTO Declaration on E-Commerce was adopted on 20 May 1998.

6. The Internet Tax Freedom Act (ITFA) was signed into law on 21 October 1998. For a summary of the ITFA, go to the home page of U.S. Representative Christopher Cox, sponsor of the bill (http://cox.house.gov/nettax/). "A Framework for Global Electronic Commerce," 1 July 1997. For an online version, see http://www.iitf.nist.gov/eleccomm/ecomm.htm.

7. For a full copy of the ACEC's report, go to www.ecommercecommission.org/report.htm.

8. You can find the directive at http://europa.eu.int/scadplus/leg/en/lvb/l32014.htm.

9. The chief of the WTO, Supachai Panitchpakdi, believes that global rules are desperately needed for Internet commerce (*New York Times,* 30 May 2001). The WTO has a group in Geneva working to update the 1992 Uruguay round-trade pact for e-commerce.

10. See http://europa.eu.int/ISPO/ecommerce/legal/legal.html#frame for documents relating to this directive.

11. One manner of e-signature enforcement involves key technology: a "private key" to encrypt messages and a "public key" so that only the intended recipient can read it. The key holder must satisfy a number of conditions to a trusted third party (usually a certification authority) that will testify to the validity of the key and the key holder's identity by signing the key. For more information on e-signatures, see http://rechten.kub.nl/simone/ds-lawsu.htm for a survey of digital signature laws or http://www.ict.etsi.fr/eessi/EESSI-homepage.htm for information about the European Electronic Signature Standardization Initiative (EESSI).

12. You can find documents describing the Safe Harbor Principles at www.ita.doc.gov/td/ecom/menu.html.

13. See www.truste.org and www.bbbonline.org for more information.

14. Both Microsoft and RealNetworks were caught collecting information about users of their software. See Courtney Macavinta, "Trust-e reports on RealNetworks as FTC examines Net privacy," C/NET News.com, 8 November 1999.

15. According to the London Chamber of Commerce, 44 percent of businesses in the United Kingdom are not executing online strategies adhering to the Data Protection Act guidelines. Forty percent of the companies surveyed did not know whether they complied with the survey, and 27 percent were concerned with regulatory issues involved in cross-border trading.

16. Source: Research by MailRound (www.mailround.com), an English marketing specialist, and analysis by Olswang (www.olswang.com), a European law firm, released on 5 September 2001. According to this study, only one U.K. office of the world's 100 leading brands using e-mail has

complied with English Companies Act (1985) that requires business communications to include company registration information.

17. "Data Privacy Issues Key to Global Business, Panel Says," *Computerworld,* 28 May 2001.

18. "Chief Privacy Officers Emerging in Response to Data-Privacy Concerns," *Computerworld,* 14 September 2000.

Notes to Chapter 6

1. As defined in Chapter 1, *internationalization* is the behind-the-scenes technical work done to enable translation and localization. This typically involves making sure that a site can support at the very least the alphabet of a target market, a problem frequently encountered by U.S.-developed software that cannot handle Japanese characters or even diacritical marks for European languages. Other internationalization tasks involve adapting systems so that instructions, error messages, currency, and measurements can be expressed differently for local markets.

2. ISO is the International Standards Organization, source of ISO 9000 and more than 13,000 standards for business, government, and society. It comprises "a network of national standards' institutes from 140 countries working in partnership with international organizations, governments, industry, business and consumer representatives."

3. Donald A. DePalma, "Strategies for Global Sites," Forrester Research, May 1998.

4. Association of National Advertisers, 1999. Cited by e-Marketer.

5. Blanche DuBois was the dysfunctional relative in Tennessee Williams' play *Streetcar Named Desire.*

Notes to Chapter 7

1. Shareware is software that its developers make available for free or voluntary payments. "Version 1.0" commercial products are usually disparaged as being full of bugs, unstable, full of proprietary interfaces, and badly documented. In software, quality is job 1.1.

2. J2EE means the Java™ 2 Platform, Enterprise Edition, from Sun Microsystems, Inc. It is a broadly accepted Java-based standard for applica-

tion development and integration. J2EE combines a variety of Java-based technologies into one architectural framework, with an application programming interface (API) for writing user and commercial applications and a compatibility test suite for testing their compliance to the standard.

3. XML, for eXtensible Markup Language, is the World Wide Web Consortium's (W3C) suggested format for structured documents and data on the Web. See www.w3.org/XML for more information.

4. DTD means "document type definition" and was popularized by systems that implemented SGML (Structured Generalized Markup Language), also known as ISO 8879. See http://www.iso.ch for more information.

5. Results from the LISA Terminology Survey. LISA stands for the Localisation Industry Standards Organization, another nonprofit organization backed by industry suppliers that evangelizes best practices, business guidelines, and multilingual communication standards for translation, localization, and globalization.

6. OSCAR expands to Open Standards for Container/Content Allowing Reuse (don't blame me for the acronym!).

7. WorldLingo survey results can be found at http://www.worldlingo.com/company_information/pr20010425_01.html.

Notes to Chapter 8

1. For an overview of the six-hats approach to communication in challenging situations, see http://members.ozemail.com.au/~caveman/Creative/Techniques/sixhats.htm.

2. Source: Fiat's vice president of corporate communications, when asked how the American and Italian systems work together, *Autoweek,* 28 August 2001.

3. As mentioned earlier, RAS means reliability, availability, and scalability, key watchwords of high-end transactional systems that run 24 hours a day, 7 days a week, 365 days a year.

4. Cable Television Advertising Bureau, http://www.cabletvadbureau.com/MMRC/.

5. "Strategy: The Canadian Marketing Report," www.strategymag.com/multiculturalmarketing.

Notes to Chapter 9

1. Shar Van Boskirk, "Driving Customers, Not Just Site Traffic," *Forrester Research,* 28 March 2001.

2. Usability Evaluation (www.cs.umd.edu/~zzj/UsabilityHome.html) provides details on the various approaches to measuring the quality of user experience.

3. RosettaNet is a nonprofit organization funded by a consortium of IT, component, and semiconductor manufacturers working to create and implement industry-wide, open e-business process standards that will align processes between supply chain partners on a global basis.

4. For more information, see the Society of Automotive Engineers' J2450 technical committee's proceedings and other details at www.sae.org/technicalcommittees/j2450p1.htm.

Notes to Chapter 10

1. Nick Bridgett, "Measuring Customer Profitability," European Centre for Customer Strategies, April 2001 (www.eccs.uk.com).

2. Frederick F. Reichheld and Thomas Teal, *The Loyalty Effect: The Hidden Force Behind Growth, Profits, and Lasting Value* (Cambridge, MA: Harvard Business School Publishing, March 1996).

INDEX